THE
BLACK
NILE

THE
BLACK
NILE

—

ONE MAN'S AMAZING JOURNEY

THROUGH PEACE AND WAR

ON THE WORLD'S LONGEST RIVER

—

DAN MORRISON

VIKING

VIKING
Published by the Penguin Group
Penguin Group (USA) Inc., 375 Hudson Street, New York, New York 10014, U.S.A.
Penguin Group (Canada), 90 Eglinton Avenue East, Suite 700, Toronto, Ontario,
Canada M4P 2Y3 (a division of Pearson Penguin Canada Inc.)
Penguin Books Ltd, 80 Strand, London WC2R 0RL, England
Penguin Ireland, 25 St. Stephen's Green, Dublin 2, Ireland
(a division of Penguin Books Ltd)
Penguin Books Australia Ltd, 250 Camberwell Road, Camberwell, Victoria 3124,
Australia (a division of Pearson Australia Group Pty Ltd)
Penguin Books India Pvt Ltd, 11 Community Centre, Panchsheel Park,
New Delhi–110 017, India
Penguin Group (NZ), 67 Apollo Drive, Rosedale, North Shore 0632, New Zealand
(a division of Pearson New Zealand Ltd)
Penguin Books (South Africa) (Pty) Ltd, 24 Sturdee Avenue, Rosebank,
Johannesburg 2196, South Africa

Penguin Books Ltd, Registered Offices: 80 Strand, London WC2R 0RL, England

First published in 2010 by Viking Penguin, a member of Penguin Group (USA) Inc.

1   3   5   7   9   10   8   6   4   2

Copyright © Dan Morrison, 2010
All rights reserved

All photographs by the author unless otherwise indicated.

LIBRARY OF CONGRESS CATALOGING-IN-PUBLICATION DATA
Morrison, Dan.
The black Nile : one man's amazing journey through peace and war on the
world's longest river / Dan Morrison.
p. cm.
ISBN 978-0-670-02198-7
1. Nile River—Description and travel.   2. Nile River Region—Description and
travel.   3. Nile River Region—Social conditions.   4. War and society—Nile River
Region.   5. Morrison, Dan—Travel—Nile River.   6. Morrison, Dan—Travel—Nile
River Region.   7. Canoes and canoeing—Nile River.   I. Title.
DT115.M66 2010
962.05'5092—dc22   2010004709

Printed in the United States of America
Designed by Nancy Resnick

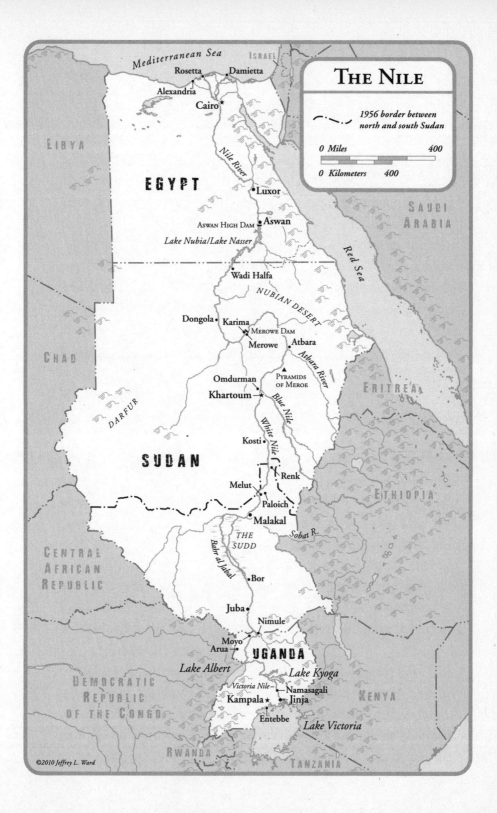

THE NILE

1956 border between
north and south Sudan

0 Miles   400

0 Kilometers   400

Mediterranean Sea

ISRAEL

Rosetta   Damietta

Alexandria

Cairo ★

LIBYA

EGYPT

Nile River

• Luxor

Aswan High Dam   • Aswan

Lake Nubia/Lake Nasser

SAUDI
ARABIA

Red Sea

• Wadi Halfa

NUBIAN DESERT

CHAD

Dongola •   • Karima

Merowe Dam
Merowe •   • Atbara

Atbara River

▲ PYRAMIDS
OF MEROE

ERITREA

DARFUR

Omdurman •
Khartoum ★

Blue Nile

White Nile

• Kosti

SUDAN

Melut •   • Renk

Paloich •
• Malakal

Sobat R.

ETHIOPIA

CENTRAL
AFRICAN
REPUBLIC

*THE
SUDD*

Bahr al Jabal

• Bor

Juba •

• Nimule

Moyo •
Arua •

UGANDA

Lake Albert

Lake Kyoga

DEMOCRATIC
REPUBLIC
OF THE CONGO

Victoria Nile • Namasagali
Kampala ★ • Jinja

• Entebbe   *Lake Victoria*

KENYA

RWANDA

TANZANIA

©2010 Jeffrey L. Ward

For Jack and Ena

ACKNOWLEDGMENTS

The author would like to thank Rebecca Friedman, Liz Van Hoose, Peter Maxwell, Judith Omondi, Naguib Amin, Violette Rychlicki, Benjamin Conable, Philip Niall, Maria Golia, Sofia Torres and Lauren Lovelace.

Special thanks to Oona Morrison and to Yossina Lopez Marrero.

PART ONE

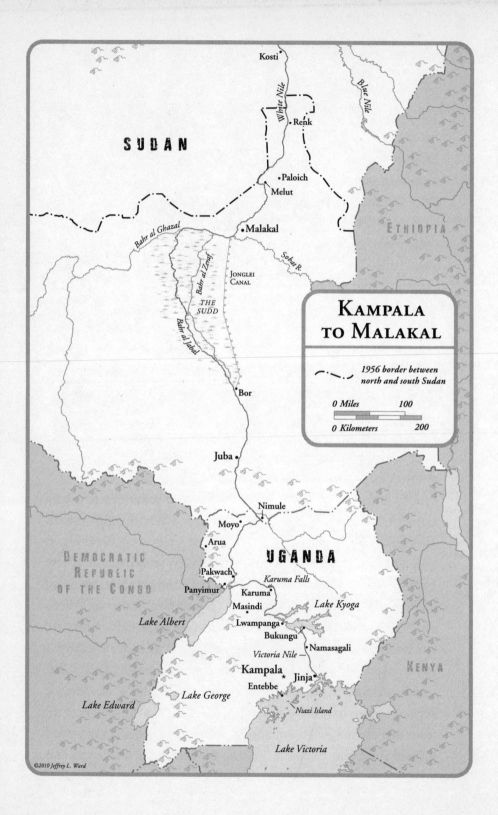

KAMPALA
TO MALAKAL

1956 border between
north and south Sudan

0 Miles   100

0 Kilometers   200

©2010 Jeffrey L. Ward

CHAPTER ONE

Ah, the Nile. What hasn't been said of it?

— Maria Golia, *Cairo: City of Sand*

The deacon grabbed me as I rounded a corner of the covered market near Old Kampala. His wide eyes were intense, wild—bereft—and they bored into mine as if we two were alone on the damp and teeming walkway, maybe alone on the earth.

I'd been searching for a bush hat among the acres of flip-flops and mounds of Chinese denim piled in the stalls of the market district; it was the last item on my list, a broad-brimmed canvas number to deflect the sun that my old blue walking cap would not, and I was about to give up when I was seized by the man in the worn black blazer and ivory shirt. He took my wrist in bony fingers, the knuckles swollen, their skin cracking, and brought his sweating face near to mine.

A stream of weekend shoppers adjusted its course around this new obstruction. A child stopped to stare and was pulled away by her mother. The deacon ignored them, just as he ignored the thunder rolling down from the hills surrounding the capital. "Do you," he panted, his pupils and nostrils dilated wide as dimes, "believe in Jesus?"

Schon Bryan, standing beside me in a sweat-blotched golf shirt and devastated Carhartt work pants, gave a snort and walked to the railing. He lit a filterless Camel, adjusted his $200 sunglasses and looked down into the scrum of buyers and hawkers one level below.

I had seen these Pentecostal preachers gyrating on street corners all over Kampala, usually in the late afternoons. It looked like an exhausting line of work. "You know," I told the deacon, twisting slowly away, hoping he would allow my arm to come along for the ride, "that's a complicated question, and I'm a little busy right now." He increased the pressure on my wrist and raised a Bible over our heads with his left hand, his breath fogging my glasses as the Muslim call to afternoon prayer began to echo from the nearby mosques. "Renounce Mohammed," he shouted in his sawdust voice. "Renounce the devil, and come now to blessed salvation."

Two women—one wearing a short stretchy neon blue skirt, the other in a longer, more traditional orange-and-black print dress with exaggerated poufs at the shoulders—watched from the doorway of a clinic selling herbal treatments for HIV. "Jesus!" the woman in the neon skirt called out. I glanced in her direction. "Save me," she cried.

"I mean no offense," I said, turning back to the deacon. "I'm just not interested. I've got something to do, and I've got to go." He slackened his grip, his pupils and nostrils contracted, and his form shifted ever so slightly from one of madman to man. He gave a short breath and asked in a matter-of-fact tone, "What have you to do?"

"I'm looking for a hat."

"But what is your purpose here? You are not a missionary. I

don't think you are an NGO. That is why the whites come. Why are you here?" A woman in a nurse's smock opened the clinic door and shouted over the market's clamor, "Godfrey! He will see you now." The deacon looked to her and again to me. "Why are you here? Tell me your purpose." He dropped my arm and lowered his Bible. It started pouring, and the market grew louder as more people pressed inside to escape the wet. Rain hammered the center skylight and the corrugated steel roof. "Tell me. I don't have long."

His simple request struck me in a way his evangelical hysteria had not. I cringed, and almost confessed, *"I'm a hack journalist with something to prove, and I've brought my best friend to Africa to keep me company while I prove it, but I'm not sure he can handle what's to come and I'm not sure I can either, and I'm terrified we're going to get our fingers and lips chopped off in the north, or that we'll be shot by bandits in southern Sudan, or that we'll be arrested and beaten for snooping around in Khartoum. I couldn't live with myself if I got Schon killed—I'd have to commit suicide."*

Instead I said, "I'll tell you," and my posture improved with each word. "I'm going down the White Nile, the length of the Nile, from Lake Victoria to the Mediterranean. I'm going to paddle a boat from Jinja to Lake Kyoga, maybe even as far as Karuma Falls, and then I'm going to trek through Murchison Park to Lake Albert, where I'll find a fisherman to take me north to Nimule and into Sudan. From there we'll follow the river to Juba, where I'll hop a barge through the Sudd marshlands—we'll fish off the side, Schon's a great fisherman—and on up to Khartoum. I'll follow the river north from there and visit the Sudanese pyramids and, hopefully, the Merowe Dam, carrying on through Nubia, past Aswan to Cairo, and then finally Rosetta. I figure I can make it in three months."

It was my hand in the air now, tracing the Nile's course from the equator to its exit in North Africa, more than three thousand miles away. The deacon ignored it, just as he ignored my flowering confidence in the plan, such as it was. His brow bundled into confusion, hurt even. "Why?"

"It's just something I've got to do. No one's made the journey in decades, at least not like this." After years as a freelance reporter, I was tired of struggling for crumbs of piecework from a fast-shrinking roster of newspapers and magazines. The hustle made me feel small. I needed to do something big, something unrelated to the American news cycle, something deep and wide and untrammeled. The Nile beckoned—not the Nile of the six-day Egyptian package tour, with its unctuous guides and sunburned Germans, but the African Nile, the one nobody hears about, the river born of giant equatorial lakes and massive continental rains a lifetime away from Cairo, a region poised unsteadily between peace and war, where decades of conflict may at last have run their course.

"Someone is paying you?" the deacon said.

"No."

"You are a student?"

"Not for years."

"Where is your boat?"

"Well, I don't actually have one yet."

The gravity lifted like the morning fog off Lake Victoria and he brightened. "*Mzungu*, that's crazy. You will be eaten by crocs. I wish you God's luck you won't be eaten. You will find your hat two buildings over, to the right, on the ground level. The hats the whites wear in the bush. Now, if you will excuse me, I am late for my drip." He walked to the clinic and said something in Luganda to the three women outside, who cackled at our impending death by crocodile.

Schon and I renewed our circuit around the market. "What was that all about?" he asked in his low baritone.

"He says," I replied, scratching my beard in the humidity, "he knows where we can find our floppy jungle hats."

"Well thank the Lord. I'm getting a little wobbly here, Maynard, and while you might be used to this volume of flip-flopping humanity and random encounters with drunken reverends or whatever that was, not to mention death-wish rides on the back of motorcycle taxis, it's getting a little much for me after twenty-six hours on a plane. Planes."

Schon's budget route had taken him from his bartending job in the piney hills of North Carolina to Uganda via the airport at Raleigh, with stops in Minneapolis, Amsterdam and Nairobi. He'd looked fine when I picked him up more than twelve hours before—rested, satisfied, humming the Meat Puppets, gobsmacked by the heat and the East African diction and the roadside casket makers. Now the man was crashing. We walked down to the narrow lanes separating the tight grid of market buildings and joined a speedy current of pedestrians, motorbikes and diesel trucks. Tens of thousands of people visited the market district each day and it seemed my feet had decided I should bump into them all. We dodged those oncoming pedestrians we could and apologized to those we couldn't, and we searched from stall to stall in the whole of the building two down to the right and found nothing at all like a bush hat. "Jesus!" one of the vendors called to me. "Osama!" shrieked another.

"I guess they don't see too many beards around here," Schon said. We forced our way back into the alley toward the road, where I flagged two boda-boda motorcycle taxis. I haggled with the drivers for the sake of self-respect as much as for frugality, and then we were off, Schon corkscrewing in his seat to gape at the giant black marabou storks flapping low and slow from parapet to light pole. The rain had turned the red clay streets to red mud streets; our teenage chauffeurs had a devil of a time getting us up the long hill of Makindye Road into Kampala's leafy southern suburbs to a crest high above the exhaust line, where each skidded to a stop. I paid the boys and we walked with care down a rutted side road to the first house on the right. We passed through the gate with a "hallo" to Sunday, the young watchman, in his blue coveralls and black gumboots, and turned up the steep stone garden stairs to the sprawling rooming house run by Claire Infield, our temporary landlady.

We entered through the homey kitchen, with its barred windows, and turned left through the dining room into a foyer, where we came to our room. I opened the padlock and Schon collapsed into the smaller of the two beds. "What time's it in America right now? Midnight?"

"The jet lag is easier if you can hold out until dark," I said. "Get you onto Africa time. Sleep when everyone else does."

He sat up and pulled off his waterlogged K-Swiss sneakers. "Morrison, I guarantee you half this town is asleep right now, and I'm about to join them unless we got something to do." He looked around the big room. "When's Noah get back? Tomorrow?"

We were bunking in the residence of my friend Noah Gottschalk, who would soon return from a visit to Florida. Claire housed a shifting roster of aid workers, do-gooders and other expatriates. Noah had been there more than a year, and his seniority earned him one of the bigger rooms. Next door was a flying instructor from Manchester, downstairs was a veteran worker for a Christian NGO, and outside held a shed with small private cells where two British legal interns bunked when they weren't working to abolish Uganda's death penalty. Noah himself worked with refugees.

"I take it I'll be on the floor once he arrives, seeing how you're the commander of this folly," Schon said, stretching his arms out and propping his head under his hands. "Fine by me. I'll take a floor in Uganda any day over a feather bed in Europe. I'm telling you, Amsterdam, walking down the aisle of the 777, I nearly swooned every third or fourth row. Europeans are pungent. I knew it would happen but there's really no preparing for it. The first one really got me. A woman. Right in the face. I was able to stop breathing just in time to reset my blood levels without serious harm. You can laugh, but I'm telling you. They just kept coming. Each rude aroma differed from the last in some way. Why was that, you suppose? Different regions of Europe? Anyway, one guy smelled exactly like rabbit shit. So, yeah, the floor will be fine."

I started unpacking the bags while Schon slept. Better, I thought, to spare him the initial anxiety. It was clear the moment he arrived that we had too much gear. Schon came off the Kenya Airways flight with three bags, a five-foot-long fishing rod case and a Wal-Mart tent the size of a surface-to-air missile. I'd arrived from Cairo with a giant black duffel containing a blue rucksack, a black paramilitary-style raid pack, a bag of medical supplies and a half dozen books, including guides to Sudan, Uganda and Egypt and some used paperbacks. My laptop had come as carry-on, along with my trusty old Nikon F2, a refurbished digital Nikon D50, a minidisk recorder, different lenses and filters, memory cards, various photo-copied book excerpts, files and cheat sheets, two small hardbound notebooks from the bindery outside the Al-Azhar mosque, a handful of Staedtler and Pentel felt-tip markers, my Thuraya satellite phone and my battered Nokia. I turned the rucksack over and spilled its contents onto the floor, then turned to Schon's gear.

He had brought all that I asked, and more. The solar char-ger (bigger than I imagined), the multivitamins, the ultraviolet SteriPen, the Katadyn water filter, the shock-resistant LaCie hard drive, three packs of brown Nat Sherman cigarettes, two Nal-gene plastic water bottles, two boxes of Ziploc bags, three crank-charged flashlights, four small Swiss Army knives, two pint bottles of Johnnie Walker Red (for minor officials in need of inducement), a liter of Johnnie Walker Black (for a major official in need of inducement), four sixteen-ounce bottles of No-Ad SPF 50 sun-screen (one of which had exploded, coating everything else) and—what the fuck was this?

"Hey, sleepy bear."

He looked up, his face saggy. "What?"

"I told you to bring bug juice, not bug spray. How are we sup-posed to carry a dozen aerosol cans more than three thousand miles?"

"We're not carrying them the whole way, jeesh. You throw 'em out when they're empty and you keep going. I know they take up some space, but I know what works."

"I'm telling you man, this won't do. And what's with the Ivory soap? You don't think they have soap in Africa?" (I too, of course, had brought my own cleanser, a small bottle of Dr. Bronner's all-natural peppermint.)

"Fuck you, Dr. Livingstone. I know what I like."

We sifted the gear for two hours, taking from and adding to the pile. Half my books and half of Schon's went under Noah's bed. So did all but three cans of bug spray, half my underwear and under-shirts, half the sunscreen, most of my pecan Luna bars, my small cotton sleep sack, a small shortwave radio, half my pocket-width reporter's notebooks and most of the batteries. Still we had too much.

I broke into the medical bags and sorted through the anti-biotics, deworming serum, malaria test kits, analgesics, anti-inflammatories, antihistamines, bandages, medical tape, two sterile intravenous kits, sterile sutures, a baby blue lice comb and a $40 super-coagulant QuickClot Battle Pack from Ranger Joe's in Columbus, Georgia. Schon stared at the minor pharmaco-poeia. "Seeing how I didn't spend eight years interning at Johns Hopkins—oh, wait, neither did you—maybe you can tell me what all those are for."

"It's mostly antibiotics, but I'd rather keep them all," I said of the mound of small cardboard boxes and silvery bubble packs. "Each does something different. Those are doxycycline, which you should have started taking yesterday, to keep malaria parasites out of your long-suffering liver. Penicillin, that's for mouth infections and fever. Cipro, that's for when I eat the wrong thing—and you know I will. Metronidazole for amoebas. And ampicillin, that's for deep abdominal wounds."

"Deep abdominal wounds."

"Yeah."

"Like in case we get shot."

"Hey," I asked, changing the subject, "what's in the tackle box?"

Schon opened the gray case, revealing five fishing rods, three reels, four spools of line, a nine-iron, a gallon Ziploc bag of scuffed golf balls, a small camp stove that ran on flammable white tablets, a metal grill, a long set of barbecue tongs, a pocketknife, a cleaver, a butcher knife, pliers and a pair of red-handled tin snips. Packs of Camel and Marlboro Medium cigarettes and a sandwich bag of toiletries filled the little gaps that remained.

"Nice packing job, eh?" He was beaming. "Every cubic inch spoken for."

"What's with the snips? You looking to install some ductwork while we're here? And what's with the golf balls?"

"I need the pliers to make my lures. I can't afford to buy 'em. Same with the snips, they're for making spoons—the shiny things that make the fish go 'Oooh.' And golf's a great game. I figure I could show some kids how to play, get some kind of poor man's golf going with the locals. Set up a mini course. Shouldn't be that tough."

Schon was not, at first or second glance, an obvious personnel choice for a trek through Africa, but he had a quality more valuable than decades of experience in the bush. Untraveled, a touch conceited, with a cloistered and underworked intelligence, he was one of the few people in the world I trusted completely. My best friend of twenty-five years would do as I asked, would speak with full candor and would watch my back as only a person who knows you can. I also secretly hoped the Nile journey would somehow restart in Schon a sly creativity that had impressed me so as a child and that had been stilled by nearly two decades of disappointment and hard living.

He apparently harbored the same ambition. Stacked to the side of the great pile of gear were three Mead five-subject notebooks. "Dude, that's a lot of paper," I said. "You can't possibly take that many notes."

"Watch me. I been doing this for the last twenty years. I have filled hundreds of these, double-sided. Couldn't stop if I tried."

"Shit, why don't you publish any of it? You've always been a good writer."

"Huh. It's a record of drunken lonely anguish, most of it. Not for general consumption. But these virgins," he said, almost hugging the notebooks, "these are going to be fun."

That night we hit the Petit Bistro for pepper steak and Nile Special beer, zeeming down the red clay back roads courtesy of the boda cartel that operated near the American club. We shot through the darkness past small shacks fronted by dirt yards and chickens and tall fine women carrying parcels on their heads. The ride seemed to be taking too long, and I was about to voice my doubts into the back of my driver's pitted helmet when the traffic of Ggaba Road came into view. He made a right into a stream of Hiace vans, bodas, and Toyota pickups and ten seconds later we were there. The ride was 3,000 shillings each, about a dollar fifty, when fair price was 2,000. We found a spot on the crowded bistro's roadside patio, near a group dinner by what I took to be an American church group. Three of the men wore matching blue oxfords and navy slacks; all the women were in long skirts, some with their arms showing, others not. None seemed to be drinking. Behind us another American man was shouting into his phone—travel plans, airport, early morning—at high aggrieved volume. "Can't place the accent, can you?" I asked Schon.

"I'm doing my best to ignore it," he said. "I came on this excursion to get away from dudes like that right there."

The man was now yelling, "Who is this? Who are you? You beeped me. Who are you? I want to know why you beeped me." Persecuted by a wrong number, he later whined for a Coke and then whined for its cancellation and not soon enough he was gone and a nice Ugandan couple sat down in his place. She ordered pork chops. They looked great. On Ggaba Road an abrasive, almost electrical sound, like a fleet of slot-car racers, grew louder until its source came into view: a man on a small 200cc motorcycle dragging forty-foot lengths of rebar. The steel rods had been bent in half, tied in an oval and lashed to the rear of his Honda. He passed us at full throttle, leaving a comet's tail of orange sparks.

The house was dark when we got back—Kampala savored its electricity for anywhere from six to twelve hours a day, and the power was still out in the morning. We took cold baths, Schon shaved and we walked down the hill to catch bodas into town, conceding most of the road to a herd of tall-horned cattle. At the City Bakery we ate meat pies and croissants and perused Kampala's three daily newspapers. Top of the heap was the *Monitor* (independent, mostly grammatical), followed by the state-owned *New Vision* (would-be independent, kind of grammatical) and the scurrilous *Red Pepper*, my guilty favorite. The *Pepper* was a classic scandal sheet: The prior month it had invited readers to send in the names of homosexuals so they might be publicly identified and thus learn the error of their ways. To the horror of many, forty-five men made the paper, listed by first name and profession. Other *Red Pepper* campaigns named alleged sugar daddies, purported lesbians, suspected sugar mamas and garden-variety cheaters, but its hunt for gays inspired real terror in a country where the president had declared homosexuals "worse than dogs and pigs" and sodomy was punishable by life in prison.

The *Pepper*'s writing was darkly lascivious; the paper's unique code name for the vagina was "Kandahar," like the city in southern Afghanistan. "Pestle," "whopper" and "shaft" denoted the penis. Intercourse itself was "shafting," "bonking" or "sexing." A typical *Pepper* story might begin like this:

MAN MASSACRES WIFE OVER KANDAHAR

Shock and fright enveloped residents of Katosi Fish landing site in Ntenjeru Sub-County when a jilted lover attacked and killed his ex-bonkmate with a panga. Ssebadduka Nankungu, a resident of Luwero Island, filled with hunger attacked Harriet Namakula and butchered her in cold blood.

Matters went out of hand when Ssebadduka failed to properly penetrate Namakula's Kandahar and cause pregnancy. Sources intimated that the love-gone-bad bonkmates had always bonked day and night with hope of getting a child but all in vain. . . .

Along the way, the *Pepper* trafficked in fantastic scoops about Uganda's political and intelligence elites that the *Monitor* and *New Vision* wouldn't touch. "I see your taste keeps getting better," Schon said, scowling up from the *Monitor*'s crossword as I chortled at the hot copy. He got up for a refill of coffee, lingering for a moment with the counter girl, and we walked onto Jinja Road in search of a ride. "That beauty had just about as much ass as you can legally carry on a frame that small," he said as we walked to the corner. "God, I love it here."

Cam McLeay leaned over my 1:800,000 scale International Travel Map of Uganda and with a ballpoint pen marked an X on the Nile an inch north of Jinja. "You got rapids up to here, mate. No point in launching before—you'll be right on the rocks." McLeay was a New Zealander, with dark eyes and short dark sun-battered hair. His handshake was crushing and his skin was weathered— the freckles seemed to have freckles of their own. He'd run rivers all over the world and now owned Uganda's top rafting company. I'd come looking for advice on how we might find a boat to pad- dle from Lake Victoria's outlet at Jinja down the White Nile to Lake Kyoga, a hundred miles north in the center of the country, and maybe even farther. The year before, McLeay helped lead an expedition that followed the Nile upriver from Egypt to its remot- est headwaters in Rwanda, using motorized rubber rafts. After get- ting through Sudan unmolested they were ambushed by Ugandan rebels inside Murchison Falls National Park, and a man was shot dead. (Months later, they restarted their journey and extended the Nile's official length by a few hundred feet.)

"I think it's a great idea, great," he said of our plan. "Just as long as you're not in a hurry. Murchison is much safer now." Peace talks had recently opened in the southern Sudanese capital of Juba between the Ugandan government and the rebels of the Lord's Resistance Army, whose grisly twenty-year insurgency had left much of Uganda's north a wasteland of refugee camps and army bases. It was their forces who had ambushed McLeay's group in Murchison. "Now, down here, in the first few days, you can just camp by the side of the river, and there's a town here"—he marked another X—"sorry, bad habit, Namasagali, where you might find a place to sleep. There's not a lot of options. Still, I don't know where you're going to find a boat. Whatever you may have thought, peo- ple don't use the Nile for transport. The river traffic facilitated the colonial cotton trade, and once that dried up, so did most of the river travel. You know, I'm having a boat built right now to port our gear from camp to camp. The old boat, the one I'm replacing, that might do the trick for your purposes. I don't know how bad off it is, but I can take you up there to have a look—I'd be happy to give it to you. The carpenter can fix it up; you'll have to pay him of course, and wait until he's finished mine—but maybe that'll fit the bill."

Cam drove us from Kampala to his work camp north of Jinja and left for other business. "That," Schon said as he drove away, "has to be the nicest man I've ever met." The work camp was on the riverbank overlooking a jagged line of rocks and whitewater that stretched the width of the river, about six hundred yards. It was our first look at the Nile since Schon's arrival, and we each stared at it for a moment without speaking. The work boat turned out to be too far gone to repair—it had rotted through in the rain and humidity. So, through Cam, I placed an order for a new one. It would take at least a week (and, after some cost overruns, about three hundred dollars) to build. Time enough to address a problem bigger than a boat: how to get into Sudan.

We returned to Kampala on a series of minibus taxis and the next day visited the Sudanese embassy to check on my visa application and to submit one for Schon. "What do you suppose the odds are these people will actually let me set foot in their country?" Schon whispered as we filled in his paperwork. Sudan's government had no love for Western visitors. Still, I hoped Schon might fly under their radar and be allowed in. I'd brought him a letter of introduction I'd begged off a friend at Flak, a nifty culture website. "With any luck, they'll think you're official enough to warrant a visa and too insignificant to be disqualified," I said.

From the tidy heights of Kampala's diplomatic quarter we rode south to the Mengo-Bakuri neighborhood and the shadow embassy of the Sudan People's Liberation Movement. The SPLM was the political arm of the rebel army whose twenty-two-year civil war with the Arab north had recently been stilled by Sudan's landmark Comprehensive Peace Agreement. After a conflict that had left two million people dead, the southern Sudanese in 2005 won autonomy, power-sharing, a cut of the oil revenues and a promise of free elections that many believed would make the autocratic rebel leader John Garang the first black president of Sudan. Then, on July 30, 2005, tragedy: Garang, flying back to Sudan from a meeting with his old friend and supporter, Ugandan president Yoweri Museveni, was lost in a helicopter crash. ("The most shocking aspect of the whole thing was that it was accidental," a Western diplomat told me at the time.) Garang's deputy, Salva Kiir Mayardit, was elevated to president of south Sudan and vice president of the troubled national unity government in Khartoum. But even now, more than a year later, the rebels were still in shock at the loss of their maximum leader.

The SPLM office in Kampala was an unmarked walled compound not far from a gas station, and it still operated as an entity separate from the Sudanese government—evidence of the southerners' virulent mistrust of their "partners" in the Arab north. This was an opening for Schon and me. The southerners were still issuing their own visas for the regions under their control, and the peace treaty had broadened that area to encompass the entire south, including cities and towns on the Nile that during the war had been in the hands of northern government forces. A southern travel pass would allow us to travel legally through the autonomous lower third of Sudan, right up to the official north-south border, regardless of whether our Sudanese visas came through or not. We sat on red cushioned armchairs in the shadow embassy's front office and stared at the framed portraits of Garang and of his successor, Salva Kiir. A beige computer sat on each of the two desks, neither with any cables, power or otherwise, attached; they were totems of the modern office. From behind a curtain we heard the sound of careful hunting and pecking on a manual typewriter.

Within an hour we each had a blue cardboard two-month pass for travel in and out of the autonomous south Sudan.

That night Schon made pasta and we joined Claire and her eleven-year-old prodigy of a daughter, Olivia, at the dining room table. We'd bought a bottle of claret on Ggaba Road; Claire, a curly-haired Briton, was pleased. Olivia was tapping on a laptop powered by the house's battery backup. It was text for a Wanted poster, part of a project at the international school where Claire was on the faculty. "Wanted by the FBI," she typed, "Funny Baboons Incorporated—for stealing the Moon." Claire was recalling the early 1990s, when armed robberies were common in Kampala. "A bullet hit just under my bedroom window and broke a clay pot," she said. "It was an enormous explosion."

"A stray bullet?" I asked.

"No, he was shooting at the house. He was down there in the garden with an AK-47. We slept under the bed in those days, but you didn't sleep. Men would come to the windows." Her voice quieted at the memory of those fearful times. "There was a mother with a little baby in her arms, my Ugandan friend Martha and her child, Jean. The baby was crying with malaria, and we didn't want the baby to cry, because people would know there was someone in the house." By the time Olivia was born, a growing economy had calmed the air of desperate menace that once ruled the streets of Kampala. She sat at the table, sucking a berry-flavored ice-lolly and writing the Wanted poster, blissfully untouched by the violence that had preceded her. She was telling Schon about her school lunches, how the teachers were served first, no matter where they stood on line, and how the larger kids pushed the smaller ones out of the way. "It's not fair, but that's how they do it," she said matter-of-factly.

"Once a man was right there at the window trying to get in," Claire said. "I screamed at him and he ran away. He had a big wrench, like this," she held her hands about a foot and a half apart, "and he just dropped it and ran away. He wanted to pry the bars open. Of course most of them use a car jack. They put it under the one bar and just lift the whole thing off. Oh—there's a nasty leaf in my wine." She'd been trimming flowers at the table in the battery-lit evening; there were fresh arrangements every day. I stepped onto the patio for a cigarette and looked at the window bars. One was twisted out of place.

"Great team, huh?" I asked Schon after they retired to their two connected rooms on the other side of the house, secure behind a solid door and a solid lock. We killed the red wine and broke into the Johnnie Walker Black, having decided its size and weight were more hindrance than boon.

"Yeah," he said, opening his journal and blowing smoke rings that disappeared over the patio railing as Ronya, the house collie mix, snored under his chair. "I wish just one of the women I know had half the personality of that kid."

The next morning Jameel Ssessgabira was waiting for us outside his blue Toyota taxi. He was reading *Bukedde*, a Luganda-language tabloid, whose cover was dominated by the oversized bosoms of a local heroine. Jameel was nearly all business—I'd hired him several times since arriving in Uganda and he displayed none of the false affection that marked other short-term work relationships. Schon got in the back and I opened the front door only to be again reminded that we were in a former Crown possession, where the steering was done on the right. With an embarrassed grin I settled into the other side, and we pulled out of Claire's driveway, past the barking Ronya (who had, so far as anyone knew, bitten only one person in her life, that being Olivia's father), and past a vacant lot with a For Sale sign that Jameel peered at wistfully while barely keeping us from sliding off the crumbling road and down an embankment.

Our destination was the Ugandan government's Water Hyacinth Control Unit, just east of Kampala, where the director, Engineer Omar Wadda, had granted us an interview. "So the dude's a
weed-whacker," Schon said from the back.

"If only," I said. "It's a serious problem. The hyacinth was nearly
the death of Lake Victoria. Nobody knows for sure how it got to
Africa from South America, but the things breed fast, die hard,
and live on shit. They double their mass every two weeks. It's part
of an environmental train wreck: The lake is full of these mutant
fish, the Nile perch, that the Brits dumped in there fifty years ago
to boost the fishing industry—"

"Which I am dying to catch one of," Schon interjected.

"—and all the perch do is eat and shit. The hyacinth love that.
Plus, more and more people are living on the lake to get a piece
of the fishing action. All their cooking fires send tiny particles
of smoke into the air, and the water vapor over the lake gathers
around the tiny bits of smoke, causing rain—but it's not mature
rain, it's a weaker rain that keeps real clouds from forming. But it's
good for the hyacinth because it's nitrogen-enriched. Meanwhile,
the people are cutting down more and more of the trees to cook
their supper. While rainfall causes things to be green, it's also true
that green—trees and grasses—sustains rain through the humidity
it creates, and with fewer trees there's less rain. And fewer clouds
mean there's more sunshine, more evaporation. It's the same phe-
nomenon that turned the Sahara from a savanna to desert."

"One hell of a Rubik's Cube," Schon said, distracted by the
relentless flow of boda-bodas, mutatu minivan taxis and lorries.
"Thanks, Perfesser."

Omar Wadda greeted us at his plain office and had us sign his
guestbook. He was a little stocky, with eyeglasses and a head of
receding white hair, and he exuded the easy competence of a career
civil servant. He'd been on the front lines of the hyacinth wars in
the 1990s, he said, when the weed covered more than ten percent of

the lake's surface, about forty-six square miles. The plant choked the shoreline—fishermen couldn't get their boats onto the water, and couldn't get them back onto land. The wind would push giant colonies of hyacinth across the lake overnight; villagers would wake up to find their landing sites transformed into green prisons. Even the cargo ports connecting Uganda, Kenya and Tanzania were closed during the worst of it. "The government resolved to tackle this through several means," Wadda said. "Biological: the use of weevils. Manual: giving hand tools, panga mostly, what you call 'machetes,' to the fishermen to cut their landing sites clear. Mechanical: using harvesters to keep the ports open. And chemical: this became controversial."

The Ugandans had introduced weevils into the lake in 1995. While the tiny insects were slow-acting, the weevils could reach where Wadda and his men could not. Wadda's men infected plants with the insects and gave them to fishermen to drop into patches of hyacinth on the open water, where the bugs spread from plant to plant, feeding on the leaves and laying eggs in the stalks. The larvae move into the roots and pupate—a cycle that happens several times and weakens the plant, until it dies and sinks into the water.

"The Americans, Japanese and the Dutch gave us the harvesters, and Egypt finally came in. They were against using herbicide on the lake, even though we had tested it and found it safe. They gave us $13.5 million to discourage the use of chemicals. They don't want that precedent on the Nile waters. The combined effort worked. By 1998 there was a collapse of the hyacinth. But now it's back. Seeds embedded in the lakeside have become exposed due to the low water levels, and have bloomed on the exposed ground." The hyacinth lowered the water level and at the same time created microenvironments that favored mosquitoes and snails, Wadda said, which in turn brought malaria and schistosomiasis, a parasitic worm.

"Is there something preventing you from using more weevils?" Schon asked.

"The weevils can't reproduce in a grounded plant," Wadda said. "The plant has to be floating for the cycle to complete. While the hyacinth reproduces quickly, it takes about five years for the weevils to catch up. We have weevil rearing sites where they are held in reserve, but it will take time to reach the numbers we need. Still, they are doing it. While we are sitting here, the weevils are working."

We drove fifteen minutes south to Port Bell, where Egyptian engineers used floating white combines to clear dense patches of the flowering aquatic plant from the shoreline. We signed the guest-book, and one of the engineers waded into the water and pulled out a hyacinth. It was an attractive plant, with a long and graceful stalk, elegant thick leaves and a purple flower. Surprisingly heavy, I thought. Wadda tore it open to expose the weevils inside. They were dark, the size of cookie crumbs, and they moved with deli-cacy across the curly brown fibers of the root bowl; farther down, the larvae were white pinheads, almost too tiny to be seen.

"Here's the thing he couldn't say," I told Schon as we drove back into town. "The rainfall is definitely off, but another reason for the lake being down is the last election. Am I right, Jameel?"

Jameel smiled behind his sunglasses. "Some say the government wanted more power before the vote and they took more water for the dam than they should have. The other countries on the lake were what? They were angry." In February 2006 the International Rivers Network had released a study showing the lake's historic low—it was down to thirty-five feet—was only partly because of drought. An analysis by the environmental group found that sixty-five percent of the lake's decline was due to the overrelease of water into two hydroelectric dams at the source of the Nile in Jinja. The sluice gates were tightened following Museveni's reelection that month, and the country's electricity supply plummeted.

"Is that why there's no power now?" Schon asked. "They're doing penance now that the old man got reelected?"

"Power might have had something to do with his reelection, but it didn't hurt that his main opponent was in jail for most of the campaign on treason and rape charges," I said. "You know—'cause treason isn't enough."

"You gotta know your audience," Schon said.

We drove back to the city and into Old Kampala, the city's Islamic and Indian quarter. Schon wanted a haircut and shave; I figured an Indian barber would have a better time with his sandy mop than an African one. The streets, traffic and buildings all were coated in red dust of the clay hills, as were the letter-sized flyers that shouted from the lampposts and walls in fifty-point bold type—"Get a Lover"; "Get a Husband"; "Get a Wife"; "Get Fat"; "For Man Vitality & Size"—each with a mobile phone number below it.

The people, however, shone—under the red dust, their clothes were immaculate, pressed, their shoes all shined. In Cairo the shoeshine men called out for customers. In Kampala men and women lined up and waited. Schon and I were invariably the most disheveled people on any sidewalk. My own appearance—the greasy long hair, the beard, the posture of a boiled shrimp, the clothes that refused to hold a crease—was strange enough that people didn't waste much time on me. Schon, however, looked normal at first glance—he looked as a *mzungu* should, with short light hair, clean cheeks and expensive shades. This first impression dissolved into confusion however as the gaze continued from Schon's face to his shirt—usually a nice short-sleeved polo from the golf resort where he tended bar—to his paint-blotted work pants and formerly white tennis shoes. We found a barber from Tamil Nadu who cut him clean under the fluorescent lights and then beat him about the head for twenty minutes, a massage that would have cost fifty dollars back home. Schon managed to flirt with the barbershop's broom girl for a moment, and we stepped out into the Kampala evening, a golden light etching the tops of the grimy cement stalls and the crumbling colonial buildings. "I could use a beer," Schon said, and suddenly there one was: two doors to the right, an outdoor café, a fridge full of bottles, sturdy plastic tables and chairs, a steel grill and a charming owner named Shems Lalji.

"So good to meet you," he said, rubbing his hands together. "It's an auspicious day, so the first round is on me." He brought out three bottles of Bell beer.

"What's the occasion?" Schon asked.

"I've just had my baby boy circumcised."

"*Mabrouk*," I said. "*Mazel tov.*"

"Thank you. And it's especially notable, because the doctor is the same man my father brought me to for the same task, back in the sixties."

I stumbled over the math. "That would make the doctor . . ."

"Eighty-one," Shems said. "I was just a boy in 1972 when we left the country; Idi Amin had expelled the Asians. But our family doctor stayed through it all, and I found him when I moved back last year, and he's still in fine shape."

"A steady hand," I said.

"A steady hand indeed. Excuse me for a moment." He got up to turn a rack of lamb on the grill.

I asked Jameel, who was twenty-five, how his generation saw Idi Amin. "He was loved at first," Jameel said. "He spoke like the people. And he built a hospital for the poor. And he made the language of the schools an African language, not English. These were good things. But he did some things that were velly bad. The Asians, they were robbing people. They had all the business. But he took everything of theirs, and other men got to have those businesses, those houses, for nothing; they did no work, and they did not know how to operate a factory, how to trade. Fifty thousand Asians were made to leave, to England, to India, to other places.

And some, they could not leave—they had no passports but the Ugandan one, they were born here. Some of these families, they went to the dam in Jinja and they what? They jumped over the side. All, including the babies. It was velly bad."

We had lamb with roasted potatoes, a right feast, while Shems told us his story. He'd grown up in Vancouver; his family were Ismaili Muslims, an ancient offshoot of Shiism. While Shems still considered himself an Ismaili, he was also a Sufi, part of a universalist strain of Islam.

"I started some restaurants in Vancouver, and they received good notices. I even published a book called *Go Ahead, Make My Curry*, but at some point I realized I wanted to come back to reclaim some of my family's properties and make a go of things." He had his café and a newly opened hotel he hoped would draw backpackers. He'd married a local woman, and now he was the father of a newly circumcised son. "*Alhamdulillah*," I said. He and Jameel laughed.

"You know Arabic?" I asked Jameel, eyeing his nearly empty beer.

"I know *alhamdulillah*," he said. "My father is a Muslim."

"That means you're Muslim, right?"

"I am Muslim," he said, regarding the label on his bottle. "Yes." It struck me: Hanging from his rearview mirror, where a Catholic might have a rosary and crucifix, was a plastic medallion depicting the Kaaba in Mecca. I'd completely missed it.

Noah Gottschalk was asleep in his bed when we returned to Claire's house that night. I seized the spare. It was time for Schon to take the floor, where he slept like a faithful hound, uncovered on a thin foam bedroll. In the morning we had breakfast on the patio and I filled Noah in on our plan. I had become taken with the idea of traveling on Lake Victoria by fishing boat from Entebbe, a half hour south of Kampala, to Jinja, where the White Nile began. "From there we'll claim our own boat, christen it with a bottle of Coke and paddle to Lake Kyoga. We'll find someone to tow the boat across Kyoga, and from there we'll paddle up to Karuma Falls."

"No we won't," Schon said.

"Or, if we're too tired, or wimpy, we'll find someone with a motor to put on the boat and putter us up to Karuma, and they'll keep the boat as payment. After Karuma, it's down to Masindi, and a hired car into Murchison Park, where the Wildlife Authority has offered us a motorboat for hire to get us to Lake Albert. From there we try to find a fisherman to take us to the Sudan border. I think it's doable," I said hopefully.

"Why are you traveling on Lake Victoria when the Nile starts at Jinja?" Noah asked, carving up a pineapple on a scuffed porcelain plate.

"I don't know, I just like the idea."

"It doesn't make sense. If you want to somehow touch the water before it becomes Nile water you could do that from anywhere. It doesn't have to be from Entebbe. Lake Victoria is big. It has its own weather. I'm just saying."

We roamed across Kampala by boda-boda as I tried to gather the elements of a decent Plan B that would get us to Sudan once Plan A proved impossible. We visited the United Nations High Commission for Refugees, which was ferrying southern Sudanese refugees back home from camps in Uganda. They would love to have us along on such a trip, the local press officer said, but the wet season was running long—no UNHCR trucks would be crossing the border for some time. A trucking company that supplied southern Sudan was more amenable. "See our agent in Koboko," the manager said, but their route went through Koboko in northern Uganda to Yei in southern Sudan, far off the Nile. The Karuma Falls and the more spectacular Murchison Falls made boating into Murchison Falls National Park impossible. At a local adventure company we learned there was no point in trying the northern overland route either—the roads were unreliable. "I wouldn't go there without two vehicles," our contact said. "One to pull the other out when it gets stuck. And it will." We would have to leave the Nile at Karuma Falls and enter Murchison Park from the south, using the established tourist route.

Then, at the Sudanese embassy, a true reversal. My three-month visa had come through, but written across it, in English and Arabic, was the following restriction: *Not valid beyond twenty-five miles of Republican Palace.* It seemed that President Bashir of Sudan had been snubbed while applying for a visa to the United States at the American consulate in Havana. Havana being distant from things Middle Eastern, the visa clerk hadn't known that sanctions in place since 1993 restricting the movement of Sudanese officials in the United States had been lifted in 2002. Bashir, who was heading to New York to attend the annual UN General Assembly, was not allowed to leave the island of Manhattan. In a fury, his government had placed similar shackles on all Americans in Sudan—diplomats, aid workers and lowly freelance journalists alike—limiting them to the capital. The restriction meant I would be traveling illegally the minute I left the south, with little hope of a reprieve if I was arrested on the way to Khartoum. We stepped outside the embassy and I let out a howl that set the marabou storks flying.

Sitting down on the embassy's front steps, I pulled out the Sudan map. "We need to reassess. At this rate," I said to Schon, "it looks like you're not getting a Sudan visa. And even if you did, it would have the same Fuck You on it that mine has. Plus, we're a week into this, and still in Kampala, and our boat isn't ready and we don't know when it will be. You've got less than seven weeks before you've got to be back to work. So you're not going to see Khartoum. That puts your end point here—Juba—or here—Malakal, the last major town in the south. It's just north of there that our blue southern travel passes become void."

"I get that," Schon said, "and I can live with it. But if you're restricted to within twenty-five miles of the outhouse, how are you going to Khartoum? I mean legally."

I didn't know. "Maybe I'll just make a run from Malakal to the capital without stopping, and then try to get the visa changed. I mean, it's a risk, but maybe a worthy one."

"Yeah," he said. "Worth a month in a Sudanese jail. You better think it over, and I mean hard."

We bodaed back to Claire's in a foul mind. At the roundabout off Queens Way, I stared glumly at the white-and-blue mutatu mini-van taxis, each with a shout-out to a team, neighborhood or deity spelled across its windshield: Arsenal, Nabinene Girls, "Maama wa Baana" (Mother and Child), a popular song by Master Parrot, Inshallah. Billboards advertising HIV treatment, marital fidelity, CelTel phones and a simple display of white text on a red background that asked, "Why are you paying a fortune for indifferent imported basmati rice when you can have . . ." The answer was obvious, at least to those who bought basmati rice.

Outside the Shoprite supermarket the dirt paths were populated by hip-high child beggars, their skin dusty and dry, their hair coarse. "Sir, sir," they called to us as we waited in traffic, their mothers or minders squatting nearby in the dirt with infants in their arms. The street was clogged with mutatus, bodas and private cars. Two small boys approached Schon's boda, calling, "Sir, sir, sir," and were interrupted by a teenage boy in a yellow soccer jersey walking the median; he threw his elbows and forearms out in a menacing gesture. One boy jumped out of the way; the other ignored him and was in turn ignored by us. The teenager was carrying a bathroom scale in both hands, face out. I realized, as we pulled away, that he sold weight. Earlier, a day or two before, a boy had approached me with a scale on the lower end of Makindye

Road and I, in a hurry, had said no thank you. I wished now I'd taken the time to stand on his scale and pay him his hundred shillings. Hustlers were everywhere in Kampala, in the best sense of the term. Boys and men and women, their arms roped with basketball jerseys, collared shirts, cardboard displays holding plastic combs and cheap manicure kits, lined the streets in the late afternoon looking for action from homebound commuters. They stood until dark.

CHAPTER TWO

We had an early breakfast of toast, juice and cigarettes on Claire's patio, serenaded by the birds and by the *shik-shik-shik* of Sunday and David, the watchmen, cutting grass under the garden trees. "There's got to be a better way," I said, as they *shik*ed forward with dutiful monotony, bent at the waist in identical blue coveralls and black rain boots, swinging their machetes at the ground. "You notice how the huts here all have dirt yards? No grass. Just a swept patch of dirt. It's like that's what makes a proper yard here. Like if everything—grass, weeds, flowers—grows with ease, just stick it in the dirt and it grows, then having an actual lawn doesn't really prove anything. But if you've got a uniformly flat patch of dirt without one unwelcome thing on it, then it shows you care.

"I don't know," I added. "I could be wrong."

Schon, reclining in a tan T-shirt with a blue bandanna around his neck, looked up from his journal—he'd already filled dozens of pages. "Oh, I'd believe it. I worked with this girl in Carolina who said her grandparents did the same thing. Every morning, grandma would be out there with a broom to sweep the entire yard. If grass came up, they pulled it. Must have been a pain in the ass when it rained."

Noah joined us, carrying a stack of books in his arms. A progressive and observant Jew, a nonsmoking vegetarian and a former intern at Human Rights Watch, he still somehow carried the look, with his hooded eyes, scraggly beard and gaunt cheekbones, of a comic book mercenary. All that was missing was the Browning automatic and an old cigar. "Hi, guys," he said. "Heading to the lake today?" He was preparing for a trip to displaced-person camps in the north and had found, on the same shelf as his Lwo-English dictionary, a copy of the Lonely Planet French phrasebook.

"Check this out," he said. "The contrasts are really something." He opened the French book. "Reading this you know exactly what the French are all about. You've got courtship: 'Would you like to go out?' 'You're a fantastic dancer.' 'Do you have a boyfriend?' Then consummation: 'Let's use a condom.' Plus, 'faster,' 'harder,' 'slower,' 'stop' and, thankfully, 'don't stop.' Then comes the fall: 'Are you seeing someone else?' 'You're just using me for sex!' 'I never want to see you again.'" He closed the book. "France is fun."

He picked up the heftier Lwo-English volume and started flipping pages at random. "'This is an arrogant and insolent talk which you should not say here.' 'Only eight children passed the examination.' 'The suffering of working as a porter does not allow me to put on weight.' 'You are a man who entices other people's women.' 'He hypnotized people and therefore stole a lot of things.' Oh my God—'Your mother has a protruding labia minora.'" He snapped the book shut. "I can't go on. They should have called this *How Not to Make Friends in Northern Uganda*."

Ronya started barking; Jameel's taxi was at the gate. We washed our dishes, grabbed our small packs and sandwiches and jogged down the garden stairs to join him. Jameel had spent time on Lake Victoria as a young man, and as we drove down the Entebbe Road, past the coffin makers and curbside furniture showrooms, he told us about fishing, East African style. There was the dragnet, where two parties standing in the shallows hauled in a U-shaped dispersion, the ropes knotted at meter intervals. It was banned—the dragnet brought up all kinds of animals that would never see market or plate—but the ban wasn't really enforced. There was tycooning, where you beat the water with a club, scaring the fish into your nets. Mukene light fishing was done at night; a lantern was placed on a float to attract the fish, which were then scooped up into mosquito netting. Two different methods were used on the Nile perch: gill nets and hooked lines. "It is a lope with hooks every thirty centimeters," he said, inverting his L's and R's like a caricature Japanese. The hooked lines were dangerous. "I have fished like this myself," he said. "You must have your hands in the light place, between the hooks. But when you bring the lope in, the fish can fight, it is very strong, and at the last minute it will pull. The hook, it can go into your neck, and the hook it can kill you."

"Sounds like a dangerous way to make a living," Schon said. "Do a lot of these fishermen know how to swim?"

"They don't swim. They drown."

After twenty minutes on the road we made a left onto a rougher track and came to a fenced-in complex. The Kasenyi landing site, just outside Entebbe, was an important node in Uganda's fish industry. We drove through the security gate, pausing briefly while a shotgun-toting guard in pressed blue khakis searched the trunk. "You see the size of that guy's Mauser?" Schon said. "I guess they take the fish business seriously here."

Jameel parked and we walked through a warren of drab shacks and wooden stalls selling insulated windbreakers, life preservers, engine parts, smoked fish and grilled sweet potatoes. In a clearing between shacks, a three-foot-high pile of tiny silver minnows gleamed like spilled treasure. They were *dagaa*, Jameel said, a high-protein staple of the Ugandan diet. Nearby, a shirtless mechanic probed the interior of a motor with the concentration of a heart surgeon. We descended onto the yellow sand beach and our first look at the broad sweep of Lake Victoria, an azure pool that rolled away forever from the shore. Dozens of long wooden plank boats sat at the water's edge, their joints sealed with strips of hammered tin and brown adhesive goo. Lean men, many wearing jerseys or shorts promoting British football clubs, lounged against the boats, smoking cigarettes and listening to a portable radio. They watched our arrival with distant curiosity. Jameel called out a greeting and a man wearing a red "Abibas" tracksuit and carrying a Donald Duck calculator and an open composition book came forward. He ignored Schon and me and, leaning against a boat, began a long conversation in Luganda with Jameel, one punctuated by frequent use of the term *mzungu* and a reasonable number of outbursts of laughter, as more fishermen joined the conversation. The news was tough. Fishing crews left Kisenyi in the evening. They set their nets and slept either in the boat or on tiny mosquito-infested islands. Jameel could not recommend joining. "It is, ah, velly velly uncomfortable."

There was, however, a nearby island where the fishermen sometimes left their nets out and returned to shore before picking up the catch hours later. A large boat was loading now to take passengers there, Jameel said, but there was no return trip until the next day, which meant he could not join us. The boat sat in the shallows taking on passengers and cargo. It looked like a tiny unfinished galleon, about thirty-five feet long, with a nine-foot beam, not so much smaller than the ships that brought Columbus across the Atlantic, or the dhows that even today linked India to Africa and Arabia.

Mr. Abibas punched his Donald Duck calculator for a moment and offered us a special one-day round trip for 900,000 shillings, more than $500, which was of course impossible. We walked back through the maze of shops and stalls to the car, gathered our small packs and walked through the sand toward the big boat, where porters wearing hot pink nylon tunics swarmed us like we were handing out green cards. Two engaged in a shoving match to get Schon's bag, each push loud as a thunderclap; these guys were strong. I sat down and started taking off my boots when a burly porter approached and dropped to one knee as if he anticipated knighthood. "He will take you," Jameel said.

"He'll take me?"

"Carry you."

"Like a damsel?" Schon asked.

We quickly agreed to portage for 500 shillings each (normal rate 200) and with an alley-oop I was sitting on the man's shoulders, my bollocks smashed against the back of his neck as he waded into the chest-high surf. I teetered over the water as he reached the boat and a half dozen hands reached out to haul me up and drop me onto a jumble of bags, canisters and other freight. (Schon insisted on walking most of the way and was hoisted aboard soaking wet.) We were the last to board and would have to stand during the journey. The boat was divided by crossbeams into six sections. The first four were built up with a wooden floor and rows of benches; the rear two were piled with cargo. I stood on the cargo in the second bay, leaning on a crossbeam, facing rows of astonished passengers. Behind me were stacks of four-foot-long synthetic gunnybags of crushed ice. At my feet were piled large clear plastic bags of bread and, to the front, red plastic cases of Ugandan beer—Pilsner, Bell and Nile Special.

It was here that I took notice of a voluptuous woman of smooth red ochre complexion seated to my left against a gunnybag. She wore a white satiny gown, her hair pulled into a tall white satiny wrap. Next to her was a thin man in a Muslim topi wearing a green leaf-patterned shirt. A bit higher, on a squat Honda diesel generator he had bought on the mainland, sat a man with a trim mustache and close-cropped hair. And next to me, competing for space on the crossbeam, was a man I took to be a member of the crew, with broad cheekbones, wide lips and a clean bald head. He watched me watching the woman.

"You want to penetrate her?" he asked.

"Excuse me?"

"You want to penetrate her? I give her to you."

"She's somebody's sister," I spat. It was ill-conceived last-second bullshit—but it was true, and it worked. He quickly changed the subject and asked if I was believing in God, and if I was Moroccan and if I liked fish. The mainland faded and the gaping passengers lost interest in the two *mzungus* and we settled into silence and watched the growing horizon. The Yamaha sliced our vessel comfortably through the silver-topped lake, immune to the smack of waves against the hull; a steady westerly wind kept us cool under the open sky even as it whipped my hair into a lopsided thicket. My neighbor the penetrator leaned forward and pulled a bottle of Pilsner from its case and, reaching back, tucked it into a gunnybag of crushed ice.

"You know," Schon said, "I think we got lucky with those dudes at the beach not wanting to take us out. Imagine a night on the water with four other guys, not being able to understand what they were saying, and them not understanding us. That would have been some real misery. Misery we're not prepared for, not really. And say the one in a million happens and the boat goes over in a storm and you and me are the only ones who know how to swim."

The penetrator pulled his now cold beer out of the gunnysack and, curling back his lips, popped the top with an ivory molar. "Jesus," I said. Schon, facing us from the opposite crossbeam, took his left hand from his lap and pulled down his lower lip to reveal a quarter-inch void. The missing tooth's counterpart on the right was capped in gold. "I lost this doing exactly what you're doing, just like that," he told the man. "This one too," he said, pointing to the gold. "It's basically a crown."

I laughed over the engine's drone. "So you couldn't learn your lesson after losing the first tooth?"

"Well, it was all cracked, but microscopically—shot through with tiny fissures that weren't really visible until I lost the other one and wised up."

We rolled across the equator under skies that I can only color September 11 blue, and the spirit remained happy even as I grew stiff from avoiding the hubcap-sized rolls lying at my feet. My left foot shared a toehold with the penetrator on a car battery. My right leg was tucked under the crossbeam and planted on a bag of ice.

The group to the left was gathered around two Nokia mobile phones, each apparently equipped with an FM tuner, listening to the Arsenal match being called in Luganda. The woman in white chatted with Schon, who crouched low to try to understand her. "They think we're coming out here because we want an island to buy," he said. "I shot that down real quick." After an hour and a half a crown of land came into view, three-quarters wooded, with large patches of what appeared to be freshly mown lawn. Below that, a brown band of huts and alleys.

"What do you call this place?" Schon asked the trim man with the mustache.

"This is Nsazi, our destination," he said. "You are English? American? I am Geoffrey Kimenke."

The village was nearly all mud-and-thatch huts, most of them standing in ragged lines back from the stony beach. I climbed off the side of the boat and onto the shoulders of a waiting brute who demanded 500 shillings. I gave him 400 when we got to the shore; he stared at the two coins and then crammed them into his pocket and bounded away. Geoffrey, our new friend, said he would help us find the village chairman, the key to smooth relations during our stay. We walked up the beach past shacks selling tea and fried dough and found the genial headman, short, meaty of hand and paunch, with a strong grip. Geoffrey introduced us and I told him our purpose. "I am a fisherman too," the chairman said, friendly and hard at the same time. "This man will help you," he said, deputizing Geoffrey, who gave him a quick double take. "I am happy you are here." Then he turned away to glad-hand some passing villagers as the sun began to set.

Geoffrey ran the village's video hall, its sole public amusement, a long weathered gray building with a chalkboard propped at the door announcing football matches and Nigerian kung-fu movies. "You will want lodging," he said. "I can help." Outside his nearby house, one of the very few with a cement foundation, his gorgeous wife, Winnie, stood wearing a red turtleneck sweater and spotless tan capri pants. As it happened she operated a rooming house. We followed them through the village maze, past the chickens, ducks, goats and pigs that competed for alley space with toddlers who crawled and bawled in the mud and scat along the way. A bare-chested boy stood in the middle of a path, gnawing the end of a tree branch he held propped in the mud before him, stripping the bark with daydreamy zeal.

Many huts were fronted by squares of grass, but these weren't lawns—the grass lay horizontal, newly cut lengths of thatch spread to dry before being woven into flat lengths of rope by women sitting on low stools. We came to a long black plankwood building with three doors on each side—Winnie's island hotel. She opened the center door, number two, popping the small padlock with a key tied to her wrist on a long faded black cord. This was the only vacant flop. "You can do with one room? That is enough?" Geoffrey said. The six-by-seven windowless cell was painted an optimistic blue, its floor covered by a thick yellow sheet of linoleum. The ceiling was a layer cake of plastic, tree branches, more plastic and corrugated metal, all covered by a moss of dusty cobwebs. A red plastic basin of dirty water sat near the door; a foam mattress occupied half the floor space. From high on the back wall a palm-sized spider watched. "It's perfect," I said. "Thanks very much."

We left Winnie to clean the room and walked back to Geoffrey's porch, where we dropped our bags and sat on a wooden bench to wait. Geoffrey left for the video hall and a group of children gathered around our newness, pushing against the porch railing and spilling up the concrete steps to almost within arm's reach. "How are you?" they cried. "I am fine, how are you?"

"You're fine, are ya?" Schon said. "Well, that's fine. I'm fine too." We did a few more rounds of that, and Schon slapped hands and fist-bumped the braver ones and then they lapsed into quiet, save a big-eyed boy whose every gesture said personality. "Do you kids like football?" I asked. They answered with silence.

"Rugby?" I boomed, overenunciating. "You kids like rugby?"

Nothing.

"That's good," Schon said. "It's a known fact that foreigners understand you better when you shout at 'em."

Quietly, I asked, "What about basketball?"

"YES!" With a single roar they came to kidly life.

"Yeah, you like basketball?"

"Where is it?" asked the fey boy. He had a pebbly voice. "Where is it? Give it to me," he said, half pirouetting, eyes fixed on our bags.

"But I don't have one," I said, despairing. "I don't have a ball." They didn't show disappointment so much as resume their studious near-silence.

Winnie returned, scattering the children with a pleasant bark, and led us back to our lodging. Stall number one, next door, was open and a woman in blue jeans and a white blouse, buxom and strong, her hair braided half in coppery red, chatted with Winnie as we stowed our gear. "Do you need water? I'll get some," Winnie said, and she disappeared. I claimed the bed and spread my sleeping bag on top of the foam mattress, the newly made sheets and the damp acrylic blanket. Schon hung his wet sneakers on a nail and unrolled his foam sleeping pad. Winnie dropped off a two-gallon plastic vegetable oil container and left for the night as a dozen children gathered close around the doorway in the fading daylight. They watched with murmured fascination as I snaked rubber tubing from the Katadyn filter into the yellow jerrican and pumped water first into my own Nalgene bottle and then into Schon's. The audience hushed when I stuck the tip of the SteriPen into my bottle and lit it up with germ-killing ultraviolet. "You notice how her clothes were all dry?" I said. "She obviously walked to the lake to refill that Crisco bottle but her clothes were all dry."

"Years of practice," Schon said. "You notice how she and Geoffrey seem to have this town sewn up tight?" Suddenly the red-braided woman from next door came screeching down the alley from the right, leaning forward in an exaggerated charge, waving a switch in her right hand. The urchins vanished in a rumble of tiny footsteps, save one toddler who, paralyzed with fear, sank shrieking to the ground, hands clawing his cheeks in an expression of impossible terror. Laughing, she lifted and carried him away. We drank some water and walked out to explore the moonlit village. The hamlet was still awake; people gathered standing and squatting by tiny shops, chatting in the paraffin lamp glow. By the shore a man worked over a charcoal griddle, rolling and pounding fresh chapatis, a flashlight held in the crook of his neck. We sat on the edge of a beached fishing boat and watched. The light would dim mid-chapati and he would shake it, recharging the battery for another two minutes, and return to work. Next to him another man grilled skewers of beef. We bought neither. At a stall farther down, I leaned on the wooden counter and bought two bags of peanuts. Inside the stall were stacks of eggs in one-foot-square cartons, bags of Ugandan UHT milk, laundry soap in long red and blue bars, cases of local beer, strips of condoms and, within pissing distance of Lake Victoria, clear blue bottles of spring water imported from China. Walking deeper into the hamlet, away from the beach, we saw a beacon. It was a wooden structure on a cement foundation, its doorway lit with bright diesel-generated light. Inside, a pool table, small counter and a couple sitting along the back wall eating fish stew. I joined a man sitting alone at another table while Schon went to the counter to buy a couple Bells. "I guess two thousand is what they tip around here," he said with a short laugh when he returned with the beer. "I waited for the change and she said that was the tip. The way she smiled at me I guess was worth an extra grand."

Our tablemate said he was from Kampala. He was in the fish business, here to buy and resell on the mainland. Nile perch sold for 2,000 shillings a kilo on the island, 2,500 in Kampala and from 3,000 to 3,700 if processed and shipped to the freezer aisles and chip shops of Europe, the United States and Asia. "Aren't stocks of perch falling?" I asked.

"It doesn't matter," he said. "With prices like these there will always be fishermen, until the last one is gone." The waitress brought a second round and popped the tops of all three bottles, throwing Schon another smile. After a couple minutes our friend noticed I was still nursing my first Bell. He took a loose bottle cap off the table, placed it on the mouth of my newly opened bottle and slammed his palm down on it. Foam erupted, rolling down to the wooden tabletop and onto my lap. He flicked away the cap and jammed a finger in, stanching the flow. The finger stayed there for a beat before he pulled it back out. The eruption resumed, and he stuck his finger back in again and we all stared at it until I said, "Here. Slowly," and gripped the bottle in one hand and his finger in the other and gradually eased the reluctant digit out of my beer. He resisted, fearing another money shot, but the slow withdrawal worked just fine.

One well-fingered beer later we were ready to leave when the chairman came in to a huzzah of laughs and handshakes. We bought him and the merchant a round, a sort of exit visa, as the chairman shouted, "I am a Frenchman! My name is François, *bonjour*!"

On the walk back to the rooming shed I peeked inside Geoffrey's darkened video hall, where about forty men sat on rough benches drinking beer and watching a Nigerian fight film. A man with a microphone stood off to the side of the television, performing simultaneous translation of the dialogue from Lagos English to Luganda. As we made our way lost through the village, our flashlights more than once fell upon naked women bathing quietly, almost furtively, crouched over plastic basins, outside their huts; one woman had an equally silent infant lying at her side. They showed neither anger nor annoyance at our intrusion, only a crouching modesty. Later, when I was lying on my sleeping bag on top of the foam mattress and acrylic blanket, burbles of delicious feminine laughter trickled in from the stalls next door. I wondered if we would be treated, if that was the word, to the sounds of human congress, but there was none that night and just as well. I needed my sleep.

With dawn came radios, washing, laughter, chastisement—a Lake Victoria morning pouring through the plank walls. I checked the skin of my hands, arms and face for insect bites and found none. All pale and smooth, save the Brillo pad beard. I pumped and zapped more drinking water by the light of the open door, where the urchin audience this time was a disappointing two. We walked to the shore and found the Muslim man we'd seen on the boat the day before strolling the beach in a knee-length lab coat, a megaphone in hand, peddling herbal medicines from a small red valise. We circled back up into the village and soon arrived at Geoffrey's place. Winnie was outside sweeping the porch in a blue pinstriped skirt and jacket over a black T-shirt on which an American flag was stretched from breast to winning breast. She called in to Geoffrey, who emerged in a burst through the curtained front doorway. He wore flat-pressed green khakis and a black T-shirt with yellow block letters across the chest that read "Soviet Collection."

"You want something? Some tea? The boats don't leave until later." We followed him deeper into the village to a small mud-and-wattle shack, outside of which a pregnant woman in a green wrap and maroon headscarf was mixing a grainy dough in a plastic washing basin. Another woman tended a pot of brown beans over a charcoal fire. We ducked inside and sat at a low table with benches on three sides. I ordered black tea.

"No milk?" Geoffrey said. "Had I known, there's a better place for black tea. Something to eat?" Our eyes bulged with panic. "Maybe just bread then." He handed the pregnant woman 5,000 shillings and she sent a girl to find us some. "There are two thousand people in this village," he said. "There were six hundred when I first came here, in 1998." Was there a school? "Yes," he said. "From last year. There was one years ago, but it didn't work. The teachers couldn't afford the island prices. But now the government has made arrangements and they can pay their expenses. We have four clinics, including prenatal." Still, the health situation was not good. "It's the water—there's no sanitation. We don't have enough influence. The government has other priorities."

"Other priorities?" Schon asked. We had earlier been directed to relieve ourselves in the woods behind the village. Judging from the number of piles I had to step around to take a private leak, it seemed everyone else here did the same. None of the homes had outhouses or latrines.

"The chairman has been elected to his post since the 1980s," Geoffrey said. "Everyone loves him. He runs unopposed. He's also elected chairman of his home village on the mainland. He owns a lot of property there."

"For a city person it's not the most comfortable place to live,"

I said. "Were you already living here when you and Winnie got married?" Out of sight, Schon's sneakered foot connected with my kneecap.

"Winnie is not my wife," Geoffrey said evenly. "My wife is in Kampala, with my two children."

Another patron came into the shack and sat at my right and was served milky tea in a brown enameled cup. I uncrossed my legs to massage my wounded knee and rammed the underside of the table, spilling everyone's tea. I pulled out my handkerchief to keep the new guy's tea out of his lap just as the cook ducked inside to serve him a bowl of beans and stretchy bread. "I can't eat around these people," he said in bitter Luganda. I stood up and let him move farther into the table, far to the left, out of harm's way. The bread arrived, one of the round loaves I'd avoided stomping the entire trip from the mainland. Geoffrey dipped his bread into his tea while I picked mine into pieces and ate without gusto. I paid for the teas, 1,800 shillings, and we followed Geoffrey to the lake. The boats, long and low, were crawling with fishermen preparing for a day on the water. Geoffrey stopped at a green boat, painted inside and out, with metal flashing nailed over its every seam. "Sure looks yon," Schon said.

"Yon? What is this, *Moby-Dick*?"

"He will take you for seven thousand," Geoffrey said. Men were tying empty UHT milk pouches to the ends of the nets. Filled with dirt and gravel, they would sink the bottom half of the nets. The top sides were similarly tied with biscuit-sized hunks of cork. "The boats will be out for a long time, with nothing for you to do. They return around seven. It will be uncomfortable."

"I wouldn't have it any other way," I said.

"They leave in ten minutes," Geoffrey said. "You will want to get your things." It was nine-thirty. We walked back to the shack and threw together our gear: a plastic shopping bag with water pump, peanut butter sandwiches and two bottles of freshly zapped

lake water. I wore my seven-pocket travel shirt, and at the last minute I grabbed a long-sleeved camp shirt and a bottle of SPF 50.

But we tarried with the packing, and by the time Schon and I
got back to the beach our boat had already left in a fit of admira-
ble, anomalous, un-Ugandan punctuality. "Well, go figure," Schon
said. "The first on-time departure in the history of Africa." Our
replacement wanted 10,000, Geoffrey said. His twenty-five-foot
boat was of raw unpainted wood, its center bays piled with a tall,
springy mound of thin-gauge monofilament netting. The top of the
Yamaha motor was missing its cover. A fuel line ran from the motor
into a yellow cooking oil container that sat upright on the floor. I
paid the owner and we gathered around the boat with half a dozen
other men and pushed it off the stones and into the dark and gentle
surf, then hopped in, Schon and I side by side on a bench near the
front. Frank, the pilot, manned the engine, and his first mate took
the prow. We buzzed south, tracking the shoreline until the island
curved away. Too soon, Victoria became choppy, and showed itself
for what it truly was, a troubled freshwater sea, bigger than all but
America's Great Lakes. The swells slapped and pounded the boat
from every direction. My left side became soaked, and my body
went cold as I tried to shield my old Nikon from the spray.

I pulled the nylon camp shirt from the plastic sack and, pride
draining with the last of my body temperature, buttoned it to the
throat, pulling the collar up around my neck. The crew, I noticed,
were wearing insulated hooded windbreakers over their bare backs.
Clouds blocked the sun, the wind picked up and I began to feel I
might as well be in a dinghy off the coast of Corsica. Or Greenland.
The swells were pushing five feet, slapping the boat at three-second
intervals. They drove my stomach somewhere near the bottom of
the lake, thirty-five feet down; bile shuffled up from those depths
to my gullet in a slow queasy two-step. Was it my imagination,
or was the water striking my side more than Schon's? I watched
him—contented, interested, comfortable—with murderous eyes.

The boat grinned forward and all evidence of land, that there had ever been such a thing as land, disappeared. One hypothermic hour later Frank cut the motor and we were instructed to move from our shared bench to the two fore positions. As Frank and the mate began feeding out the net, the sun finally showed itself, and the saliva jets came on, priming a backward pump. I slipped off my glasses and bent at the chest over the side and cast my tea, bread and tiny kernels of dried corn into Lake Victoria. "You feel bad?" Frank said.

"He's fine, just a little seasick," Schon said brightly. "You see, he's just not used to the water. Gotta get his sea legs," he said, with extra burring gusto on the "sea." I wiped my mouth and beard with a handkerchief, rolled back onto my bench and tried to breathe my eyes, ears and stomach into agreement. "Hurling like a supermodel," Schon chuckled. "That's all right. I've spent a lot more time on the water than you. Fact, went out on my brother's boat, the *Talley-Ho*, just last week. An oldie but a goodie. Goes forty miles an hour and pulverizes the kidneys in just five minutes. So we go to the Outer Banks, and I hook a beauty of a mackerel, and at the last second, just as I'm reeling her in, a shark comes and takes half of it. Big shark. Anyway, just keep your eyes open and your head up. And try to focus on the horizon. That's about all you can do. You'll be fine."

The men continued doling net into the lake, orange cord suspended by the cork, blue cord weighed down by the milk bags, forming a barrier that would stretch more than a hundred yards through Africa's great lake. I tried to fix my eyes on the sky and gave another retch. "Here," Schon said. "You need to eat. Get something in your belly." He pulled a Ziploc bag out of the yellow plastic sack and tore off a piece of peanut butter and honey on brown bread. "I really don't," I said.

"Just try a little," he said, and I did. It was drier than a gravedigger's callus, drier than Kalahari sand, drier than the queen's perm. It was the driest food in the world. I washed it down without chewing, the Nalgene plastic stench burning my nose. "No good will come of this," I said.

Water poured into the boat from several unplugged seams, including a quarter-inch gash at Schon's feet. Frank tossed me a cut-down cooking oil container and gestured to the growing pool. I bent down to bail and the horizon rocked even more as I dipped the container into the swaying boat and dumped the water. Again I went over, sending my sandwich into the lake, feeding foam to the Nile perch, tilapia and tiny silver *dagaa*. Between gasps, I could hear the clicking of my best friend's digital camera. "Now that's what I call chumming," he said with a laugh, as I prayed for some rare freshwater shark to break the surface and relieve him of his arm. "That's enough," Schon said as I heaved away. "I mean it, that's enough."

"I don't really have a choice."

"You do. Take it from me. I used to be a drunk. There's a point where your mind can take over. It's mind over matter." I thought perhaps a change of vantage would help and so I half rose and half crawled toward the left-hand side of my bench just as a thick swell struck the boat. It rolled hard, nearly capsizing, the port-hand gunwale brushing the lake surface. "Whoa!" we all shouted and I lunged back to the right where I belonged. "Sorry about that," I said, resetting myself as Frank glowered, the first mate avoided my eye, and Schon smiled in wonder. "Man, you just about did it. Just about put us in the drink."

It took about an hour for Frank and the mate to finish paying out the net. They took turns with the paddle to keep the drifting boat broadside to the wind, staying perpendicular to the net. Then the first mate crawled forward and, standing in the bow, lifted and threw the anchor—a gunnybag full of stones—over the side. The rope whipped after it for a very long time. Whatever the official water readings, this slice of the lake seemed miles deep. Now it was time to wait. We shifted places again: me at the rear, on the left; Schon at the next bench, on the right; Frank in the middle; and the mate at the front, where he stripped to his undershorts and began washing his clothes against the wooden hull.

The iron gray sky had burned away, replaced by a poisoningly clear sun and a few cotton-wadded clouds. Slumped against the side, my ears and stomach swimming in mercury, I watched the clouds for ducks, woodpeckers, Varga girls, antelope. Exhaustion pushed me low into the boat, but the deeper I slouched the more difficult it was to focus on the horizon, which disappeared every two seconds with the rhythm of the lake. The tardy sun bored through my tinted lenses. I pulled my hat low and squirted more SPF 50 onto my face. Dreams came—short, detailed, intense narratives that ended with each new jostle. I was aware of my hands and lips warming and then cooking in the daylight. It was a comfort. A white heron with a long pointy beak and the palest of yellow eyes, sensing no threat whatsoever, landed on my calf and stayed there a moment before moving on to a solid wooden perch near my feet. "Please don't crap on me," I said telepathically, and the heron answered, "No promises." While I had my sickness to keep me company, Schon was left alone to look at the sky and the lake and at me and Frank and the mate. His eyes darkened with boredom as the hours slowly lapped by. "I wish I'd brought a rod out," he said. "At least I could pretend I was doing something."

After the mate had finished his laundry and laid his slacks and shirt on the side to dry, he and Frank shared a pot of stew that had been tucked under a small alcove at the prow and had somehow remained untoppled through the chopping waves and my near-capsizing. Then the mate lay down on his back in the bilge and went to sleep. At about 6 p.m., seven hours after we'd left the island, they started bringing in the catch. The first mate stood and hauled up the anchor and then the nets. For forty-five minutes he pulled, bringing up perch after perch. While the fish grew to more than five feet, none of these was longer than fifteen inches—evidence of overfishing that had reduced the lake's stocks by more than half. Each perch had its mouth open, with an enormous swollen tongue protruding between upper and lower fangs. They appeared to be smaller than the legal limit. The Nsazi fishermen were, as the Ugandan government later put it, "especially notorious in fishing malpractices." There were a few catfish in the nets as well. The mate, with biceps like mangos, broke their dorsal spines against the side of the boat, the sound oddly affecting, before throwing them in a separate pile, for the local market. Frank took over the net work, moving slower than the mate did, and after another forty-five minutes they were done. Frank ripped the motor to life and we throttled back toward Nsazi as the sun dipped into the western horizon. We motored in the refreshingly cool moonlight while low clouds advanced from the east. "Sonny," I told Schon. "I think we're gonna make it."

"I do believe you're right," he said. "My ass has never hurt so bad. It's beyond pain. The whole ass just gave up about four hours ago, shut itself down and tried to fall off." At this the motor sputtered and died, and Schon's eyes widened into yellow orbs of panic. "You did this, Morrison. You had to jinx us. Now we're gonna have to sleep out here."

Frank tried rip-starting the engine a few times and then peered into the plastic fuel bottle and found it empty. He and the mate had no choice but to paddle the boat home for two hours as the clouds gained on us, their mass lit up by trapezoidal flashes of lightning. We crunched onto the stony beach just as the rain started to fall in earnest. I tipped them 500 shillings each, took the gear and stumbled back to the shack for an hour of coma while Schon went in search of a meal. "How you feeling, boss?" Schon said as he came in.

"Much improved," I murmured, eyes closed. "Though I could use a toothbrush."

"I went to the place we were at last night. They were serving this guy liquor in a plastic bag. Some local moonshine."

"You didn't."

"Oh, I didn't. But it was interesting."

"It's waragi, banana hooch. Or millet. Or cassava. Whatever's around," I said, sinking back to sleep. "Sold by the bottle or the bag. They drink a lot in Uganda. More per capita than anywhere. More than Ireland. More than Russia. I had thought waragi was a local take on arak. That when Samuel Baker led the Egyptians down here in the nineteenth century they brought their own booze, and the Ugandans adopted the name. It's raki in Greece, arak in Turkey, Syria and Egypt. Waragi sounded like a reasonable adaptation. But it's not."

"Of course it's not," Schon said. "You think these people can't have their own name for booze? They need to get it from Egypt?"

"Not from Egypt," I replied, grateful for not having been an Egyptian conscript sent away from home under British command to claim central Africa for the khedive. "England. The local name, the original name, is *enguli*. During World War II the Brits down here were cut off from the motherland and they couldn't get any more Gordon's or Plymouth. So they made do with the local hooch and called it 'war gin.' War gin became waragi. You know," I added, "I think I've had my fill of Lake Victoria. Let's just start this trip at Jinja."

"You suffered like a champion out there," Schon said, switching off his flashlight. "Not one complaint. I'll be sure to mention that when I'm showing the pictures around."

CHAPTER THREE

A chainsaw," the bartender was telling Schon. "This is a weapon of mass destruction."

He swabbed the dark wooden counter with a rag, pulled open the clouded glass door of the refrigerator behind him, grabbed two Nile Specials and set them down in front of us. He'd popped the caps along the way, with the speed and invisibility of a cardsharp; a cool mist rose from the sweating bottles, just like in beer commercials the world over. "And I'll tell you this," he said. "A net isn't much better."

"What's that?" I asked, looking up from my map and notebook. "Chainsaws?" We'd been in Uganda for weeks; my initial burst of confident activity had curdled to boredom and dread as we waited for the boat to be built. My mountain of Ugandan shillings was eroding, and my fancy digital Nikon had dropped dead, fried by a bad battery. Its replacement, a small Canon point-and-shoot, had cost $700, twice the going rate in America. Told our craft would be finished in a matter of days, we left the comfort of Claire's rooming house and Kampala's hilly suburbs for a campsite on the Nile's eastern bank a few miles north of Jinja. But the boat refused to be ready, and our stay at the campsite had stretched to nearly a week.

The bartender poured drinks for a tattooed couple from Wales and turned back to Schon. "Nobody had a chainsaw when I was a boy. The forest had always been there, it was vast compared to a little village, and nobody thought a forest could ever run out of trees. My father sent me to university in Kenya, and my eyes were really opened. When I came back to Uganda—my father took sick and I am the eldest—I tried to tell people that the forest isn't forever, that there is an end to it, that others have seen this end and now they are suffering. But the village didn't hear me. My family didn't hear me."

A white movie screen hung from the ceiling, and a heavy-metal soundtrack accompanied clips of helmeted thrillseekers crashing over the Nile rapids in big orange rafts, as lifeguards paddled around them in fleet kayaks. Like Uganda's forests, the rapids too would soon disappear. A new hydroelectric dam was slated to be built on the Bujagali Falls, just north of Jinja, altering—or erasing—the whitewater. The adventure operators suspected new rapids would appear farther downriver once the new dam was raised, but no one knew for sure if this would happen. It was a small price, the authorities said, for beefing up Uganda's power grid; the country was still producing the same amount of electricity that it had in the early 1960s.

But the bartender's mind was on more weighty matters than the possible demise of recreational rafting. "It's the same on the lake," he said. "Fishermen just won't believe that Victoria can be overfished, even when the evidence is in their nets. My brother is a fisherman. He waved me off when I tried to tell him. In the early eighties my father and another man were the only people in the village with money. Only their boats had motors and they could go deeper into the lake and catch more fish. The others all rowed. Today, almost everybody has a motor. And the fish are nearly gone.

Mass destruction. They cleared the forests on the Ssese Islands for palm plantations. Now Museveni has given the Mabira Forest to Asians so they can farm sugarcane. And they wonder why we are in drought."

Late next morning, Schon and I took bodas into Jinja in search of paddles for our still unfinished boat. The driver slowed as we approached a group of small boys—the oldest was maybe eight—gathered on either side of the dirt road. They were using their hands to pack soil into some of the deeper ruts, and they raised a thin, knotted clothesline across our path—a symbolic roadblock—and called out for tips. The boda drivers roared over the string and kept going, as Schon turned back in his seat for a last look.

"I guess those kids we saw back there don't go to school," he said as we settled into a table at a café on the sleepy town's main street. "They're just starting universal primary education here," I replied. "It's going to be a while before it reaches the whole country."

I ordered "river chips," slices of fried liver, while Schon went with the more conservative eggs and hash browns. "This coffee," he said, looking at his mug with raised eyebrows, "is strong as lye. You could clean an engine block with it." My chips came promptly, still sizzling in their basket, but Schon's eggs appeared to have been lost. We read old copies of the *Monitor* and *New Vision* and watched the bicycles and bodas churn up dust on the nearly vacant sunny street.

"I've got a lead on where we can get our paddles," I said. "The night watchman at the campsite says there's a fishing village on the lakeshore, just a couple miles south of here. It'll make a nice walk."

Schon set down his crossword. "A nice walk. You know I have the hip sockets of a seventy-year-old. Anyway, I'm not going to be in any shape to go anywhere if I don't get my eggs. Miss?" He waved to the waitress. "Do you happen to know where my eggs are?" She looked at him without speaking, and Schon said, "Eggs? Breakfast?" The waitress turned and pointed without speaking to the counter inside the restaurant, on which sat a large white plate. "Are those mine?" Schon said. "Can I have them, please?" She left and returned with the plate, which held two now cold fried eggs and a pile of cold oily potatoes. Schon looked at her with dull anger, shook some salt onto the eggs and cleaned the plate without speaking, daubing the last bits of ketchup with crusts of thin white toast.

"You all right?" I said. "We'll find a good lunch someplace. Don't worry about it."

Schon wiped the corners of his mouth, tossed the paper napkin onto his plate and tapped out a Camel, lips pursed like he'd eaten a lemon. "I came here in part to figure out why things are like they are. I mean, you invited me and I came, and maybe I'll actually get to fish one time. But I wanted to know why things are different." He lit the cigarette and looked at the street. "It's because of the people. Things are different here because the people are different. Not the environment, or the weather, or the geography or anything. The people. If things are going to be better, you have to want them to be better. I'm not sure I see that. They seem to be fine with the way things are. And so, I guess, they're fine. Why do foreign people try to come in and impose on them to advance technologically, economically, medically, morally, whatever, when they just want to be peasants? Or maybe the way to put it is: They are peasants, and they don't have a burning desire to be anything more, or anything else. Maybe 'more' is the wrong word."

I squirmed in my chair. "That's quite an assessment to come out of one plate of cold eggs," I said. "This place has had more war than countries ten times its size. Wars tend to set you back."

"Come on, Morrison. People should live how they want, not how other people—richer people, well-intentioned people—want them to. I just think, from what I've seen, that Ugandans seem to like how they're living. And yes, it's a way that results in me getting cold eggs in a restaurant where the total number of customers is you and me."

We walked through Jinja. The colonial city of factories, mills and breweries had become all but a ghost town after Amin expelled the Indians. Leaving town we passed a dead railroad spur and descended into a rough and dirty fishing village, a more advanced and prosperous version of the one we'd visited on Nsazi Island. There were more stores, more toddy shops, more restaurants. It appeared to traffic not only in fish but in five-foot-long burlap sacks of charcoal, presumably a product of Victoria's myriad and rapidly deforesting islands. The shops sold netting, hooks, line, floats, big and bulky life preservers that would be far too hot to wear on the river, wood caulk and small-gauge nails, but they didn't sell paddles. After half an hour of walking up and down the forty-yard main drag, we found an old woman with three hand-carved paddles, each different from the other. They were about five feet long, hewn out of planks and cut down to teardrop-shaped blades with long rounded handles. She would part with them, a young boy said, for 15,000 shillings.

"Fifteen seems high," I said. "What about seven?"

The old woman was under five feet tall and was built like a fireplug, with a blue kerchief on her head, an ankle-length brown dress and plastic flip-flops worn thin as leaves. The corner of her wide mouth held a stubby unlit corncob pipe. She stood fast.

"She says she want fifteen thousand. That's all she take."

"Eight?"

A few words flew in Luganda. "Fifteen."

I was impressed. Schon and I each lit a cigarette, and we looked at the paddles and looked at the ground and looked at the ground some more and we didn't speak. I examined my Sportsman cigarette; they burned quickly. As the ash raced toward the filter I

looked at the old woman, then at the paddles and back at the cigarette, and a few more words of Luganda were exchanged. "She will
agree to eleven thousand," the boy said.

"Marvelous." We carried the three heavy paddles back up the
hill and walked again into Jinja, collecting stares along the way.
"Well done," Schon said. "Your hardball tactics have saved the
mission a dollar and a half."

That evening at the campsite, during a meal of pepper steak,
rice and beer, I received a call from Richard Landy, one of Cam
McLeay's lieutenants. The boat at last was ready. We toasted our
turning luck and I left the table to gather our laundry from the
campsite's clothesline in the mosquitoed evening light. Schon was
gone, probably in the washroom, when I returned. Next to the
overfull ashtray and four empty beer bottles, his notebook lay
open. *I promise and swear that I don't think it's a stupid thing
to do,* he had written. *But I can't stave off a sense of foreboding.
Please don't let us turn that goddam boat over. Please don't let us
turn that goddam boat over. Please don't let us turn that goddam
boat over. Please.*

At eight the next morning, Landy picked us up in a yellow Isuzu
flatbed truck. We sat with him in the cab and drove north to the
work site at Kalagala, where our boat lay on its side in a puddle.
Our handsome craft was made of double layers of one-inch plank
board and it was about twenty feet long, three feet at its widest.
The wet planks were horizontal bands of light brown and yellow.
Strips of tin and rubber were glued and hammered over some of
the wider seams. The keel was a length of hand-hewn four-by-four,
and the prow had been carved into the rough shape of a keystone,
the better for tying up. Nearby lay the ruined craft Cam McLeay
had first offered us and another new boat, this one covered in a
blue tarpaulin.

A crew of men arrived in another truck and a dozen of them
lifted our boat and slid it onto the flatbed, stern first. I doled out

cash to each of the hands while Schon smoked a cigarette, and then we got back into the cab with Landy and set out for our launch site, downriver of the cruelest rapids. Landy was talking about how he got his name (he drove the company Land Rover), about the time Prince William had come with a few friends to shoot the rapids ("A very fine man; he treats everyone equally"), and about possible repercussions of the Bujagali Dam ("Frankly, we may be screwed"), when Schon looked at his watch and said, "Damn. We're even ahead of schedule." I smiled, content. The Nile waited to carry us north from its source, off the grid and into freedom. A heartbeat later the Isuzu started sputtering and knocking, and Landy cut the engine and pulled over. He pulled a lever and tipped the cab forward to reveal the engine underneath. We had broken an injector bolt. Our ride was over.

We waited by the side of the road while Landy hitched a ride back to Jinja on a passing motorcycle. There were four or five houses nearby, enough to provide a dozen children who gawked and asked for money and posed and shone for Schon's camera. An older girl, maybe fourteen, bald and in a yellow dress, stopped in front of us and asked, "Can you give me money? I am an orphan." I gave her a few shillings. "Nice," Schon said. "Now we're gonna have a whole village of orphans coming to us for your bleeding-heart money."

"Yeah," I said. "You're probably right." But no one else approached.

We split a pineapple and drank from our water bottles and three hours later Landy reappeared in another Isuzu truck, with more men. They backed the new Isuzu up to the old and transferred the boat and we set off again and made five minutes of progress before Schon realized we'd forgotten the paddles. He and another man went on bodas to collect them and we all met an hour later at the launch point, a mud flat descended from dense scrub where the water was wide and shallow and calm. Landy drove part of the way down and we carried the boat to the water like pallbearers. We loaded our bags, stepped inside, and they pushed us onto the river before an audience of children in threadbare clothes, Schon in the rear seat piloting, me near the middle, water at my feet. Why was there water at my feet? Maybe the seams needed to swell. That was it—the timbers would swell, and that would seal off the water. I was still in my boots; there hadn't been time to change to sandals.

I gripped my paddle, left hand at the top, right hand near the middle, and dipped the blade into the water, just like when I was a boy at Camp Berry in the eighties. And so we slid away. Very soon, we were alone on the silent river, paddling down the middle of the Nile, arcing toward one bank and then the other. Dense scrub ran to the shore, interrupted sometimes by plots of maize and other crops. Hyacinth clung like plaque to the riverbank and forests of papyrus began to appear as well, tall green stalks, each topped with a thick pom of fine green threads that shimmered with rainbow hues.

It was nearly four in the afternoon in late September. I was wearing what would become my basic uniform for the rest of the journey: green work pants and a dirty camp shirt with too many pockets. A Leatherman tool and a nylon camera case hung from the right side of my black leather money belt, with three hundred dollars inside the hidden compartment. On my head sat, embarrassingly, a flaccid-brimmed bush cap that a tailor in Kampala had made for me after we'd found none in the markets. My boots—my boots were wet. "We're sinking," I said. It wasn't true, but water was filling the floor at a steady rate. I could actually see it rushing in through several seams and cracks. "Take it easy," Schon said. "Every boat takes on a little water. Lean up there and open my pack. I got a present for ya." Squeezed under the top flap of his rucksack was a yellow plastic cooking oil container. "God, that's great thinking," I said. "You've saved us."

"Thanks," Schon said. "Picked it up when we went back for the paddles. Better'n using our hats. So don't just sit there. Bitch seat gets to bail." I cut the top off the bottle, scooped out two inches of water and resumed paddling. The boat felt solid, steady. The river itself was slow; the clear water offered no help. We moved with the illusion of speed under long tufted clouds and light blue sky. Fish jumped and preened and splashed at every turn, mocking Schon and his arsenal of rods and lures. "You wanna skip lunch?" I asked. "Make up for lost time?"

"Fine by me. I'm just glad to finally be on the water." He sang Willie Nelson, tweaking the lyrics:

On the road again,
Drinking Miller, smoking killer
With my friends . . .

Within forty-five minutes we reached the first set of rapids, shards of white cascading down what appeared to be a shallow descent. We pulled the boat over to the eastern bank and evaluated. "It doesn't look like much," I said.

"I know," Schon said, squinting. "I think we shoot for the middle there. The water looks faster on the sides. Whatever you do, just keep paddling. You don't want to fight the current, just keep some control when it takes you. Keep paddling. You've been on boats before, you know what to do."

"Well, in the Boy Scouts."

"That's the last time you paddled a boat? The Boy Scouts?"

"Wait," I said, searching my memory as we bobbed in the hyacinth. "There was another time. Yeah, my honeymoon. We went out on the lake in Central Park. There were turtles basking in the sun. And a stork."

"A stork. Really? Can we do this now?"

We did, shooting the rapid with much splash and paddle,

dodging half-submerged rocks, cutting through the rough waters and reaching the calm with hardly a drop of doubt.

"Now that was fun." I laughed. "For all the leaking, this boat is rock steady. I want to do that again."

"And we will," Schon said, not laughing at all. "According to Cam, there's another set ahead of us. If you'll recall, he also told us to drag this monster overland." I had forgotten that. Still, we'd easily passed the first test.

We soon reached the next set of rapids and even in the distance it looked another species. We paddled to the western bank and drove the boat onto a sandbar. Schon got out, waded through the hyacinth and climbed some boulders for a better look. Ten long minutes later he was back. "What do you think?" I said. He frowned and ran both hands up over his forehead and down his scalp. "Let's go out a little so you can see what I'm talking about." We paddled a few yards into the river and stopped.

"You see that shit right there?" Schon said over my shoulder. "We don't want anything to do with that."

"What shit?"

He raised his paddle out of the water and jabbed it in at a band of livid white that stretched nearly from bank to bank forty yards downriver. "You don't see that white sploshy mess, right there? We gotta go around it. So we're gonna cut across to the other side and go into that roundabout there, that eddy, and hopefully the current will let us past the worst of it. There's a gap, about twenty feet, that looks calmer, and that's what we're aiming for. The main thing is, we don't want the boat to get turned sideways. Whatever happens, keep the boat straight."

We drove hard across the river, aiming for the gentle pool that would ease us around the angry rocks and broken current, a polite evasion of the riot next door. We hacked at the water, digging deep, and the quiet Nile became loud and then deafening as the river at first nudged and then hurled us off course and dead into the whitewater. The boat started to spin and rock in the three-foot chop, soaking us and the gear. I paddled in reverse to try to point the nose forward, to no effect, and within seconds the boat was thrown sideways down the rapid, a five-foot drop, landing beneath the rocks with a tooth-rattling thump. Water poured into the boat as we spun counterclockwise and glanced first off one boulder and then another. The water, surprisingly cold, bit at my calves and still more crashed in as we ricocheted through the foam and roar.

I thought, *We're going to lose our stuff.*

I thought, *My wife will be angry when I'm dead.*

I paddled harder, looking for calm. "Hit the bail," Schon said. "Hit the bail!" We were riding low; the water inside now approached my knees. I grabbed the plastic bail and started flinging water overboard while Schon straightened the boat and piloted us past a last boulder and into mellower waters. We paddled hard for a minute and then let the becalmed river take over. Schon stretched out his legs and pulled out a pack of Camels. He plucked out four in a row and dropped them overboard until he reached a dry one, and then felt around for matches. I took a lighter from my shirt pocket, shook the water out and flicked the wheel. We drifted like that for a while, Schon dropping a stroke here and there to keep us in the middle of the river, while I flicked and flicked the lighter until the flint dried and it finally produced flame.

At dusk we came upon puzzling signs of modernity: a clearing on the right, cement pylons rising like stairs from the muddy shallows, and, suspended across the river a hundred feet in the air, two steel cables. "What do you suppose that is?" I said.

"I don't know," Schon said from behind me. "Looks like a ski lift, almost." We beached the boat and I walked up a rocky embankment to a grassy hillside in search of someone of authority. I found him in Pamba Luca, the local watchman. "Of course you can sleep here," he said. "You have nothing to worry about. I am just leaving, but you are welcome." The site, he said, was a Nile measuring station operated by the Ugandan government. The stairlike pylons we had seen were marked at centimeter intervals, but the water level was lower than the lowest hash mark. The steel lines supported a capsule-shaped cable car that was presently moored to a metal tower fifty yards back from the river's edge. "That," said Luca, "has not been used for some time."

We pitched the tent in the grass and changed out of our wet clothes. As a light rain drummed on the nylon roof, I devoured a can of sardines in oil with some Ritz-like crackers manufactured in the United Arab Emirates, saltines being all but unknown in Uganda. Schon ate half a can of processed chicken that recalled nothing so much as dog food. "You know, I'm tempted to celebrate our survival with one of those Johnnie Walkers," I said. While a full-length mirror was not around to confirm it, I was sure my body was rippling with newly defined muscles. I felt lean and strong. "At this rate," I said, "I don't see why we couldn't paddle this thing all the way to Karuma Falls. We might not even need an engine."

"Riiiight," Schon said, bending the metal lid back over the uneaten portion of his canned chicken. "We'll see how you feel in the morning, when your body's had time to consider the day's abuse."

I lay down, passed out instantly, and dreamed I was editing news stories on an old Atex machine, rewriting crime briefs on a tiny green screen, before the dawn of the Internet.

The dream ended abruptly: There was someone outside the tent. Many voices, several lights bobbing in the darkness through the wall of the tent. "Hello?" I called out.

"We are the LC."

The LC? Local Council? Last Chance? "Just a moment." I dressed, grabbed a flashlight, unzipped the oval nylon door and stepped out. Seven people, including the deputy district chairman, were gathered around the tent. Two held dim old flashlights; one carried what appeared to be a rectangular paraffin lantern that glowed like an anemic firefly. "We are from the LC," the only woman said. "Luca has told us of a visitor. We must give the approval. We must register you." They had all, including a club-footed man named Ibrahim, walked miles in the rain to fulfill their civic duty and vet the strangers on their shore. I shook hands with each, and showed them my Ugandan press card and my old New York press card and my old Indian press card, and then found my Egyptian press card, and at this critical mass of identification they were satisfied. Someone pulled a guestbook out of a plastic shopping bag and I signed for myself and for Schon as a storm of moths and other insects, drawn by the intense white beam of my flashlight's LED bulb, blocked my vision and filled my mouth and nostrils and ears. "So very good to meet you all," I coughed. "Thanks so much. Thank you."

I woke up slowly to rainfall and the voices of two men talking in the distance, followed by the now familiar sound of bailing, the scrape of plastic against wood, followed by weak splash—scrape, pour, scrape, pour. I squinted, as if that would improve my hearing. "Are they bailing our boat?"

"I hope so," Schon said.

I pulled on my green rain poncho and went out for a look. Two men had just finished bailing a fifteen-foot dugout canoe. I called good morning to them and to a small girl who stood at the water's edge in a too-big canvas mackintosh, the cuffs turned back to her elbows, the hem at her ankles. She held a yellow jerrican in one hand and a plastic soda bottle in the other. Sent to fetch water, she lingered now by the river's edge watching the drizzle. The fishermen apparently were waiting for the rain to stop. A few minutes

later it did, and they were on their way. Our departure would take
a bit longer. I changed back into my soaked pants, put on a dry
shirt and bagged the rest of the wet items.

Luca appeared with a few boys while I was bailing rainwater
out of the boat. They helped me load the gear while Schon struck
the tent. "Luca," I said. "Have you ever seen the river this low?"

He pushed back his straw hat and folded his arms over his sweat-
shirt, a purple number that showed the silhouettes of three men on
snowmobiles under the slogan "Snow Fun." "I have worked for the
water ministry since 1982. I have been on measuring expeditions
all over Uganda—Masindi, Karuma, Nimule, Arua. It was a privilege to be taken on these journeys with the engineers. But I missed
my village and my family. So I asked my boss and he made me mea-
surement officer here at Mbulamuti. Now I am happy."

"And the water level?"

"The river has never been this low."

We were standing beside the bow of the now packed boat.
Schon tapped out a Camel, his first of the day. "Do you smoke?" I
asked Luca, and he said no, just as Schon let out a burst of hacking coughs. "I'm glad to hear it," I said. We shook hands again,
bade goodbye to the crowd of boys and pushed off. Soon after, I
pumped and sterilized some river water, bailed the leaky bottom
and started paddling. We pushed for several hours, slowing when
we saw fishermen in their dugout canoes, twice reversing the boat
after we were snagged in their net lines.

"Man, I would kill for a country ham and egg biscuit from Bis-
cuitville," Schon said. "I get that with hash browns and a Mountain Dew, because I've already had my coffee at that point."

Late that morning I saw a six-foot fan of ripples emerge from
the water's ice-smooth surface far ahead of us. For a moment it
appeared the ripple was advancing on the boat like some kind of
river beast. It was, for a second, unbearably peaceful, transport-
ingly strange. Only at the last moment, as the pace of the river

suddenly quickened, did the trap become visible in the clear water. "Rock!" With an awful crunching sound and a lateral shake we were pinned sideways by the river against a barely submerged yellow boulder embedded with tiny pocks of green algae.

"Are we whole?" Schon said. "Did it crack?"

I looked down and felt around the floor and the right side. "Everything's smooth," I said.

"Well thank God for that." We started to pry, or try to pry, the boat off of the rock, but it was no use. The paddles would have splintered—they were no match for the cumulative weight of the river. "I'm going to get out and push it," I said.

"No-You-Are-Not," Schon replied.

"Fine." I wedged my paddle between the boulder and the boat and tried again, putting as much of my weight on it as I dared while Schon churned the water with his paddle.

"I'm getting out," he said.

"What's the difference?"

"What?"

"Between you and me," I said. "Why are you getting out?"

"First of all, I'm stronger. And my seat's in the back, so I can push her off and still have time to get back in once she's free."

Yeah, I wanted to say. *But it's my boat and my trip, and if one of us is going to drown it probably should be me.*

Instead, I said, "Do it."

Schon eased himself out of the boat and crouched on the rock, water racing over his ankles. He gripped the right side with both hands and started to push. I sat on the left side of my bench and flayed the water while Schon rocked and pushed the gunwale for ten minutes until the boat abruptly slipped away from its snag and glided off the boulder. Staring forward, afraid of striking another rock, I heard a thump as Schon jumped in behind. We were away.

"God as my witness," I said. "I'll never make fun of beer muscle again."

Over time it seemed we were wasting effort. Two people paddling seemed only slightly faster than one. We were looping down the river, wide arcs that were, I felt, adding miles to our journey. I paddled at a nearly regular pace on the right side while Schon hit the left. He would switch to the right to compensate when we went off course, but it seemed it was always two or three strokes later than it should have been. There were enough clouds to keep the sun from being oppressive, but already there was a sense of sameness, a sort of visual tinnitus: flat water, hyacinth and papyrus—forevermore.

Around eleven-thirty, just as Schon started making noises about lunch, we spotted a landing site on the western bank of a wide curve in the river. We drove for it, and what appeared to be the roofs of at least half a dozen huts. It seemed to take a long time, but soon I could make out a line of women doing laundry on the beach. To their immediate left, men were clearing a twenty-yard stretch of land, whacking away the papyrus with pangas and burning the plot's two trees. We nosed into the landing site to a chorus of laughter from the women as they bent at the waist, slapping laundry against the water. I walked up the bank and bought five orange-sized fried dough balls and a couple of Cokes. The man who'd escorted me into the village then asked if I would buy him a generator. Back at the boat, Schon was buying two pineapples from a boy. He paid 1,000 shillings, about fifty cents, and the kid's face lit up.

I was in the pilot's seat now. "I actually prefer riding bitch," Schon said. "Less thinking involved. You can actually let your mind wander." We pushed off and the boat immediately started looping across the water. "I resign my commission," I cried, but soon enough I got the hang of it, aiming the key at a distant point and holding to it with two or three strokes on the right and then one or two on the left. We never once had the wind at our back—only dead water and headwinds bearing down for hours and hours, as Schon bailed the boat and pumped drinking water. It was actually easier to pilot alone, but it wasn't nearly as fast. The front seat was the muscle, the rear provided direction.

Around four o'clock, Schon suggested we find a place to make camp. "It gets dark so fast out here—I don't want to be caught on the water when it happens," he said. We'd been paddling slow through extremely shallow water, two feet deep and dead still. On the eastern bank eight hundred yards away, we spied what appeared to be a tall cement pier or bulkhead, and behind that houses, proper houses with a distinctly industrial look. "I think that's Namasagali," Schon said.

I disagreed. It was an old commercial farm of some kind, I said, not a town. We would waste an hour getting there that we could spend driving for the real Namasagali. "It's the only example of man-made anything we've seen since lunch," he said. "Now, I love our little boat, but I don't want to have to sleep in it."

We paddled slow and careful through the shallow water and beached the boat just north of the concrete bulkhead, a ten-foot-high wall rising from the banks of the Nile. I walked up a weedy slope, past a rusted steam-powered crane sitting on grass-choked double rails, toward a small cinderblock house that in America might be found inside a state park—a seasonal residence for rangers, or a bunkhouse for scouts or teenage cadets. I knocked on a green wooden door and waited. It opened just enough to reveal an inch of pale face, punctuated by a faded blue-gray eye. "Oh, good afternoon," the sliver said. The door opened wider to reveal Simon Downie, warden of Namasagali College. He pushed up his bifocals. "You'd better come inside."

He was a left-behinder, a British teacher who had refused to escape even during the worst of the Idi Amin years. "I don't have a good answer as to why I remained. I suppose I was curious as to how things would turn out," Simon said after serving us tea inside his book-filled living room, the coffee table covered with old magazines and yellowed correspondence. "Darling," he called over his shoulder, past the kitchen into what I assumed was the bedroom. He got up and went into the room. "They're journalists, from America." His muffled voice had the tone of a parent to a recalcitrant child or, as I surmised in Simon's case, a husband to an annoyed wife. "They've come down from Jinja in a canoe."

Simon returned. "She's just finishing her meditation. In time I came to see there was more for me here than in England. I've got a sister, and that's about it. I've been here at Namasagali more than thirty years, been deputy headmaster, headmaster, vice chancellor and now I'm the warden." He pushed his bifocals up the bridge of his nose and pulled a guestbook from the drawer of a maroon credenza. "Our enrollment was once quite high. We were away from most of the fighting during the difficult years and the campus was seen as something of a haven. We're mainly a teachers' college these days. Now that the country has stabilized we have many fewer students and fewer resources. Jon Snow, surely you've heard of him, from Channel Four, used to teach here. He's a real friend of the school, he came last year for a report on malaria and in January with a load of donated bed nets for the villagers. I want to show this campus is still important, that it is of interest to important people like Jon Snow, like yourselves." He opened the book and held it out, and I dutifully filled in the blanks and passed it back after tucking two of my business cards inside.

"I remember other Nile travelers," Simon said. "There was a group that came up from Egypt; they had run into trouble in Murchison Park. And, years ago, in 1987, a Swiss kayaker came here, out of his mind from the sun, really far gone. He stayed a few days and went on. They found his traveler's checks in Arua and his clothes in Nimule, but he wasn't seen again."

We tied up the boat and carried our bags down the campus's neat dirt paths to an empty dormitory building, tipping the grounds-keeper on the way. While Simon was a high-ranking administrator, he needed the groundskeeper's cooperation to shelter us in the dusty abandoned dormitory, where scavengers had made off with the drainpipes and the flagpole had to be kept under lock and key.

Simon led us on a tour of the peaceful campus—apparently we had arrived between terms. The small windowpanes of the chemistry lab were broken; the supply shelves had been cleared of whatever the thieves could reach through the bars. Elsewhere, the corrugated roofs were rusting; the whitewashed concrete-block walls were peeling and turning brown from the rain and humidity.

Still, that which could be achieved through labor, like landscaping and other basic maintenance, seemed to have been accomplished. Money was missing, not industry. The buildings needed paint; broken windowpanes went unrepaired or were replaced by scraps of wood. As we walked through the campus, past the dingy library and the orchards and the parade ground, I could almost see Simon's old students leaving the morning assembly for class, the girls in red dresses, the boys in their white shirts and khaki shorts, good kids sent to this oasis for a structured and humane education away from the brigandage and gunfire. The school's motto was "Strive Regardless."

A notice from the headmaster posted to a bulletin board a month earlier addressed "GRAZING OF ANIMALS (CATTLE, SHEEP, GOATS) ON SCHOOL COMPOUND."

> I wish to bring it to your attention that Village community neighbouring Namasagali College have made it a habit to bring their animals, especially cattle, to graze on the school compound and the orchard garden. The animals are doing a lot of danger to the school in the following ways:

—they make the compound dirty with cowdung

—they destroy newly planted trees and flowers

—they eat clothes, soap etc in students dormitories
and teachers quarters

Let this letter act as a warning to those who bring
animals in the school compound.

Animals arrested will be tagged with the school farm
yellow tag and kept on the school farm.

Please let the village community be informed always
in local council meetings.

The college was founded in 1965, three years after Uganda's
independence, by the Mill Hill Missionaries, a British Roman Catholic order. The campus was the former headquarters of the Busoga
Railway. "The steamers from Masindi would land here and the
freight would go down to Jinja on rolling stock," Simon told us.
"There was a chain of ports and railroads connecting Mombasa
with the Congo and Sudan. But it all disintegrated quite quickly
with the floods of 1962, and then of course the years of fighting."

Simon led us through the campus into a nearby village for a
beer, and back down to the steam crane on the shore. "We used to
hold student regattas here, the different houses racing each other,"
he said. "All kinds of competitions. The boys would swim across
the river and back."

Clouds the color of steel pressed down on us. I could see thun-
derheads across the river and, behind them, small panes of orange
sunset. Three boys were wading in the river to the left of the bulkhead, where they pushed yellow jerricans beneath the surface and
then lugged the heavy containers home.

When we stopped at Simon's the next morning before setting
out, his wife came out of the bedroom to greet us. She was a Ugandan academic, attractive, much younger than Simon and barely

friendly. She held in her lap a copy of Els de Temmerman's *Aboke Girls*, about the mass kidnapping of 139 girls from a Catholic boarding school by the Lord's Resistance Army, and thrust it at me soon after we sat down. "Do you know about the abductions of the LRA?" she said. "If you are going to the north, you should educate yourself and pursue this subject. I suggest you read this book."

"I'm familiar with the subject," I said. The LRA, led by the enigmatic Joseph Kony, had turned much of Uganda's north, traditionally the country's breadbasket, into a wasteland of refugee camps, fallow fields and army checkpoints.

"Have you read *Aboke Girls*?"

"I haven't. I was in Gulu and Kitgum last spring, and I visited a couple camps. I even met some of Kony's wives."

"Victims," she shot back. Most girls in LRA custody became forced concubines.

"Victims, absolutely, unquestionably," I replied. "Though they do refer to themselves as his wives." So too did members of their community, often without pity for the horrors these girls had been through.

"Would you like some more tea?" Simon interrupted. "Darling, perhaps you'll put on more water while I show them the medallions from the old Egyptian Irrigation Department."

For decades in the late nineteenth century and the first half of the twentieth, Britain had controlled the White Nile through its colonial rule over East Africa and its de facto control of Egypt. Egyptian engineers like the hyacinth-slayers Schon and I met outside Kampala had been preceded by Britons who'd set up more than a dozen measuring stations along the river. Mbulamuti, where we'd spent our first night on the Nile, was one such station. Britain's interest was more than scientific: The Nile fed Egypt's cotton crop, much of which found its way to British textile mills. The medallion Simon produced had been pried off a dead piece of port machinery.

It was an iron oval cast with the letters "EID" at its center and a serial number, 800, stamped below, a tiny relic of empire.

We made a cool getaway from our genial host and hauled our bags to the boat. It was exactly where we had left it, looking good, with a few inches of rainwater on the floor. Something was different, but I couldn't put my finger on it. Schon came down the hill with his backpack and fishing case. "Shit," he said. "Somebody stole our rope."

"Who were those wives you were talking about? This the same guys that shot up Cam's group?" Schon asked, pumping and zapping fresh drinking water while I paddled the boat.

"Same outfit," I said. "The Lord's Resistance Army. They've been fighting since Museveni took power. A lot of the northern tribes had backed the losing side—Museveni is a southerner. Near the end of the war in 1986, some of Museveni's allies raided the northern tribes, stealing tons of cattle, basically taking their collective savings. So the northerners lost power and they lost their wealth and they were petrified of being wiped out in revenge for earlier massacres."

"Payback's a bitch," Schon said.

"Exactly. So out of this panic comes these spiritual movements that combine local religion with some warped ideas of Christianity and the one that survived was Joseph Kony's group, the Lord's Resistance Army. The LRA said they were fighting for the Acholi tribe, but when the Acholis didn't support them, they started going after their own people—mutilations, looting, that kind of thing. But their signature is kidnapping children, mostly children, and turning them into fighters and slaves. The girls become sex captives. We're talking more than twenty thousand people abducted."

"And then those kids kidnap other kids? Is that it?" Schon said.

"Worse," I said. "Some are forced to kill their parents, or to kill their brothers or sisters. The LRA owns them after that. And get this: They think Kony has superpowers. I talked to some guys—adults—who'd been kidnapped and escaped and they believed Kony was still watching them. Even talking about it made them nervous. They thought he could kill them long-distance."

Kony had taken dozens of girls as his concubines and forced the "marriage" of thousands more to his officers and soldiers. I was on an assignment for an American newsmagazine when I met a few escapees at St. Monica's, a church-run boarding school in Gulu, a depressed northern city located fifty miles off the Nile. Evelyn Amony had been kidnapped at twelve and became a nanny in Kony's household. Three years later, he informed her she would be his next wife. She was beaten by cadres with long bamboo poles when she refused, and soon enough she agreed. Evelyn bore Kony three daughters before she escaped with them in 2004.

Evelyn's story contained within it echoes of the centuries-old conflict over the identity of the people of the Nile Valley. She lived with Kony in Juba, in southern Sudan, where the Islamist regime provided the LRA with protection and weapons, a reprisal against Museveni for his support of the rebel Sudan People's Liberation Army. Evelyn's oldest child was born in an army garrison in Juba during a visit to the city by Sudan's president, Omar Hassan al-Bashir. Bashir, she said, stopped in to congratulate Kony and was given the honor of naming the baby. He called her Fatima, for the Prophet Mohammed's daughter. After Evelyn escaped, the nuns at St. Monica's renamed the girl, christening her Bakhita, for the patron saint of Sudan, a slave from Darfur whose story has sharp resonance for Sudan's black Christians. Captured by Arab raiders in the late 1870s at the age of eight, Josephine Bakhita was sold into bondage, forced to convert to Islam and was resold four times at slave markets in El Obeid and Khartoum before finding refuge with the family of an Italian diplomat. In 1896, she joined the Canossian Sisters, an order of nuns in Venice, and she was canonized in 2000.

Before her death, Josephine Bakhita said that, given the chance, she would thank her captors and tormenters because their actions had led her to Christ. I doubted the girls I'd met at St. Monica's would ever say the same thing.

"So this LRA business has been going on for twenty years and nobody's stopped it?" Schon asked. "That, in my book, says somebody in charge just doesn't care enough."

On this, our third day on the Nile, the river grew wider and deeper, but the current remained just as slow, the wind just as relentless. The receding shoreline made me uneasy. The river wasn't just broadening; there were floating islands of papyrus and hyacinth to paddle around, and inlets that dead-ended into backwaters indistinguishable from the river's free-flowing channels. There was a fat one on the map I had taken to calling "the Abscess," a three- or four-mile eddy that I feared getting lost in, though I couldn't tell how far downriver it lay. At noon we paddled to the side of the Nile, nudging the boat against the papyrus that choked the shore, and shared a can of tuna and some crackers. "You know where we are?" Schon asked.

"Nope."

"Any way of finding out?"

We took a GPS point off the satellite phone and tried comparing the reading with the faint lines on my tourist map. "I think we're at the first 'I' in the Victoria Nile," I said, about forty miles south of Lake Kyoga. "No way we're reaching Kyoga today."

"Where are we gonna bunk tonight, then?" Schon said. "We'd have to hack through this papyrus just to get to land—that's a day's work right there. And god knows what's in the water waiting for us while we do it."

"We could tie up to the papyrus and sleep in the boat."

"You know my feelings on that," he said tersely.

"Let's just keep pushing and see what we find."

I smeared more sun cream onto my cheeks and forearms and feet, splashed water onto my pants to keep my legs cool and cleaned my eyeglasses with a lens cloth from my shirt pocket. We drove on for hours, singing Warren Zevon songs to break the boredom. I talked about my hero, the writer Murray Kempton. Schon talked about his, the horror director Rob Zombie, and all the while my paddle grew heavier, and my muscles, which had felt like coiled pythons the day before, revealed themselves as useless sleeves of cement.

With dusk approaching we found ourselves a lonesome mile from either shore when Schon spied something moving in the distance. "Get the binoculars," I said.

He pulled a small pair of field glasses from my raid pack. "It's a boat," Schon said. "Bigger than ours, maybe twice as big. It's got people in it. And a bicycle. It's ferrying people across." He lowered the binocs. "That means there's something on each side." We aimed for that spot and then looked to each shore. To the west we could make out what appeared to be a small settlement—a handful of small corrugated steel roofs. I squinted through the binoculars to the east and saw real buildings, smaller than those at Namasagali, sitting above a crowded landing site. "Maybe it's an old way station," Schon said, "an old cotton port or something."

Squinting further, I could make out two-story brick buildings. "Dude," I said, "this could be a real town. Maybe they've got Indians. Indian food, a real hotel." I hooked us to the right and we pushed for an hour against the wind. But as we got closer the proper brick buildings disappeared from view. The town's landing site looked different from all the others we'd seen. It was wet. No dry red earth or pebble beach, no stores or shops, just a collection of boats nosed into black mud and deep green vegetation. We slid onto shore, but the keel never scraped land. I stepped out of the boat, and onto nothing solid; my foot sank into muck.

The women here were laughing, wailing, at our arrival, in a

tone different from what I'd heard in other villages. It sounded like they were watching a cow escape slaughter, only to be run down, tied and butchered. We sloshed through the muck onto land and asked where we could find the village chairman. No one seemed to speak English. The spongy ground gently rocked with the pace of the river, and I felt a hint of vertigo. "This is wrong," I said. "What's wrong with this place?"

"We're standing on pad," Schon said.

"Pad?"

"We're floating."

A large fishing boat landed and six crew members got out. They ignored us and started down a path through a jungle of papyrus and hyacinth. I followed them into the village across a hundred yards of sponge, stepping where possible on solid papyrus roots, some of them arm-thick. The track appeared to have been cleared by machete and trampled flat by use. My village of two-story hotels had been a mirage. This village, Ksike, was made up of a few one-room brick shops, a pair of tired wooden restaurants and a welter of mud shacks and driftwood homes.

The local chairman, whose name was Hazrat, showed me a patch of dirt where we could pitch our tent. I asked for two boys to help with the baggage. "How much will you pay them?" Hazrat asked. I offered two hundred shillings each and then reoffered at five hundred, mindful of the growing darkness. He agreed and passed me to the care of Yusuf, a local man who lived nearby. I gathered the two helpers and we walked back to the boat in pitch darkness. The boys, eager and utterly familiar with the route, got far ahead of me and I lost track of their footsteps. Twice on the way I broke through the pad up to my ankles, each time pulling my feet free against a giant wet suction.

Twenty feet from the boat I really broke through, a solid stomp that plunged my right leg past the knee into warm and gritty protosoil. I pulled back, clenching my foot to keep my sandal on as a passing local took my arm and pulled. I knew I could escape if I left the sandal behind but I was unwilling to surrender it and so kept my toes and foot flexed. He pulled and pulled and finally my foot came free, bringing with it a splash of black slime that hit my Good Samaritan square in the eyes.

"Sorry, thank you, sorry," I said, and offered my arm in a stupid gesture. He made a disgusted noise and was rid of me. Schon and I loaded our two helpers with baggage. I leaned down to check the floor of the boat for loose gear and when I looked up again the boys were already away. I grabbed my raid pack, the food bag and my boots. Another boy, one we hadn't seen before, strapped on Schon's backpack. Schon grabbed the paddles and his own black bag. "Is that everything?" I asked.

"Yeah," Schon said, walking gingerly, with speed, to keep up with the last boy. We left behind a bag of bananas that had been floating in bilge, and the last of our pineapples, tucked into the bow, dry. Twenty-five steps later I was again thigh-deep in pad. I pulled out, got onto my knees, and reached back into the hole down to my shoulder to recover my sandal. The soil was wet, warm, scratchy, filthy, alive—the quick of creation. We got to the village and I tried in the dark to pick our two helpers out of the gathering crowd. I found them and gave them a thousand-shilling note to split. "Where's the other guy? I asked. "Where's the other guy who helped us?"

"That's me," said a man in his forties.

"No it isn't," I said, a little too seriously. "Where's the third guy?"

"It's this guy," Yusuf said with a laugh. "He just made himself young for the job." I never saw the kid again, and if we did and didn't recognize him, he never asked for a dime even though two of his neighbors had been paid a swamp king's ransom.

"You got the water bottles?" Schon asked.

"I've got my bottle in the food bag. I thought you said we had everything."

"I thought you had both our bottles," he said. "You know it's not going to be there in the morning."

I went back for the bottle while Schon pitched the tent, passing two groups of people cautiously making their way from the landing site while carrying bags, babies and two bicycles. One man broke through to his green khaki hip and pulled himself out with barely a hint of annoyance. I crashed through twice more and entered the village cursing and hating. My legs and arms were covered in black granular slime. Schon stood outside the tent, handing out Marlboros to the congregation. "Can I get one of those?" I said, and quietly smoked, a filthy scarecrow pitched outside an orange-domed tent.

We asked Yusuf where we could buy a jerrican of water. "I will give you," he said. Schon went inside to change his clothes while I smoked and tried to relax, gently pushing aside children so they wouldn't be burned as they crowded the tent four deep trying for a look inside. Yusuf returned with a jerrican and asked, "Do you have drinking water?"

"I have a filter. We'll pump it straight from the can."

"This water is not fit to drink," he said. "Although some do." He disappeared again and returned with a cold sixteen-ounce bottle of boiled water. I passed it to Schon through the zippered door and he filtered it out of caution and handed me my bottle of peppermint soap. Yusuf led me to a bathing spot thirty yards away, behind a hut. "You can step here," he said, pointing to a white flat stone. I took off my tan nylon shirt and laid it on the ground, squirted soap into an orange basin and tried washing my feet. Impossible. I took off the undershirt and washed my arms and face, put the undershirt back on, and carried my camp shirt back to the tent. "We need more water," Schon said.

"I don't think it will be forthcoming," I said.

"We need more water," he repeated.

"Yusuf," I said, "can we have more water?" He paused, took the empty bottle away and came back with it half full.

Schon left to wash while I went inside the tent and, staying near the doorway, emptied my pockets, tossing the squeeze bottle of Purell and a wad of Ugandan cash toward the back, then changed into shorts. Surveying myself in the torchlight, I saw my feet were still black. I did the best I could with Handi-Wipes, slipped on a pair of dirty socks to keep from fouling my sleeping bag and promptly passed out.

"Where are your sandals?" Schon asked.

"Outside," I said, asleep.

"Not for long."

I sat up and pulled them inside. "You know," I said in the quiet, "when I kept falling through, all I could think was, 'How can people live like this?' And then I realized, they can live like this because they have to. They have no choice. They live as they must."

"They do so have a choice," Schon said, suddenly angry. "Of course they have a choice. Bunch of guys could get together and dig up a bunch of dirt and fill that fucking bog. Stone Age tools. You cut that shit down, you get everybody together and you carry dirt from the town and you fill it in. Human beings been doing it for thousands of years. They'd rather come home and fuck off."

I woke up to rain followed by bright sunlight, radio, roosters, children singing, the silhouettes of children clumping around the tent like gnats on a lantern. I slept some more, stirred and changed into clean underwear, khaki shorts and a cotton long-sleeved shirt—no point in fouling two sets of pants in this hell-swamp. After a Luna bar breakfast ("Nutrition for Women"), I left Schon to strike the tent and found Yusuf rolling chapatis in one of the restaurants. "Yusuf," I said. "May we give you a gift?"

"Yes," he said, avoiding my eyes. I handed him one of the crank-charged flashlights, which also, I learned, could be used to charge mobile phones. He suppressed a grin and said a demure thank-you and went back to his work.

We walked in safety back to the boat. In the daylight the route was nearly free of hazard. The bananas, the pineapple and—curses—the bail were all gone. Schon went back to ask Yusuf for a new one and returned with a sixteen-ounce container. I said good morning to a group of young men sitting on the side of a large boat to our left, two of them wearing brilliant white-collared dress shirts. It was a paradox that would endure over the next thousand miles: People were cleanest in the dirtiest of places. I handed out three Sportsman cigarettes; the boy first in line tried to pocket them all until I made him share.

We paddled our asses off, past exhaustion. I made a wrong turn out of Mudville, and we became snared in the Abscess, wasting an hour of time and undernourished effort. My contribution was all but limited to maintaining our course while Schon kept us moving, scraping his paddle's long wooden handle along the side of the boat in a steady labored rhythm. The heat came, and the sun. I never changed into my long pants and collared shirt—the boat was too unstable. By the time we broke for lunch, the map said we had paddled twenty-five miles, but it felt like fifty.

The Nile opens wide at Lake Kyoga, wide enough for us to waste hours on another wrong turn, paddling through two-foot waves, zigzagging around floating islands of hyacinth, wildgrass and even shrubbery, on which white herons sat like jealous monarchs.

The only consolation for the painful monotony of chopping against the elements was the sight of others doing the same thing, though the local craft seemed lighter than ours. These were lake boats, uniformly painted a weathered green, with registration numbers on their sides. When at last we rounded the final point and officially entered the lake, we came upon groups of naked men hanging off their boats as they bathed in the shade of the woods running to the water's edge. Two canoes approached and passed us, paddled by strong men who stared at our piles of gear.

Closer to the landing site, women and girls stood in the lake, dresses tied around their thighs, as they fetched water and washed clothes. My gaze lit upon a small girl, maybe ten or eleven, struggling to submerge a jerrican half her size; she covered her pubis with her hand as we passed. Then came the landing site. We sliced through shallow dark water, ignoring the hoots from the shore, and nosed between two canoes. "Not here. It's not safe," a man in a mauve shirt called out. "Put the boat over there," he said, pointing farther down the eighty-yard beach. Schon got out without speaking and, waist deep, pushed the boat away and pulled it by the prow to the appointed spot. He looked like a refugee. As I stepped out of the boat, the man said, "I am the police. I am the OC in this village. Identify yourself and state your business here."

The OC, or officer in charge, was tall and strapping. To his right, shorter and with a fuller belly, was Ronald, the village chairman. They engaged in a brief skirmish for possession of the two *mzungus*. "It is not safe to camp here," the OC said. "You can put your tent at our barracks."

"I will help you find a hotel," Ronald said.

Schon looked from the cop to the politician and said to me, quietly, wearily, "I don't want to sleep at the police station. I'm just not comfortable with that. Go with the other dude. We don't need the police."

I thanked the OC for his offer and said to Ronald, "Let's take a walk."

He led me to his office, a bare shack on a cement foundation at the far end of the landing site. "Sit down," he said, presenting the guestbook. I squatted on a tiny bench, low and narrow as if made for small children, the only furniture in the room besides his wooden desk and chair. "I would like very much to help you so that your visit is a pleasant and safe one," Ronald said. "As you can see, we are a very poor village. Do you want to make a contribution?"

I said I would, once our arrangements were set, and this satisfied him.

We walked down the dirt main street of this town of seven hundred people, past a sign announcing a Ugandan-German roads project, past a gray disintegrating colonial-era cinema hall and down a tight alley into a splay of bandas and wooden shacks. We reached two gray stucco buildings, each with eight doors facing a narrow courtyard: Ronald's chosen hotel. "It is the best in Bukungu," he said.

The proprietress, Zenya, was sitting in the dirt while a man and a woman on stools wove red extensions into her hair. Ronald said something to her in Lusoga, and she got up without a smile and opened the padlock on a room. It was an unpainted cell, seven by seven feet, with a single barred window, wooden shutters and a corrugated steel roof. With her hair half in tight braids, the other half a chaos of black-and-red frizz, she reluctantly agreed to add a second bed as long as I paid for two rooms.

Schon had pressed two boys into service, and they arrived pushing our gear in wooden wheelbarrows the locals used to porter jerricans of water into town from the lake. "Good man," I said. "What are we paying these guys?"

"Three hundred each," he said, about fifteen cents apiece.

I emptied my pockets and found nothing but a sweaty fold of 10,000- and 20,000-shilling notes and two coins, a 500 and a 100. At the sight of the bankroll, the older boy decided to renegotiate, and there followed a bitter, mutually incomprehensible argument, during which his younger colleague kept a hopeful silence.

Ronald intervened and ordered the boy to give *me* four hundred. "Now," the chairman said. "Give him five hundred and you'll be finished."

"But that's only a hundred," I said. I pointed to the smaller kid, barefoot and in tattered slacks, whose eyes moved from me to the chairman. "And what about him?"

"He doesn't matter. He is satisfied."

"But it should be equal."

"He is satisfied. Don't worry about him."

I tried to make it work, and failed. Ronald ordered the boys back to the lake. We gave him his "contribution," 10,000 shillings, and I locked up our room.

We left our unsmiling innkeeper for one of the town's three restaurants and had an exhausted meal of chicken, yellow sweet potatoes, beans, rice and two Cokes each. Prepared food had never tasted so good. Back at the hotel, we piled our gear against the door (it had no latch) and slept like dead people.

We would linger in Bukungu for three days of recovery. Schon was in especially bad shape. His hands trembled when he lit his cigarettes. His pen trembled when he scribbled in his notebook. He moved like a sloth to breakfast our first morning and, unrefreshed, moved like a sloth back to our lodgings to sleep until evening. While he snored on his foam mattress and surprisingly clean sheets, I took the room's water jug, a towel and my shaving kit and walked past the scattered condom wrappers and empty waragi bags to the hotel's backyard for some overdue ablutions. "Good morning," I said to Zenya, who sat on a stool in the shade of the courtyard peeling a bucket of potatoes. She didn't answer. I unhooked the wire latch on the outhouse door, pulled it shut behind me, unbuckled my belt and squatted over the fragrant pit. As I balanced there, trying to keep my Handi-Wipes from falling in, I watched through the flies and the gaps in the plank wall as Zenya came out the hotel's back fence door, stepped over a trash-filled puddle and entered the bathing enclosure next door to the latrine. There she hiked her skirt, sank to her haunches and pissed like a racehorse. The stream gathered between her feet and ran under the door and into the trash puddle outside. She stood up, let down her skirt and walked back to the potatoes. I decided to hold off on bathing for another day or so.

We had seen, standing out among the fleet of wooden crescents at the landing site, a fiberglass boat with a big Evinrude engine. It belonged, Ronald said, to the marine police who patrolled Lake Kyoga. After a full day of torpor Schon and I mustered the strength to investigate. The corporal from the marine police was reading a five-month-old copy of the *New Vision* when we knocked on his open door. His unit was unconnected to the police camp where Schon and I had been offered camping space, and he dropped the newspaper in surprise as we walked in. I explained that we were looking for passage to Lwampanga, forty miles away, across the Nile on the western corner of Lake Kyoga. "Our boat is too small for these waters, but we're thinking you could tow it." The corporal squinted and pored over my map in his darkened office. He nearly sniffed it as if he were, for the first time, face-to-face with a graphical representation of his navigable world.

"Lwampanga is another district," he said. "It will cost two hundred thousand. Fuel charges are very expensive." He took the map to the back door to examine in the sunlight. "No Kayago, no Tomba," he said, frowning. "This is not a very good map." I had feared this: Our map was decades old. Sites that had been important in the 1960s were no longer notable. New towns had risen or had taken prominence.

Teasingly, I asked, "Can I see yours?"

"I don't have a map," he said, ignoring the bait, "but I know where everything is. I am the OC at this station. Acting OC. The OC has gone to the Darfur."

"Gone to the what?"

"He has gone to Darfur, in Sudan."

"Ah, I was in Darfur in February," I said. "I saw many Ugandan police and soldiers there with the African Union." He wasn't interested, and was probably cursing the OC's luck in scoring a good international stipend.

"I just can't pay two hundred thousand," I said.

"Good luck to you," he replied, watching his lottery ticket blow away.

We found passage across the lake to Kayago, thirty miles away, on the northwestern shore, on a forty-five-foot vessel commanded by the owner's fourteen-year-old son, Ashraf. The boat was painted Islamic green and declared in foot-high white letters, written across the hull, "CALL ME WHAT YOU WANT—ALLAH KNOWS MY NAME." Instead of towing our craft, Ashraf ordered it raised out of the water and set astride his ferry's eight-foot beam. Younger than the other crewmen, he called the shots and counted the money.

Some of the other passengers made camp in the shade of our boat as we crossed the water under open blue skies. I used the occasion to inspect the bottom and sides for cracks and found many, circling the bigger ones with a pen, including a nail hole that went clean through both layers of plank. "Hey," I said quietly as I dug through my bag for a tube of Shoe Goo. "You notice how many Muslims we're meeting on the water?"

"Nope."

"I'm telling you, compared with Kampala, compared with Jinja, it seems like every other person we meet here is Muslim. What's up with that?" I squeezed adhesive into the nail hole and moved on to some of the bigger gashes.

"Well, why do people take on one religion or another?" Schon said. "It's usually because someone tells 'em to."

It made sense. The Philippines didn't become Catholic through the gentle persuasion of the Word. And most African Americans were Protestants because it was the religion of the people who'd enslaved their ancestors. But while Arabs had conducted slave raids in eastern Africa for much of the nineteenth century, they didn't conquer Uganda. Perhaps these Ugandan Muslims' forebears had converted in the late 1800s, when expeditionary forces from Egypt came up the Nile to claim the region for Cairo. An Egyptian soldier garrisoned in a heathen land thousands of miles from home would likely take a local wife. Even if she didn't adopt Islam, their children would be born Muslims; it was a patrilineal religion.

Ashraf, our lanky young captain, sat reclined on a crossbeam in a red Sean Jean jersey, wide-legged blue jeans and a worn straw hat held tight to his head by a black chinstrap. He watched the horizon in laconic satisfaction. Someday, all this would be his.

From Kayago we made a short hop by ferry to Lwampanga, the last major village before Lake Kyoga and its smaller northern neighbor, Lake Kwania, tapered off and the Nile resumed. Our boat was lashed alongside for this journey and loaded with sugarcane and a foot-pedal sewing machine.

In Lwampanga we established a base near what passed for the center of town and went looking for a man and a motor. One hundred and fifty kilometers downriver was Karuma Falls, where the Nile made a steep descent into Murchison Falls National Park, a 23,600-square-mile preserve of elephants, buffalo, hippos, crocs and lions reclaiming their territory after three decades of rampant poaching. We hoped to take our boat, with a hired motor and pilot, north to Karuma and then travel southwest by bus to the city of Masindi, the sole launching point for expeditions into Murchison Park. Once there, I would rent a boat from the Wildlife Authority to take us downriver from the spectacular Murchison Falls to Wanseko on the shore of Lake Albert.

This plan was contingent on a lot of things, the first being the notion that we could find someone willing to slap their Yamaha onto our boat. We'd met a pleasant, circumspect man named Surolou Bosco on the trip from Kayago who thought he could help. "I am a pilot," Bosco said. "I will speak with my employer."

We were staying in a two-room suite with metal spring beds located next to a small general store and a pair of toddy shops. Schon's room opened into our landlady's dirt yard and the shacks where she and her extended family lived. Mine opened onto an unpainted porch where, each day, a barber set up shop with a straight razor, a mildewed shaving brush, a small gasoline generator and a pair of electric clippers.

At three minutes to six on our first morning there I woke to pounding on Schon's door. "I am Bosco. Alo! Alo!" It didn't sound like Bosco. Confused, I opened my own door, found no one there, and lay back down. I got up again, walked to Schon's door, realized I was still in my underpants and went back to dress. Schon meanwhile extricated himself from the tangle of his mosquito net and answered the summons. Towering over the doorway was a man I didn't know, and standing behind him was Bosco. I pulled a swallow from my water bottle and dragged three stools into Schon's room.

The big man sat. "I am going to Kampala now," he said. "I need money, two hundred thousand." It was the same fee the marine corporal had asked in Bukungu.

"You're going to Kampala?" I said, groggy.

"Kampala, yes. I need two hundred thousand."

"What is your name, sir?"

"I am Lutalo Joseph. I am the owner of the boat."

"So you want two hundred thousand. That takes us where?"

"Two hundred thousand. Bosco will take you."

I pulled my document bag out of the raid pack. "Let's go in here," I said, and spread the map on my bed. I pointed out a possible route. "Lwampanga to Maiyuge. That's two hundred thousand? It seems like a lot."

Lutalo Joseph stared at the map in the same way the marine police corporal had, nostrils flaring at the sight of it. He held firm on two hundred thousand. I said to Schon, "So a deuce will get us to Maiyuge, near Masindi Port," the Nile crossing where steamers had once dropped goods and people bound for the city of Masindi, twenty miles inland.

"Ah!" Joseph said. "It is near Masindi Port!"

"How much to get us to Atura, here," I said, holding the flashlight with one hand and pointing my pen with the other. It was twice the distance to Atura, located just south of Karuma Falls, as it was to Maiyuge.

"Three hundred thousand."

"So Bosco will take us and our canoe to Atura for three hundred thousand."

"Yes, three hundred thousand."

"What if I give you my boat? A trade. An exchange."

"No change. Three hundred thousand."

"But what if I leave my boat with you, to keep? It's a new boat, built just last week." There followed a long conversation between Bosco and Lutalo.

"I don't want a boat," he said. Was that beer on his breath? "I want money."

"But it's a beautiful boat," I said. "Bosco will tell you."

He laughed. "I need money, three hundred thousand." He left to make a phone call and then poked his head through the door. "I have to leave and will return at nine tonight." And then he and Bosco were gone.

"What do you think are the chances?" Schon asked.

"I don't know." I yawned. "Pretty slim. We'd have to pay him with a hundred-dollar bill, with the balance in local cash. I don't even have the sense he understands where we want to go. And there's no guarantee he won't come back here asking for a million dollars, or for a house in Hollywood. I'll tell you something else. All those meat dinners and Cokes are catching up with us. We're probably down to sixty thousand shillings, maybe less. Nobody's going to be able to change dollars in this burg. It looks like we'll be getting by on beans and chapatis until we can find some more shillings." I yawned again. Talking about money made me sleepy.

We never saw Lutalu again. Over the next four days we wandered over and back through Lwampanga looking for a way to continue our journey on the river. I went to see the local Beach Management Unit—each village on the water had one to regulate the fishing trade—and explained our plan to its chairman, Hassan Keto. "Find Bosco," he said. "There are many motors in the village, but very few skilled mariners."

"We met him," I said. "Bosco is good. Bosco is serious."

"He is more than serious," Keto said.

"His employer appears to be serious about different things," I said, and Keto nodded.

We were sitting on lawn chairs under a big shade tree drinking black sweet tea. Keto and his colleagues gathered for a sidebar and then he turned back to us. "You can leave your boat here and we will take care of it for you. You can take it when you come back."

"But we're not coming back."

"We will care for it while you're gone."

Schon and I walked glumly back into town, past the village square—an intersection of dirt roads—past our hotel and the gas station with its two hand-cranked pumps, to our favorite restaurant. "The thing is," Schon said, "I like those guys. It's too bad they're trying to take our boat."

That night I got a call on my cell phone from Lutalo Joseph. The price to Maiyuge was now 400,000 shillings, he said, about $170. "Joseph," I said, "I'll walk to Maiyuge before I pay four hundred thousand." Every dime counted: There wasn't an ATM or a credit card machine for the next two thousand miles; our purse was finite. There would be no motor excursion down the river. It was time to cut our dear boat loose.

The next day Schon and I walked the length of Lwampanga town looking for a buyer, ignoring the children as they screamed *"mzungu!"* at the sight of us. "You know, I can't help but feel a little miffed when they shout that," Schon said. For lunch we sat at the crossroads drinking Fantas and smoking and watched big trucks rumble into town to pick up loads of iced fish for market. The village was a collection point for fresh tilapia. Ice came up from Kampala in giant plastic containers. Fish were caught in the lake, packed and shipped out. But the trucks, I noticed, were heading west out of the village, toward the relatively poor Masindi, not south to Kampala, the country's biggest city and its biggest market for food and produce.

This detail vexed me nearly as much as the problem of the boat. As Schon and I watched another lorry drive into town from the landing site and turn onto the western road, I grabbed a thin gray-haired man as he walked past in three-quarter pants, an oversized Milwaukee Brewers T-shirt and flip-flops. "Excuse me, sir," I said. He stopped and looked up from me to Schon with curiosity and maybe a pinch of fear in his watery eyes, the dark brown irises waning to blue. "I'm sorry to bother you, but do you know where those trucks are going?"

"They go to Sudan," he said, and added, "They take fish."

"To Sudan?"

"To Gulu, and then to Sudan, to Juba," he answered. "You are here to buy fish?"

"God, no," I said. "Sudan. That's odd."

"There is money in the Sudan now. That is what people say. They buy fish. And vegetables." I had heard complaints in Kampala that food prices had more than doubled. Juba, newly infused with foreign aid dollars, appeared to be vacuuming up Uganda's produce.

"Are you a fisherman?" I asked our informant.

He lowered his eyes, bashful. "I am a painter. A housepainter. I am Albino." Albino was nearing fifty and looked past sixty. I didn't imagine there was much work for a housepainter in Lwampanga, or any other village in rural Uganda. We invited him for tea and he declined and carried on to the east side of town.

There wasn't much in the way of consumer goods in Lwampanga, or in any of the other tiny towns we lit upon. The little wood-and-brick shops sold two varieties of dried beans, cassava flour, maize flour, strips of rubber and tin for sealing boat joints, nylon rope and sometimes some monofilament netting. Also soda, and candy bars, and lots of laundry detergent, as well as shoe polish, tooth-paste and hair extensions. There were two sizes of paraffin lamps, both fashioned from tin oil cans, that used clothesline for a wick. One of these, a tiny lamp the size of an inkwell, was blown from my windowsill onto the porch early one morning as I slept. It was gone by eight when I went to retrieve it.

Over four eternal days in Lwampanga we were repeatedly mistaken for missionaries ("because most of your tribe, when they come here, it is to preach God's word") and for fish buyers ("because most whites, when they come here, it is to buy fish"), but no one seemed to take us seriously as boat sellers. There was no mystery why: The banks of the lake were crowded with boats, many of them rotting in the muck. Our craft, a twenty-foot river canoe, was insufficient to its location. The local boats were bigger, more seaworthy, and could hold larger crews and more fish. Still, I couldn't bring myself to abandon our trusty launch. "I paid nearly three hundred dollars. The wood is worth at least a hundred. Not that I want her cannibalized."

"Seems wrong to ditch it," Schon said. "Feels like we'd be losing and someone else would be winning. I don't know who that is, that's just how it feels. So I've been thinking: Why don't we give it to the poorest fucker in town, who we both just happen to know?" That night, by flashlight and candle, Schon wrote out in block letters a fake bill of sale that transferred ownership of our boat to Albino for the princely sum of 1,000 shillings and we both signed it.

We walked in dusk and light rain to the "nice" section of town, stopping to chat with Hassan and the others at the Beach Management Unit. Fifty yards later we were on the outskirts. I asked a man walking by for help, and he led us two hundred yards farther outside town and then down a path to a settlement of twig huts. Clouds were moving in, dark clouds that blotted out the moonlight. "Wait," he said. The man pulled a wooden chair over and ran to a nearby hut to bring another. "Sit." He then spoke through the door of the nearest hut and Albino came out blinking in the dark.

"Albino," I said. "Schon and I are leaving early tomorrow, and we can't bring our boat with us. Would you like to have it? It's smaller than the lake boats, but I'm sure you can use it somehow. It would be our pleasure for you to have it."

He said the clearest words of our short acquaintanceship: "Yes, please."

Schon presented the bill of sale. "It says a thousand but that's fake." Albino nodded and smiled. We told him where the boat was beached and he nodded as if he already knew.

Pats of heavy rain started cratering the dirt. We took a few photos and did a round of handshakes and made a quick exit. As Schon and I fumbled down the dirt path, Albino and our guide broke into happy congratulatory laughter. Schon smiled. "Let's hope this one goes unpunished, at least for the next twelve hours."

We packed and after a fitful sleep I got up at four-thirty and walked out the back door, past the chicken coops and the padlocked

latrine, to piss against a tree bracketed by two snoring black hogs.
I tiptoed back through the mud, mindful of waking the swine,
and went to the crossroads to secure us seats on the morning taxi
out of town, the first in a chain of minibuses that would take us
to Karuma. Two Hiace taxis were parked against a shop at the
edge of the square, but there was no sign of life. I smoked a couple cigarettes and watched the overbearing congregation of stars
and the light of a high-flying jet. It must be making for Nairobi,
I thought, or maybe Johannesburg. But the blinking plane didn't
seem to advance. It moved but it did not progress. Was I misseeing?
I tried to measure the aircraft's progress against another star, and
another, and another. It was, I realized, a satellite in geostationary
orbit, forever falling behind and catching up to its assigned position in the heavens.

The Karuma Falls sent the Nile crashing over fifteen feet of rock, a
noisy if humdrum descent compared with the great falls of Africa,
so unspectacular that the British explorer Hannington Speke—
the first to declare Lake Victoria as the source of the Nile—didn't
even bother to name it for one of his illustrious countrymen. Still,
the eternal turbulence of the water sluicing through its ravine had
a hypnotic quality and the memory of our fearful dousing that
first day on the Nile was still fresh. From here, the river flowed
into Murchison Falls National Park, where Cam McLeay's team
had been ambushed by the Lord's Resistance Army the previous
year. The power of that moving water hadn't escaped the government's notice. There were plans to build another hydroelectric dam
at Karuma now that security had returned. We watched the Nile
rumble for half an hour and then picked up our bags and hiked the
two-mile trail back through fields and bush to the road.

Karuma town was nothing more than a strip of shops and vendors where buses and mutatus traded passengers. The falls still

roaring in our ears, we walked to a restaurant and fell into conversation with Ali, the proprietor, over a lean piece of chicken, a
chapati and black tea served in deep red melmac mugs that read in
familiar white script, "Coca-Cola, Vladivostok Bottling Co."

Ali said he was from Arua near the Congo border. Arua had
boomed during the 1990s, when Uganda's army invaded its cha-
otic western neighbor and looted untold millions in timber and
diamonds—this while the LRA was wreaking havoc on Uganda's north. "I came here fifteen years ago," Ali said. "Karuma was
nothing then." Schon raised his eyebrows at "then." Ali had had
four wives and sixteen children, not counting the six who died as
youngsters. "I'm so sorry," I said, wincing at the magnitude of his
loss.

"It was a long time ago," he said, puzzled by my concern. "Are
you married?" he asked. "How long?"

Six years, no children, I told him, adding, "But that will probably change next year."

"How do you know?"

"What?"

"How do you know it will change? It is on God's hands."

"Well, some practices will start and others will stop," I said.

He gasped. "It's wrong. You are killing the eggs, the sperm."

"You know," I said, "the female body ejects its egg every
month."

"Yes," he said, gripping the table's edge, "but the sperm! They
must move freely. You mustn't hold them back. It's murder!"

We crept our way west in a series of minibus taxis. At Masindi I
received a depressing call from the Wildlife Authority: The Nile
was low inside Murchison Park; their boat was grounded. Transport into Murchison would cost two hundred dollars, with no
guarantee we could leave by water. I scratched the park off my

itinerary, and we kept moving overland through Biso, Bulisa, Wanseko. These rides ranged from cramped to apocalyptically, dangerously uncomfortable. During one six-hour segment, Schon and I were packed with twenty-nine other people in a minivan with a maximum capacity of sixteen. "We are human beings!" an aggrieved man shouted as passengers twenty-six and twenty-seven were stuffed aboard by the driver and his two helpers. We banged along the road, the sweltering van's sliding windows—closed for the dust—rattling in their tracks. Schon and I were seated over the rear axle, packs on our laps, a howling infant to my left, her mother using one arm to brace against the seat in front of her while the hungry baby tried to nurse and was thrown off the breast with each new impact.

Still, the countryside was beautiful. "All the landlocked amenities," Schon marveled. "Mountains, hills, plains, savanna, rivers, forest. Real nice. The bigger farms are pretty too, pretty as any I've seen. Even the villages are cute—from a distance."

Two days after leaving Karuma, riding almost comfortably in the front of a Hiace van, we left the plateau of central Uganda and descended into the Western Rift Valley. Here the sun felt kinder, the air smelled cooler and soon the steely surface of Lake Albert came into view with the Blue Mountains of the Congo rising up on the other side.

We crossed Lake Albert in a wooden boat—the government-operated diesel ferry was grounded in its berth due to the low water level—and were stopped by Michael, an officer from the police Special Branch, when we stepped onto the beach at Panyimur. The village was just miles from the Congo border, and Ugandan and Congolese troops had recently skirmished in a growing dispute over who owned the oil that had recently been discovered under the lake. The secret policeman, satisfied that we were neither geologists nor mercenaries in the pay of Kinshasa, found us a hotel and agreed to look for boats that might be heading north toward

Sudan. "It is unlikely," Michael said, "extremely unlikely that I will succeed."

We spent the night at the Marine Boys guesthouse in Panyimur, sweating on spent foam mattresses while a crowd of more than a hundred gathered on rows of benches in the hotel courtyard. The front half of the courtyard watched Congolese music videos on a generator-powered television. The other half of the audience watched a qualifying match for the European Cup. Both groups cheered with gusto for most of the night. Sometime around eleven our door opened and Michael entered without knocking, joined by Apolo and Henry, two officers from Uganda's Internal Security Organization. These domestic spies couldn't find us a boat—"No one is traveling as you wish to travel," Michael said—but they had a solution. "Henry here will drive you tomorrow to Pakwach," Apolo said. "There you will take a bus to Moyo."

"At Moyo you will take a mutatu to Panjala," Henry said. "From Panjala boats go to Nimule and Sudan." We chatted for a few minutes and then they all left. No one asked for a dime.

"Those guys are a big help," Schon said as he pulled his waistband away from his belly and poured a healthy dose of Gold Bond powder into his shorts. "Maybe I'm being paranoid, but I still felt like they were checking us out, waiting for one of us to screw up and reveal our secret plan." The night went on forever, mosquitoes buzzing my ears, impervious to my slaps. At five in the morning the staff started cleaning up. They bellowed at one another and noisily stacked the wooden benches. Cocks were crowing, dogs were barking and somewhere in the courtyard a baby coughed and coughed and wailed in discomfort and fear and never was a soothing voice heard.

A couple hours later we loaded our gear into Henry's Toyota station wagon and made the drive north to Pakwach. "I monitor everything," Henry said, "everything related to internal security—economic, political, criminal. If local officials are not doing their job, if there is corruption, I report that too. Whatever can lead to instability or revolt." The Lord's Resistance Army wasn't a factor in northwest Uganda, but the region was home to an alphabet soup of tiny rebel groups based in the Congo.

"Do you read the *Red Pepper*?" I asked. The papers that week had been aflame with the story of a prominent evangelical pastor who had divorced his wife after a public tribunal in which she confessed to carrying on an affair with a lowly street vendor. "I would have thought twice if she had committed adultery with tycoons in Kampala," the pastor had told Uganda's press corps, "but not a chapati baker. I would have appreciated that maybe she was tempted by money."

"The *Red Pepper*?" Henry said, swerving around a motorbike. "Not frequently."

"Because I was just wondering—what's their batting average? What percentage of their intel stories are actually accurate?"

"In my opinion, forty percent," he said. "It is best not to take the Ugandan newspapers too seriously." That was easy for him to say. The Internal Security Organization, the military and the police and spy agencies had worked closely with the president's campaign to ensure the boss's reelection. They ran secret jails inside Kampala stocked with dozens of political prisoners. Of course he wasn't fond of newspapers.

Delivered to Pakwach by the friendly spy, we bused to Arua and spent the night in a hotel where we washed our clothes in the sink, ate omelets in a proper restaurant and were awakened at three in the morning by amplified chanting and drums banging outside our window. A parade was wending its way through the city's red mud streets. We walked onto our balcony and tried to track the group as it snaked through Arua's small colonial-era downtown. Fattened by the war in the Congo, the city of twenty-nine thousand was now booming as a base for aid agencies working in eastern Congo and the remote southeast of Sudan—though here, as in the rest of Uganda, food prices were on the rise. "A wedding?" Schon said of the racket. "Isn't it kind of early?"

We smoked in the morning air and listened to the happy clamor and in time I was able to make out that the leader, a gray-bearded black man wearing a short black fez and carrying a bullhorn, was shouting in Arabic. The Muslim holy month of Ramadan had begun. The parade was meant to wake stragglers so they might have a last meal before the sun rose.

In the morning, unrested, we caught a minivan to Moyo, thirty-six hours of hard driving and two breakdowns that left us at a sleepy administrative center just a few miles from the Sudanese border. Moyo's taxis congregated outside a circular park, gone now to dirt and a single defiant tree. It was the first planned attempt at civic beauty we had seen since leaving Jinja. Schon, slouched and puffy-eyed, looked like a vagabond. But I had a surprise waiting. "Take care of the bags, I gotta do something," I said, and stepped away from the throngs to make a phone call. When I returned, Schon was fending off taxi offers, trying to keep would-be porters from grabbing our baggage.

"Where are we going?" he asked.

"Just hold on," I said.

Ten minutes later a clean, white and comparably massive Toyota Land Cruiser pulled up to the park, its polished chrome bumper and door handles shining like parts of an alien machine. I waved to the driver and he got out with a broad smile. "See that?" I told Schon. "That's our ride."

"You are shitting me."

Away from the taxi stand the town, a former link in Uganda's chain of cotton-growing centers, was broad and pretty, the most kept I'd seen in Uganda. Tall old trees—some crowned by swarms of tiny bats—shaded dozens of stately administrative buildings,

including a 150-bed public hospital. The driver turned from the
hard clay road onto a paved drive and dropped us at the door of
the United Nations High Commission for Refugees, where we met
our benefactor.

Tarek Muftic, the local UNHCR representative, had agreed
through the organization's spokesman in Kampala to put us up.
Tens of thousands of Sudanese had taken refuge in Uganda during the civil war. Now the agency was slowly moving them back—
some after more than a decade away—to villages that lacked many
of the conveniences of a well-run, internationally funded camp.
Once the muddy tracks of southern Sudan dried out, trucks would
again be transporting refugees to their villages of distant memory. "The first thing we do is take the community leaders back to
see the location—a 'go-see,' we call it," Tarek said. "They tell the
camp what they've seen, what it's lacking, and then they decide
whether to return."

A career UNHCR man from Bosnia, Tarek was a former refugee himself, though he now lived in relative splendor in a two-
bedroom house with a big yard, a diesel generator and satellite
television. He had a slightly distracted air, with a buildup of hard
wax in his ears that caused him to miss half of what was said in
conversation and to keep his television and car radio on at blister-
ing volumes. Olive oil—doctor's orders—seeped from his ears and
down his jawline. Tarek's guestroom was clean and quiet, and his
housekeeper washed and pressed our laundry, while his cook prepared us pleasant meals. Two days of such luxury and we were
strong again.

CHAPTER FOUR

We said grateful goodbyes to Tarek and took a two-hour taxi ride down a series of progressively smaller trails, to the riverside hamlet of Panjala, where I hired a boat downriver to Nimule, at the border of Sudan and Uganda. The sole passengers in a green thirty-five-footer, we were back on the Nile, happily so, slipping past floating baubles of hyacinth, with elephant grass, rocks and trees lining the shore on our left and familiar miles of papyrus jungle bending to the breeze on the right. Schon looked wistfully down at his scuffed and unopened fishing case. "They got electric catfish up here," he said. "Three hundred fifty volts, generated by electrolytes in the chest. They shock their prey and eat it. And they communicate with electricity too. Maybe I can still get a line in." Half an hour into the ride, the pilot warned us to put our cameras down. We were nearly there.

The Nimule landing was a crumbling concrete dock haunted by the mournful rusted skeleton of a long-ago destroyed customs house. We entered a small guard shack, where a young man, a teenager really, sat behind a wooden table; an AK-47 with a weathered wooden stock leaned casually against the wall behind his chair.

His desk was decorated with a handkerchief-sized flag of the Government of South Sudan and on the back wall were framed photographs of the late John Garang and of Salva Kiir.

"Hi," I said, puzzled. "This is Sudan?"

"Yes," the teenager said from behind his sunglasses. "This is New Sudan."

"Sudan."

"Yes, Sudan."

I breathed with the same vertigo I'd felt on the floating pad outside Ksike. "But the map shows Nimule in Uganda, not Sudan."

"I don't know about any map," he said, his voice rising. "This is Sudan." Schon looked at me in alarm. "Do you have papers?" the gunsel demanded. "What is your business?" Apparently my maps were wrong. Uganda might be home to a border crossing called Nimule, but the town itself and the river port were squarely in Sudan. The young guard may have been new to his job, but he carried the easy contempt of border agents everywhere. We unzipped our bags and handed over our passports and our blue SPLM travel passes, as I recovered my composure and summoned the smiling bonhomie that had carried me past suspicious border agents in Pakistan and Afghanistan. Schon, conditioned by his years as a champion alcoholic and the collisions with authority native to such a vocation, maintained a humble and diffident silence. The young gatekeeper hunched over our passports, paging mine from front to back, stamped our blue travel cards and leaned back on his chair. "So. This is New Sudan checkpoint. What can you give me?" I looked at Schon, who had involuntarily raised an eyebrow. What did we have for him? "You must have something for me inside those bags."

My stomach churned and then the churning stopped. "I'll tell you what," I said. "As you can see from my documents, I'm an American journalist. I would hate, just hate, to have to write about how the new Sudan looks a lot like the old one. Was this

Dr. Garang's vision? Bribes for boy soldiers? A lot of Americans have given a lot of money—millions, tens of millions—to help the people of south Sudan. I'm sure they would like to know how that money's being spent."

He smiled a hating smile and twisted a pen in his long fingers, and an adult voice came through the barred window and said, "Let them pass." It was the boy's superior, a tall and skinny man, gap-toothed and wearing horn-rimmed glasses, a worn T-shirt, green army pants and flip-flops. "Where are you staying in Nimule?" he asked. I told him the name of an American aid group; a friend of a friend had arranged for us to spend the night at their compound. "When is your car coming?" he said.

There was no car. I didn't know a soul at the place—the plans had been made by my contacts in Kampala. We would walk, I said. How far could it be? We hired two boys with bicycles to help us port the gear, the bigger bags balanced across their seats, and started up the grass-lined road from the checkpoint. The landscape was the same as in northern Uganda but it was clear we were in a different country: A little boy chasing a metal hoop took one look at the two whites and shouted in Arabic, "*Khawaja!*" Two hours later we limped through the gates of the aid group's compound; it was located miles outside town. It hadn't occurred to me to check.

In the morning we caught a ride into Nimule, a longtime SPLA stronghold. The town had forty-five thousand people, almost half of them refugees, most of them living in broad neighborhoods of grass-roofed mud huts. Downtown was a collection of one-story cement and brick shops and warehouses clustered on the Juba road. Nimule had been cut off from the rest of the south for much of the war; in some respects it had become an annex of Uganda. Ugandan shillings were as prevalent as Sudanese dinars and the local mobile phone network, Gemtel, was Ugandan as well. The easy Nile we had crossed to reach Sudan turned livid north of Nimule in a rolling set of unpassable rapids; for half a century technocrats had dreamed of raising a dam there to electrify the south. For now, they were still struggling with basic roads and sanitation.

Schon and I had missed the daily bus to Juba, a hundred miles to the north, so I hired a truck driver to take us. He was hauling cement, part of a growing trade with Uganda. The border, closed for most of the civil war, had been thrown open, and Juba was rich in dollars, thanks to the Comprehensive Peace Agreement and the United Nations peace mission. The same cash gravity that drew fresh tilapia from Lake Kyoga was now carrying us up the Nimule road. But it wasn't carrying us very quickly. The route out of Nimule included a fair number of hills, and we ground up it like we were carrying, well, cement. Our wheelman rarely made it into third gear as we ascended hills covered in speckled green scrub and passed stretches of roadway lined with signs warning of land mines and clusters of burnt-out armored vehicles.

We'd considered paying 30,000 Ugandan shillings each to make the journey in the back of a flatbed truck before I flagged down our current chauffeur. The flatbed came barreling up behind us now, spewing a long tail of dust, and passed us on the left, leaving nothing to spare on the one-lane road (a reasonable course considering the land mines). It clipped off our passenger-side mirror and would have taken my elbow too if I hadn't pulled it back. Our driver, hunched over the steering wheel, sucked his teeth in annoyance and said nothing. Still, I didn't envy the poor souls in the back of the flatbed standing in the open with goats and chickens for company, and I made the mistake of saying so. Right then our truck started misbehaving, the steering suddenly loose, clunky and loud. The driver eased us down the hill and pulled over in front of a short row of shops, shimmied underneath and came out with the top half of a sheared bolt from the steering linkage. Schon and I settled under a band of shade outside an empty roadhouse while the driver caught a southbound minivan. Our truck wasn't the only patient in this roadside ward. Another lorry, an old British model, sat with its hood up, two members of the crew asleep underneath, while a Ugandan man in torn blue coveralls and flip-flops fixed a crack in the radiator. He said his name was Chibsi Cola, and he was welding the radiator using a car battery, jumper cables and what appeared to be the lead slug core of a nine-volt transistor battery. "I used to be a soldier in the presidential guard during the time of Obote," he said. "It was high life. We trained in Zimbabwe. We trained in Korea, the North Korea."

"What was that like?" I asked.

"Oh, it was very different," he said, squinting against the tiny bursts of yellow sparks. "Their tactics involved using lots of ropes and rappeling; we hadn't trained in ropes before." What about Korea? "I didn't see Korea. I saw an army base where they were training us. I think in that country they eat lots of cabbage." He'd fled in 1986 after Obote was overthrown, and lived in a refugee camp in Zambia for nearly a decade before returning to Uganda. Now he drove a truck. "It could be worse," he said. "I was sure they would kill me when I came back. They had invited us, yes, with amnesty. But you never can know."

Five hours after he left us, our driver reappeared and installed the new steering bolt. We piled into the cab of the truck—Schon, the driver, his assistant and me—only to find we had additional company. Reclined in the back of the cab was a plump Ugandan schoolmistress, Viola Saonko. The driver had picked her up in Nimule, another paying passenger. Viola was one of hundreds of Ugandans taking advantage of the wide-open southern economy. She sold truckloads of Ugandan vegetables in Juba and also owned a tanker truck that peddled water.

"So how's business?" I asked.

"Business is very good," she purred. "These Sudanese, they

don't know business. They have got nothing. We bring everything they need."

The challenge of surviving Juba, with an economy geared toward aid workers and diplomats living off generous per diems, would be more punishing than the heat. Most foreigners lived in deluxe tented camps where the accommodations started at a hundred dollars a night and rocketed up from there. There was little public transport, and a car and driver cost a hundred dollars a day. But I had an advantage that I hoped would save a fortune. My friend Greg, a Cairo-based expatriate, had recently been appointed chief of mission for a small NGO in Juba. Greg was stranded in Egypt, a victim of the same diplomatic pissing match that had spoiled my Sudan visa, but he had left instructions that Schon and I could stay at his organization's new guesthouse.

We crawled north, through landscape that *National Geographic* and *Wild Kingdom* had taught us to recognize as classic Africa savanna, all of us sitting tight in the musky cab. Soldiers from the SPLA stopped us at several checkpoints, and we could see units of the Ugandan People's Defense Force as well, deployed into Sudan to track the dreadlocked child soldiers of the Lord's Resistance Army. Juba was hosting peace talks between the Ugandan government and the LRA, and fear and paranoia were high on both sides: The LRA, gathered for the first time at two camps in south Sudan, feared they would be massacred by Ugandan forces. The Ugandans and the southern Sudanese feared the LRA would rampage if they didn't get their way at the negotiating table. It made for a lot of armament.

The truck pushed on over the long-suffering road, rarely reaching thirty miles an hour, as the orange sun disappeared behind the scraggly hilltops. Well into nighttime, my satellite phone started buzzing with text messages: Greg's logistics man, Samuel, was getting worried. He came in his Land Cruiser to retrieve us, and we met on the road fifteen miles outside town. Samuel, tall, thin and strong in a white short-sleeved shirt, grabbed my arm like we were family and ushered me into the front seat.

The cruiser was a workingman's cousin to the plush model Tarek drove; manual windows, no chrome, two rows of bench seats running along the sides in the back. We brought Viola with us and picked up half a dozen hitchhikers on the way, and nine hours after leaving Nimule, we finally reached home. A slice of heaven just off Juba Day Road, the compound had solar- and generator-powered lights, wireless satellite Internet during the day, unlimited tea, Nescafé and bottled water, and a bathroom that was cleaned each and every afternoon. We bunked for two happy nights in the quarters of a staffer who was away in the field before moving across the road to a less cozy nest. The workmen renovating Greg's guesthouse were far behind schedule, so we pitched our now moldy tent on the concrete floor of the house amid piles of construction debris.

"Still," I said as I unrolled my sleeping bag and jealously eyed Schon's foam pad, "it beats paying."

"If you say so. It's your dime. Your back, too."

Juba was a spread-out, starved and broken-down colonial construct straining under the weight of thousands of returning refugees and newly arrived aid workers, a bullet-pocked village of 160,000 people with seven miles of paved road, down from the sixteen miles the British had laid. The entire south, a region the size of Nigeria, had just sixteen miles of blacktop and since independence had known even fewer years of peace: a small interval between the first civil war (1955–1972) and the even more destructive second civil war (1983–2005). There simply hadn't been enough time for development to take hold. A government-controlled garrison during the civil war, Juba had been constantly under siege by the SPLA. Now it was crawling with fighters from the victorious rebel army. But the liberators and the liberated appeared to have an uneasy relationship. Not far from our guesthouse, the burnt shell of a new Toyota Hilux pickup sat overturned. The driver, an officer fresh out of the bush, had struck and killed a child from one of the refugee camps that lined the road. Residents had poured out of the nearby huts and beaten the driver nearly to death.

I converted some of my cash to dinars at a dry goods store, and we walked the two miles downtown for a breakfast of fried liver, toast and fresh mango juice. I left to look for a newspaper, and Schon had a sour look on his face when I got back. "Here's something I do not understand," he said as I sat down. "They put in flush toilets that are designed for the user to sit on, and there is never a goddamn toilet seat on them. And I want to know why. Do people steal them?"

"Most people don't have toilets," I said. "Why steal a toilet seat?"

"People will steal pretty much anything, whether they can use it or not," he said, stubbing out and then relighting his cigarette. "Do they put the crapper in, and they don't know to put a seat on it? Did they not order toilet seats with the toilets? Can you not get them here? Why doesn't anybody raise hell about it? And, if they deliberately leave the seats off, why would they do that?"

"Travel constipation?" I asked. "This ought to help your bowels move." I showed him the front page of the *Juba Post*: More than forty travelers had been murdered in attacks on the Nimule road the night we arrived in Juba. Some were burned alive, others had their eyes gouged out before they were shot dead. No wonder Samuel had been anxious to get us into town. The road was now closed, and the peace talks were in jeopardy—Uganda blamed the LRA, and the LRA, hysterically, blamed Museveni's army. Salva Kiir, the southern Sudanese president, had spent his first year in power working to unify the south's more than ninety different tribes and factions. He had brought a powerful rival of the SPLA into the fold and had forcibly disarmed feared bands of cattle raiders who terrorized the grazing grounds of the sprawling Upper Nile region northeast of Juba. In the summer of 2006, he turned his government's attention to the Lord's Resistance Army. The LRA, under pressure from Ugandan forces, had spilled back over the border into Sudan's Equatoria region, transplanting its reign of terror to the newly autonomous south. For the sake of his own people, Kiir decided to host marathon peace talks between the madmen of the LRA and the Ugandan government. Now the talks had hit a rough patch, and it appeared that the road massacres were a demonstration by the LRA of its enduring capacity for mayhem.

Amid this chaos, I remained that rarest of creatures in Sudan, a walking *khawaja*. Tromping through the Equatorian heat, my city-boy lope evolved into an energy-efficient torrent of short choppy steps. Schon and I would wake at seven, run across the street to shower before Greg's staff arrived, walk downtown for breakfast and the papers, and then walk back across town, past the hospital, the Konyo Konyo market, the cluster of dead armored vehicles—remnants of the SPLA's failed 1992 assaults—and the old Ottoman mosque, across the red dust field behind the Islamic school, to the Juba port. The site was called a port because boats and barges tied up there, but there was no infrastructure to speak of, just a cluster of flat steel barges and the boats that pushed them.

There, under the shade of towering mango trees and doum palms, Jecob Daniel Djadobe, the Sudan River Transport Corporation's local agent, sat sipping tea at a card table with a group of customs clerks and policemen. "In one week, the barge will go," Djadobe said amiably. He said this every day for five days, as Schon's patience and stamina were pummeled by the sun, the red dust, the constant walking and the heavy rainstorms, which made his joints ache like those of an old person. Schon's fishing case remained unopened. I had imagined back in Kampala that we might fish from the side of our boat, or off the banks of Lake

Kyoga or above Karuma Falls, but that was before we understood the labor and discomfort of traveling rough. Schon might have put a line in the water from the Nile's banks in Juba, but that would have killed hours of my own time—he was too inexperienced to just leave alone by the water.

When we weren't haunting the port, we were interviewing Sudanese bureaucrats and aid officials for a basic understanding of the massive effort to turn the south into something like a state after nearly fifty years of war and underdevelopment. Their stories depressed, thrilled and depressed again.

"You never talk about reconstruction in south Sudan," said one. "It's construction. There are no war-damaged schools or hospitals—there were never any to begin with."

"There's an acute housing shortage," said another. "The judges of our high court are right now living in a barracks. But the education ministry—that's a fantastic ministry. School enrollment has doubled in the last year to more than 750,000. And we've immunized a million and a half children for measles—that's the main killer."

"This is the worst place in the world to grow up," said a third. "Highest under-five mortality anywhere—one in four die before their fifth birthday. Highest maternal mortality. A girl child here has a nine times better chance of dying in childbirth than of finishing primary school."

I was ill at ease with the people of Juba. The impossibly tall Dinka soldiers and the Equatorian refugees—Azandes, Acholis and Mandaris—might have been Martians. Their world—one of decades-long conflict, biblical suffering and enduring tribal tradition—was completely different from anything I had encountered before. I had more in common with residents of Kampala than either of us had with the people of south Sudan. It lacked the British Commonwealth veneer that added a pinch of familiarity to so much of Africa and South Asia. There was grief in the air, and madness too. Late one night, as Schon and I walked home from visiting the LRA peace talks at the Juba Raha hotel, a movement in the dark caught the corner of my eye and I jerked to the left to face it, my hands tingling, my stomach catching that cold-water splash that says, *You, laddie. You may be dead.* Standing a few feet away on the slope of a drainage ditch, a naked old man leveled an imaginary Kalashnikov and silently tracked our course along the baked mud road, arms jerking with each phantom shot and recoil, his gritted teeth reflecting moonlight.

"Jesus Christ, it is hot. Hot," Schon said, chugging a glass of salted Tang. It was our fifth night in Juba. We were sitting by the water tank in the gravel backyard at Greg's office compound, watching our clothes dry on the line. Schon had made pasta and an oily homemade sauce on the night watchman's butane stove. In our struggle to save money, it was our third such supper in as many days. He drained some water off the top of the sauce, set the pan back on the burner, mopped his brow with a bandanna and sat next to me on a plastic lawn chair. "I've got to level with you," he said. "I'm pretty near miserable. This may be the most interesting place we've been so far, but . . . These walks are a bastard. Even with all the water I'm drinking, every day I get a headache. This might not be for me anymore."

He had been putting off this talk, and so had I. Schon wasn't a drag on me—yet. But the day was fast coming. Everything I'd heard about Malakal led me to expect a malarial tinderbox. The war wasn't quite finished in Upper Nile state—antagonistic militias stewed in camps while their leaders grappled for political power. Clans and tribes were fighting over issues remote to the actual civil war, but their battles added to the region's insecurity. "I know you're beat," I said. "Give it another day, and if there's no boat north we'll get you back to Kampala and onto a plane. You said it yourself—this is the most interesting place we've been."

Schon got up and returned with two plates of spaghetti and still-watery sauce. "At this point," he said softly, "my body's so worn out that the important stuff just kind of washes past me. But I'll tell you what. I'll never look at home the same way again. I'll never look at education the same way again. That's what's been missing here, the whole way, from Kampala to Juba. It's education. How are you supposed to want something if you've never seen it? And we totally take that for granted. I do, anyway. So, yeah, let's give it another day, but not much more than that. 'Cause I am tired."

Two mornings later, we arrived at the bus depot and learned the Nimule road had been closed again thanks to new attacks east of the Nile. The direct bus to Kampala, which usually made the 350-mile trip in less than twenty-four hours, wasn't running. The only alternative was the western route, down tracks that made the Nimule road look like Interstate 80: Juba to Yei down to Kaya, right near the Congo border, then south into Uganda. A ticket would be waiting in Kampala. Schon had two and a half days to make his flight, an easy enough feat with the Nimule road open. Now it would be a race. I looked at my haggard friend, his tortured sneakers, his two packs and the fishing case (which he had taken to calling "this goddamn thing") and wondered if he would make it.

"Excuse me, did I hear you say you are traveling to Kampala?" He was a Kenyan in his early twenties, about Schon's height, with short receding hair and wire-rimmed spectacles with lenses barely bigger than his eyes. "I am also going to Kampala. Shall we find some new transport?" Carrington Ochieng Oudah had been a bookkeeper at a politically wired oil company that had set up shop in Juba; he was heading home to Nairobi after six months in the southern capital. He knew the route. He had a cell phone. His only luggage was a small roller bag. And he looked strong. My anxiety lifted at the sight of him. They struck up what appeared to be an instant friendship, two dudes with someplace to be and a lot of miles to get there. As they squeezed into a minivan, I handed Schon two hundred dollars and a fistful of dinars and shillings and took a last photograph of them.

"You stay in touch," I said. "Carrington, he'll pay you for the minutes, just make sure he calls me."

"Don't worry about a thing," Schon said. "We'll talk to you from the road. Right? In a few days I'll be at the pyramids and a few days after that I'll be back at the bar, serving the rich and nameless. Then," he added, "I'm going fishing." I stepped back from the van, the driver started the engine and they were gone.

I was now alone in a town where I had no friends. Schon had uncomplainingly played the role of cook and quartermaster, shopping for the vegetables and pasta and Tang that made up so much of our daily diet. The common gear that we'd both carried had accrued to me alone; my bags had never been heavier.

On the other end of the balance sheet, my daily budget doubled the moment he and Carrington drove off. I could now afford to spend twenty dollars a day on food and smokes, which meant a daily luncheon at the United Nations compound's afternoon buffet, a twelve-dollar feast that included multiple entrees, salad, dessert, fruit punch, purified water and tea, all of it eaten under a big white tent where BBC News was often on television. It quickly became the high point of my day.

I resumed my visits to the port, and still couldn't get a straight answer about the next barge north. I was walking back through the Konyo Konyo market when a familiar voice called out, "*Mzungu!* You are here!" It was Viola Saonko, our fellow passenger from the ride to Juba, her head poking out the window of a white Isuzu tanker truck. She was heading to the Nile to fill up. Viola made room and I climbed in. On a mud flat south of the port, a half dozen cast iron diesel pumps were lined up along the water, each with a thick plastic hose sticking into the air. Viola's driver backed the truck up to a pump. A shirtless boy grabbed the cast iron wheel with both hands and threw his body downward, the greasy gears turned, the old pump chuckled to life and in short order Viola's tank was filled with seven hundred liters of Nile water. She paid the pump's owner a thousand dinars—around five dollars—hitched up her black cotton dress and climbed into the cab.

"I want to show you something," Viola said, and pointed the driver toward a nearby refugee settlement. These were villages within the city, established decades before by people fleeing the war in the countryside. The truck wended through the round thatched-roof tukuls, toward the sound of drumming. In a clearing, an intersection of two dirt roads, fifty or more half-naked people were dancing, an unorganized dipping and bouncing, to a steady beat hammered on animal-skin drums and a metal oil can. This was no celebration—their expressions were grim, their skin covered in ash. The old women wore what appeared to be donated brassieres, most of them in shades of pink and purple. "You see!" Viola said, her eyes shining. "Look at that." She pointed. "They are naked! They are savages."

I was mortified. "Viola, I think this is a funeral."

"Yes! And they go naked at the funeral, just drumming and drumming. I heard a story that the first baby they have, they take and kill it. After seeing this, who can doubt?"

The mourners had been at it for some time; tracks of sweat cut through the ash on their legs and torsos. They ignored us even as Viola ordered her driver to make another pass through the outdoor wake. "Please," I said. "Do we have to look at this? Let's just go." Viola said something in Luganda, and we drove away.

"They don't have God, no morality," she explained. "They should be made to wear clothes."

"You know," I said, "it wasn't so long ago that Europeans were saying the same things about Ugandans."

"But I am Baganda," she said. "We wore garments of barkcloth. We are a moral people."

"Is that why there's so much HIV in Uganda?"

"That we got from you."

An hour later, Viola's water had been pumped into the black plastic tank of a local family's brick-walled compound and she had pocketed 10,500 dinars, a 950 percent windfall. Juba's sixty-year-old municipal water system had been built for a population of seventeen thousand. Everyone else relied on water portered directly from the Nile. "In Kampala, you have to steal if you want to make a hundred dollars a day," she said with a laugh. "Here I get twice that." We promised to keep in touch and I jumped out of the truck, while Viola turned back to the Nile for a refill.

Conflict was already brewing between the locals and the entrepreneurs from Uganda and Kenya. There were stories of shakedowns and robberies. Meanwhile, the Arab traders—who had thrived during the war, along with their partners in the Sudanese army—were now on the defensive. Their supply chain from the north—they got their goods by barge—couldn't compete with the land route from Uganda. Many northern traders had been burned out in rioting that ensued after Garang died. Now the *jallaba* were being called to pay ever more serious debts: The week Schon left, three Arab traders were found dead on a mountainside outside Juba, bound and shot execution style. It was no robbery—they still had money in their pockets.

But it would take more than a few murders to erase the Arab stamp on Juba. While the amplified call to prayer had been turned down to modest volume by SPLM order, Arabic was still the common tongue of the south. It was the language members of different tribes used to communicate, so ingrained that the city had its own Arabic dialect, with its own dictionaries. I was speaking with a twenty-three-year-old United Nations employee, a crucifix-wearing Dinka refugee, when she received a phone call informing her that she would soon be returning to her home a hundred miles to the north after fifteen years away. "So you're finally going back?" I asked. She clasped her hands together and said, "*Inshallah.*" English was the official language of the new government, but its capital remained the southernmost Arabic-speaking city in the world.

I devoted the first hours after Schon and Carrington left to administrative work. Greg's second in command, an officious Sudanese with a love for Big Ten college football, had grown tired of the moochers in his midst, so I set to inquiring around town about affordable lodging. By nightfall, with no word from the travelers, I was pacing and chain-smoking. By morning, lying alone on the floor of the construction site—more comfortable now that Schon had left me his foam pad—I had gnawed off my fingernails and much of the finger flesh as well. There were reasonable explanations for the lack of contact: Sudan's mobile phone network was more than oversubscribed, and it grew weaker the farther south you went; fewer than one in five calls actually connected. Carrington's phone might have run out of minutes. His battery could have died. I opened my Sudan map and noticed for the first time the Yei route's proximity to Garamba National Park in the Congo. Garamba was where Joseph Kony hung his hat, along with a few hundred crack LRA troops. Later that morning, I confided my worry to a Kenyan agricultural specialist at Greg's office, who asked, "Why didn't he fly straight to Nairobi?"

"It's three hundred dollars from Juba to Nairobi," I said, "and then another six hundred to Cairo."

"Your institution doesn't have a budget for air travel?"

"We don't have an institution. It's a self-funded project."

The Kenyan cocked his head and seemed to shrink from me. "No affiliation?"

"None."

"This is Sudan. The roads are dangerous," the Kenyan said coldly. He saw my face turning ashen—Schon had been my best friend since fourth grade—and added, "I am sure he will be fine."

Thirty-six hours after they left, I got the email message I'd been waiting for.

> O.K.
>
> *Sorry for the delay. We just got to Arua. And yes, it was the single most fucked-up and physically ruinous goddamn trip I hope I ever have to endure. Not too much trouble w/government or militaries. Just extremely tough to get here. I'm still with Carrington. Numerous minibuses and backs of flatbed trucks and a nice, brisk eight-hour walk. Roads washed out, hundreds of trucks backed up, some turned over in the mud.*
>
> *I'll describe later, when we get to Kampala. Carrington went and sold his phone to some dude because there was a profit in it for him. Not because he's inconsiderate of me, but because he's addicted to making a profit. He's a good kid. Weren't for him, I'd likely not have made it.*
>
> *I got the flight information. Should be smooth sailing from here. Unless I really am cursed. In which case . . .*
>
> *It's good to be desperate once in a while. Gives you an appreciation of the looks on people's faces when they're desperate and you're not.*

At this, my own desperation eased. Schon was on his way home, but I was still stuck in Juba.

Most residents of Juba, like the refugees Viola had been mocking, lived in tukuls, low round thatched-roof huts hidden behind reed fences. There were few latrines and almost no running water. The children ran down the roads playing with clattering push-toys fashioned out of plastic castoffs: soda bottles, small laundry detergent tubs and colorful lids carved into crude gears. There was no shortage of raw materials—trash was everywhere in Juba. The people lived on *ful*—stewed fava beans, a staple in Sudan and Egypt—and whatever handouts their communities could cadge from the World Food Program and other agencies. Those who couldn't afford the beans themselves subsisted on whatever protein might be found in *ful* water, the leftover broth. It wasn't that vegetables and fish weren't arriving daily from Uganda; it was that no one could afford them who wasn't on a foreign payroll. The thousands working for the United Nations and other humanitarian and development groups drove the price of garlic and tomatoes higher than what you'd pay in New York or London. Their Sudanese staffers were invariably former refugees who had lived and been educated in camps in Kenya or Uganda. They were the southerners with modern administrative skills. Those who'd stayed behind and endured the fighting and famine had little to offer. They might take jobs as menials and washerwomen at one of the tented camps that housed the foreigners, or as laborers on a construction project.

The foreigners lived in tiny container apartments or in canvas tents that cost more than a hundred dollars a day. For that they received shelter, electricity, three hot meals, bleached drinking water, clean toilets, showers and laundry service, though the Sudanese women refused to wash men's or women's undergarments. Each foreigner washed his or her own drawers and hung them to dry outside their billet. Thus each tent advertised the gender and girth of its occupant.

Soon after Schon left, I struck out for Palica, a run-down guest-house operated by Juba's biggest Roman Catholic church. Even at thirty-five dollars a night, the place was a godsend; I had a dusty private room with a real if ancient mattress and actual 1960s shower stalls. The church had been a bastion of peaceful opposition to the north during the long years of civil war. Now, with freedom at hand, it found itself at odds with Juba's new dispensation. The SPLA was grabbing land outside the city for new facilities; villagers and their clergy were beaten and arrested when they protested. Local journalists, many of whom had written for church publications during the war, were now being hauled before SPLA commissars to explain their reporting on the southern army's abuses.

"These conflicts will pass away," Marian Okumu, a laywoman at the church, said one morning. "We pray it is growing pains. Before, you could not do anything. You could only smile during the day and cry in the night because the Arabs killed your brother. You cannot have funeral. You are not allowed to even mourn."

The terror reached a high point in the summer of 1992, when the SPLA twice took, but could not hold, the city. "We went to sleep praying they would be here when we woke," Okumu said. "We were very annoyed when they failed."

Annoyed, and frightened. "The government arrested three hundred police and soldiers," said Robert Kundi, a police constable I'd met while trying to secure an interview with Salva Kiir and his vice president. "All were slaughtered." We were sitting in Robert's home, a messy wooden shack, not much bigger than an office cubicle, where he slept alone on a foam mattress under a leaky tarpaulin-covered roof. Robert had a house nearby, a fair-sized tukul, but he'd given that to his brother. "My children have left and my wife is dead," he said. "My brother and his family need it more than I do."

Robert had somehow evaded the death lists in 1992, when every southerner in government service was suspected of treason, but his turn came in 1995, when he was arrested and taken to the notorious White House, an army-run torture center. "I knew I was dead," he said. "They killed thirty men every night I was there. They tied their arms with wire, put them in a trench and buried them alive with a grader. Every night."

"Good God," I said. "What would the men say while this was happening?"

He looked at me blankly. "They said, 'Please don't bury me alive.' I will never forget the sound of the grader. They kept me twenty-one days and then let me go. I don't know why. I kept a journal of that and all the things that happened during the war."

"You know, and I don't want to be too forward, but is there any chance you would let me read through your diaries from that time?" Unlike South Africa, Liberia and other countries racked by civil war, Sudan hadn't set up a truth commission to air the sins of the combatants. Neither the SPLA nor its adversaries in Khartoum were much for self-criticism. In another country priests, imams and tribal holy men would have been saying prayers at the edge of the White House's mass graves, and forensic teams would have been exhuming the bodies for identification. Here, the dead stayed buried, and no one wanted the testimony of the survivors.

"My brother burned all the notebooks," Robert said.

"He was being overprotective? He didn't want you to dwell on the trauma?"

Robert set his tea down on the wood pallet floor. "My brother burns things. He is mentally ill."

CHAPTER FIVE

Fiscal discipline was lost as a second week in Juba bled into a third. In addition to my $35-a-night room at Palica and the $12 UN lunch, I added dinner at Juba's sole pizza parlor, the Café de Paris, where a plate of spaghetti and tomato sauce started at $10, not counting the beer and South African wine. Such luxuries were necessary, I told myself, a fattening up before the river barge left, whenever that would be. In a land largely without roads, the barges were the major economic lifeline, pushed and dragged downriver by diesel-powered flatboats that were villages unto themselves. Each of these vast cargo trays was covered by a convex corrugated metal lid. Dense townships of plastic huts and lean-tos, cooking fires and tea ladies grew on these sun-hot slopes, and I was anxious to join them for passage to Malakal. I bought heavy sackloads of canned food and sweet crackers, a bucket and rope to haul water and a new bottle of iodine for the inevitable cuts to my feet and hands. I wondered how I would possibly carry it all. I wondered if Schon's Wal-Mart tent would slide into the drink while I slept. Until that moment of truth, I felt I deserved my pizza and wine.

I was bent over my notebook at the café late one night when

an accented voice called my name. It wasn't the first phantom I'd heard address me in my solitude. But this one called out again, and I looked up to see the Gallic handsomeness of Alexandre Godard squinting at me from a table across the room. I'd met Alexandre at the very beginning of my journey, on the flight from Cairo to Uganda. We were somewhere over Sudan in a nearly empty plane when he turned back in his seat and said, "Excuse me, I don't wish to bother you, but do you know of any hotels that are not too expensive in Kampala?" He was a Parisian photojournalist, an impetuous one it seemed. When news broke that the LRA leader Joseph Kony might be making a public appearance, Alexandre had jumped the first flight he could find in hopes of shooting the ruthless enigma. I'd given Alexandre a ride into Kampala, me with my hundred pounds of contingency planning, him with just two small carry-ons—one filled entirely with black-and-white film and two Leica cameras—and dropped him at the door of Kampala's seedy Tourist Hotel, where a sign ordered patrons to leave their "arms and ammunitions" outside. "It's the only place I know," I'd said in apology. "It's a little rough."

Alexandre hadn't batted an eye. "It will be fine."

Now, two and a half months later and three hundred miles north of Kampala, he was waving me over to his table. "Ah, so you made it, Dan! The Nile, you are doing it?"

"I'm almost doing it," I replied. "My barge north keeps getting delayed. It's been weeks. I'm dying here."

Alexandre nodded, and looked down to focus on some stray morsel on his plate. "There is another barge," he said finally. "Not the government one. A humanitarian group. They are going to Ethiopia on the Sobat River. I am taking it in two days. It is not my invitation to make, Dan, but I will ask the one who has brought me on. Come here tomorrow night. You will definitely find me here—I am sleeping on the roof."

I wasn't sure how close the Sobat River was to Malakal; that it wasn't in Juba was all I needed to know. Two days later I woke late and stepped out of the guesthouse, through the gate into the lane with its tall old trees, past the men's dormitory with its drumming and hymns and onto the Juba road. It was a pleasant eighty degrees. I walked past the radio station and the mosque to the dusty parade ground, where police were being drilled in the arcane art of parallel parking.

I turned onto a side street and found Alexandre riding in the back of a dented old Land Cruiser pickup, bracing himself on the roll bar, a few duffels and rucksacks at his feet. As I jogged over to him, the truck stopped and a small pale wraith of a man in wraparound sunglasses exited the driver's side and walked into a building. A bearded, ginger-haired young man came out of the passenger side, Matthew LeRiche, Alexandre's ticket north. He wore a plaid nylon camp shirt and a tan canvas cap, browned by years of sweat, that read in embroidered letters, "Explore Newfoundland, Inc."

"Hey, good to meet you, Alex told me you might be coming along," he said. "More the merrier."

"I don't want to intrude on your deal," I said. "Another interloper might be one too many."

"I've learned it's always easier to ask forgiveness than to ask permission." Matthew grinned. "So you might as well come along. Besides, the barge is owned by NPA, Norwegian People's Aid, and John's brother runs the NPA show in Sudan. With him lurking about they're not likely to say no. We're off to the port now, should be leaving this afternoon. I've been waiting a month for this." The wraith—John, apparently—came out of the building, got into the cab without speaking and started the engine. I climbed into the back with Alexandre and we bumped down the familiar route to the port.

"Thank you, Alex," I said, and I meant it. Whatever was coming, he could have had it exclusive. Instead he'd brought me along.

"That's all right," he replied. "I would not have liked to leave you stranded."

I had seen the NPA barge but, assuming all the boats were controlled by the River Transport Corp., I hadn't inquired about it. She was a flat-bottomed self-propelled craft, about thirty by seventy feet. The pilothouse, clad in green fiberglass siding, sat directly atop the engine room, with four windows overlooking the canopy-shaded deck. The flag of the new south—the Sudanese tricolor remixed to represent the new dispensation with the black band on top, red band in the center and a green Islamic band on the bottom, all set against a blue triangle—fluttered ragged from the roof. Hanging below that was the flag of NPA, three human figures locking arms around a green cross. A big spotlight sat on the roof, as did a .50-caliber heavy machine gun.

We sat in a circle of white chairs under the trees and waited for the head of the local NPA office to arrive. "So," I said to Matthew, "what's the plan? I don't see any of these cargo flats lashed to our barge. What's it carrying, besides us?"

"It's an experiment," Matthew said. "They want to see if they can deliver relief along the Nile and then up the Sobat to refugees in Gambella in Ethiopia. It's extremely remote and very expensive to supply, so if the barge can do it, they'll be able to expand their aid and do it cheaper. The only other way is by air. I'm supposed to be in London, finishing my PhD, but I can't resist a last fling, especially on this barge.

"It's a special barge," he added. "It has a special history. They're going up to Bor to pick up some JIU for security, and after that it's on to Malakal."

The JIUs, or Joint Integrated Units, were an optimistic feature of the north-south peace treaty. The agreement stipulated that Sudan would have two armies—the Sudanese Armed Forces, controlled by Khartoum, and the Sudan People's Liberation Army, controlled by Juba. The JIUs were staffed with soldiers from both forces. Historically, such integration schemes, in which former enemies don the same uniform and forget all that spilled blood, take years, decades even, to reach peaceful fruition, and so far the JIUs were following that precedent. SAF and SPLA soldiers in the same JIU typically bunked, ate and trained in separate camps, or on opposite sides of the same camp. The week before, a southern JIU soldier had been shot dead by his southern platoonmates after he suggested they bring plates of food to their northern counterparts who had just broken the Ramadan fast. The Upper Nile region was still dangerous—it was home to recalcitrant militias and warring clans. But I doubted these forces were the answer.

"Aren't JIUs a bad idea?" I asked. "Angry, unstable?"

"These are Cirillo's guys," Matthew said of the platoon that would be guarding the barge. "They're pretty reliable." Thomas Cirillo Sowaka was an important southern officer who commanded one of the better-equipped JIUs. The apple-cheeked Canadian appeared to have deep connections in the SPLA. Before I could ask Matthew about this familiarity, he slouched in his chair, his eyelids fluttered, the whites of his eyes appeared and he went to sleep. I'd never seen a man fall so swiftly from full to suspended animation.

I passed a couple hours sipping tea and chatting with the policemen billeted at the port. The middle of the grove was temporary home to a small camp of families waiting for barges north. They lived under tarpaulin lean-tos with their children and bedrolls and jerricans; tiny shops selling tea and smokes and hot snacks had grown around the camp to make it a proper little village. Near the water's edge, pale John was in quiet smiling conversation with an extremely tall, thin and dark-skinned man wrapped in a deep red tartan shawl. The man carried a spear with a long steel blade at the top. He was a picture of grace.

"That guy looked positively Maasai," I told John when he came back.

"That's because he is."

"There are Maasai in Sudan? I thought they lived down in Kenya and Tanzania."

"He's from Kenya," John said, a bit of Scotland in his voice, a ton of Africa in his many wrinkles. "He walked here. They do that sometimes, just set off and walk, take a little work where they can find it and keep going. They're the greatest. I love them."

"And you were speaking—"

"Swahili," he said, the *of course* unstated. "So you want to join them on the barge, eh?" he said. "Shouldn't be much trouble." The late morning turned to afternoon and soon the local NPA boss appeared and gave his permission. An hour later the captain, Moses Moel Anyong, arrived at port and Matthew pulled me over to introduce us. The captain was tall, not a giant, at least a decade older than me, with a long face and downturned lips. He had the personal gravity of a man accustomed to being obeyed; this despite the Eminem T-shirt. The captain looked at me without warmth and said, "In two hours we leave."

I hitched a ride into town and was dropped at the guesthouse with ninety minutes to go. I collected my things, stuffing, unstuffing, cursing and stuffing again until I had four bags: rucksack, raid pack, tent and a sack of food. I quick-marched down the hallway to the office to settle up, found it empty, turned away and ran into Father James, who was in charge of the Palica center, and Marian Okumu. "You can fix your accounts with Marian, and then I will drive you to the port," he said.

Ten minutes later I ran into the courtyard and saw through the fence that the priest's red pickup truck was gone. "Where did he go?" I wailed to no one in particular. "He said he'd take me. The boat leaves in an hour."

A thickset nun in gray and black habit sat by the gate in animated conversation with three or four lay people. Someone had just dropped a bit of good news. "*AlHAMdullilah!*" she cried, slapping her thighs.

I interrupted. "Excuse me, do you know where Father James went?"

"You sit," she said in her sandy voice. "He will be back at three." I remained standing in the confected hope that he would return, and when that hope dissolved my curses became steadily less sotto and more voce. There was a white sedan parked outside near the gate.

"Whose car is that?" I asked, and one of the laypeople pointed to a young man sitting with the nun. "Can you take me to the port?"

"Thirty thousand," he said.

"Three thousand?" Fifteen years had passed since the dinar had replaced the old Sudanese pound, but northerners and southerners alike still quoted prices in the latter, adding an extra zero. "Three thousand is too high. I'm just going to the port."

"Eh!" he said, his lip curled in disgust. "Petrol is expensive. It's sixteen thousand a gallon."

"It may be sixteen hundred a gallon," I said, again fixing his decimals, "but you're not burning a gallon to go to the port, it's just two miles."

The nun and the driver both started shouting, the young man reiterating the price of gas, while the nun castigated me for quoting the prices in the actual currency of Sudan. "The thousand system is the system of the north!" she said. "We don't recognize it. We don't recognize it."

"So the pound system isn't from Khartoum?" I asked. "Where did it come from, Angola?" and at that she blew up.

"You are trying to dominate us!" she shrieked. "You and your white-man reasoning—you want to dominate. I have been to America, it is very expensive. African people have to pay lots of money. You should pay too. They work like slaves. It is slavery!"

I modulated my tone and was able to talk the angry bride of Christ down to twenty-five hundred, beat back a last-minute rally in which she said the driver would cost extra and waited for the young man to finish his bottomless mango drink. I picked up the gear and followed him out the gate. He passed the old sedan and opened the door of the sister's new Mitsubishi Pajero. He drove without speaking and I arrived at the port with fifteen minutes to spare to find Matt and Alex sitting exactly where I'd left them. The captain had gone for more ammunition.

By six o'clock it was clear we weren't going anywhere. John got me a bed at the NPA guesthouse, I walked to the United Nations compound for dinner and later caught up with Matthew and Alexandre at Café de Paris, where the Canadian lolled into a mini-coma the moment conversation lagged, only to spring again to life when an interesting or important point came up. It was a satisfying last night in town.

We met at the port the next morning and waited again until early afternoon, when Moses came off the barge and waved us over. In the cool darkness of the canvas-roofed cargo area we stashed our gear—Alexandre's two small bags, Matthew's rubberized waterproof duffel and my four albatrosses. The place was packed nearly full with boxes, bags of maize flour, slick yellow jerricans of cooking oil, flats of gluco-biscuits and the stripped body of a white Land Cruiser. Two tight paths ran down the length of the musty enclosure to the engine room, with its immaculate twin diesel motors, and a narrow walkway connected the port and starboard sides. To the right was a small metal workbench; to the left, a steel ladder. A crewman directed us up, past the shallow landing and the door to the pilothouse, to the roof, where a few men in fatigues sat cross-legged around the .50-cal.

"You wait here," he said, and we did, watching as dozens of passengers were squeezed on board for the ride downriver. I tried to count them as they came on and lost track. I tried again later that evening, but each family had sequestered itself quietly on the nooks and ridges of the stacked cargo like discreet cliff dwellers. A floating repair platform—a kind of mini-barge—about fifteen by thirty feet was lashed to the right side, the words "RED CROSS II" stenciled in stubby capitals on its side. This was piled with a wooden bedframe and headboard, a half dozen wooden benches and scores of stavelike lengths of sugarcane.

"This is nice, eh?" Alexandre said. "We have the best seats, with the best view." It was true. Twenty feet above the Nile banks the mango and doum leaves shushed in a slow wind and the water seemed to breathe. Two hours after we'd come aboard, the engines turned over and a crewman dislodged the mooring, a steel pike and cable, wedged into the crook of an old mango tree. We inched away from the shore, pivoted to face north, and began moving at a crawl, slowly gaining steam. My skin sang at the new breeze, the dustless air. We passed the riverside camps where aid workers drank cocktails by the Nile and soon the city was behind us, followed by the site of Gondokoro, Juba's predecessor, a trading post where African slaves were assembled for shipment downriver to the markets of Shendi and Cairo. There was nothing on the patch of bush to suggest the commerce in humans that had taken place there.

The sprawl of tukuls gave way to scrub and big sky. A man came up the ladder, not quite as lean or as tall as Moses or the other crewmen, his face softer. "How are you?" he said, trading handshakes. "I am Michael, the radio operator. The captain says you will sleep up here tonight. Is that all right? You won't fall off?"

The roof would indeed be crowded; a solar panel the size of a desktop ate up some of the space, as did the machine gun. "It's heaven up here," Matthew said. "Besides, I'll make sure to sleep in the middle."

"We'll be fine," I said. "It's perfect."

Michael stayed to chat. He was forty-one. He held the rank of sergeant major, and had been a soldier since he was seventeen. A Dinka from Duk Fawil in the Dinka heartland, he'd been readying to leave home for university when the civil war started in 1983. He'd been assigned to the barge for nearly fourteen years, and was apparently the most educated member of the crew. Like them, he was both a soldier of the Sudan People's Liberation Army and an employee of Norwegian People's Aid. "You're with both," I said.

"Yes, both," he answered.

"And therein," Matthew said, the narcolepsy taking temporary leave of him, "lies an interesting story."

"See, back in '91, some of the worst days of the war, the Red Cross had a small river barge running out of Bor, delivering aid inside the Sudd marshlands to the Dinkas in Jonglei state. It's pretty impenetrable, as you know, and was more so during the war. The barge had a limited capacity, so they had a new one, which could hold sixty tons, specially built in England, shipped over to Mombasa in pieces and trucked into Bor, where they assembled it. The government saw this, and they—not unreasonably—lost their minds, thinking it would be used to move rebel armor down the Nile. So they banned the Red Cross from operating it. And it sat there. The Red Cross is completely nonpolitical, and they couldn't risk their operations elsewhere in Sudan by defying Khartoum over the barge. Meanwhile the SPLA was getting ready to just seize it, 'cause there's a famine going on, and the people need food. And the government is sending Antonovs over Bor to try and bomb the thing to the bottom of the Nile, but the bombs get caught in the wind and keep missing the mark.

"The solution was this: If the Red Cross isn't allowed to take sides—can't even brook the appearance of taking sides—why not give the barge to an organization that can? That's where NPA comes in. While the rest of the aid community was bending over backwards to appear impartial, NPA said, 'The hell with it. We're on the side of the people, and in south Sudan, that's the SPLA.' They're a bit different from the other groups, they're an outgrowth of the Norwegian labor party and the trade unions, so there's that militant aspect the other groups don't have."

While the United Nations and the aid groups operated only where Khartoum allowed them, an arrangement that favored the north and its southern proxies, NPA's staffers worked only in rebel-held areas, and in close coordination with the SPLA's social services wing. They abandoned the Jonglei region when the fighting got too hot, but the aid vessel's crew of Dinka fighters did not, and it became, for a time, a warship. Then it was camouflaged and hidden away for years inside the vast Sudd marshlands, where it awaited its next act. After the peace treaty was signed, NPA returned to the Sudd, bestowed seven years of back pay on the crew and reclaimed the barge as a humanitarian vessel.

I asked Michael if the barge had ever been involved in combat. "In 1992," he said with a faint smile, "we ambushed a *jallaba* steamer full of reinforcements. I will show you when we reach the place."

We retrieved our sleeping gear from the cliff dwellers and made camp on the roof along with two crewmen. The sun took hours to set, casting sky and river in a single blue penumbra. When at last it disappeared, the barge's spotlight came on, a bolt of semi-solid white light that zigzagged over the water's surface in search of sandbars and thick patches of hyacinth. We dined on canned tuna and bread, and a crewman brought us lengths of sugarcane to strip and chew for dessert. Sometime around midnight the barge stopped at a patch of bare dirt and a stand of trees on the western bank. The anchor pike was driven into the ground and most of the passengers and cargo were off-loaded into the inky night to walk to their homes in the roadless hinterlands. I stayed on the roof, wetted the exterior of my sleeping bag with insect repellent and slept as the spotlight drew armies of flying bugs into its siren beam.

I woke the next morning to a slight chill and the sound of Alexandre and Matthew conversing in French. They hadn't yet risen; Matthew was still in his sleeping bag atop a thin inflatable sleeping pad, and Alexandre, who didn't carry a sleeping bag, was wrapped in a windbreaker. I sat up, pulled my eyeglasses from my shirt pocket, wiped the lenses with a handkerchief and did a double take. "Hey man," I said to Matthew. "What's with your face?"

"What?"

"Your lip. It's—it's big."

He felt around his mustache and beard and winced as his fingers prodded his lower lip, which had overnight swollen to twice its size. "Got a mirror?" I opened the raid pack and handed him mine. "I guess something stung me. My mouth's kind of numb, come to think of it." He beamed. "Maybe I'll discover a new disease."

"You can always submit yourself as a case study if your research doesn't work out," I said. "And what is your research, by the way?"

"War Studies, King's College," he said. "I'm looking at the impact of humanitarianism on the civil war."

"So this isn't your first time in Sudan."

"I've been coming since 2003," Matthew said, "interviewing commanders, aid officials, the like. Got enough for a pretty good history of the war. But the dissertation's the main thing. What about you, Alex? First time?"

"I have been in the north," Alexandre said, plucking a tiny toothbrush and a minuscule tube of paste from his wallet-sized shaving kit. "I have driven down from Ethiopia into Blue Nile state. From there I went north and went on the ferry from Port Sudan across the Red Sea to Saudi Arabia. It was years ago. I had a

Land Cruiser, a very good model, the old HJ60, and I had a small, how do you say—*un fusil à canon scié?*"

"A shotgun?" Matthew said.

"Shotgun." Alexandre nodded. "But cut down. Sawn off." He held his hands about two feet apart. "I had the gun wrapped in black paper on a little shelf, here, at the ceiling. For protection. And when I got to Jeddah, they kept the car overnight for customs police to search it. I thought I was finished. Dead. My life in a Saudi Arabian prison." He laughed.

"So what happened?" Matthew said, still checking his lip in the mirror.

"I went to the port the next day, the officer came and threw me the keys and I drove to Jordan like nothing was wrong. They didn't find it. I don't know if they even looked."

Alexandre had been an architect before falling hard for photography. He worked mostly for international charities, documenting their overseas work, and when he wasn't doing that he traveled to satisfy his wanderlust. He'd driven across the Middle East and North Africa and had been as far south as Madagascar. A purist, he refused to make the switch to digital. "I have to make the image myself, with my own eye," he said. "I produce the negative with my own hands and the prints the same way too, in my own darkroom. They are always making bigger sensors for the digital cameras, but these still cannot record the same information that the silver bromide crystals can hold on a roll of film."

Michael, the radio operator, appeared at the top of the ladder bearing thin loaves of bread, like frankfurter buns, and a box of Egyptian-made sesame halvah bars. Another crewman handed up a pot of sugary black tea. As we breakfasted the scrub trees and bushes began to fade from the shore and the way ahead became flat as glass, the current imperceptible, the land increasingly defined by forests of papyrus that dwarfed what Schon and I had paddled through in Uganda. The single river divided into meandering channels that the crew read from memory.

We were approaching the Sudd. For thousands of years this giant swamp—more than fifty thousand square miles, as big as England—had repelled invaders from the lands to the north. The British explorer Samuel Baker described it as "a vast sea of papyrus ferns and rotting vegetation, and in that fetid heat there is a spawning tropical life that can hardly have altered very much since the beginning of the world." In AD 61 the Roman emperor Nero, who controlled Egypt, dispatched troops up the river to find the source of the Nile. They returned with reports of "immense marshes" that were too dense for all but the smallest of one-man canoes. It wasn't until eighteen hundred years later that a Turkish naval captain, operating under orders from the Egyptian ruler Mohammed Ali, was able to penetrate the swamp, reaching as far as Gondokoro. Slaves and ivory were soon flowing north on the Nile. This was the beginning of what Dinka lore calls the time when "the world was spoiled."

And still something about the swamp was remarkably unspoiled. Later that first morning, we passed a man-made clearing in the papyrus on the western bank, a floating homestead with a reed-roofed tukul, a small black dugout canoe, racks for drying fish, rows of cultivated sorghum and a naked family of four standing by the river's edge watching us pass. They were all—mother, father, son and young daughter—leaner than lean, rippled with muscles, with posture to make a yogi envious. They stood in a row and waved with open smiles like the goodest people in Creation and Michael grabbed two bars of halvah and hurled them over the water and onto their floating patch, calling out something in Dinka.

While Alexandre prowled the barge with his Leicas, Matthew and I climbed down for a look at the pilothouse. It was a shallow bridge, painted white, with just a few simple instruments and enough room for a man to stand at the steering wheel without his back touching the wall. There were two wheels, actually—one for each engine—and when the barge bottomed out on a sandbar the crewmen would stand side by side cranking the wheels and goosing the throttles in unison to Moses's barked instructions. Behind them were two doors leading to the private cabins of the captain and the chief engineer, to their left, a small table with a radio, Michael's station. From the windows we could see, at the very front of the barge, a crewman in green coveralls delicately probing the depth of the river with a fifteen-foot wooden pole, much like they did on the Mississippi in Mark Twain's day.

We passed the time chewing sugarcane and dangling our feet in the water. Very late in the afternoon, I spied a blanket of smoke ahead on the eastern bank, a Cairo-like haze hovering over an acre of cleared land. "What is that?" I said.

"Cattle camp," Matthew replied. I had read about cattle camps but hadn't yet seen one. A hundred pale, tall-horned zebu cows had been tied to stakes for the night by their young wardens, two boys not older than twelve. One boy wore a tiny red Speedo, the other, yellow shorts and an undershirt just a little dirtier than the one on my back. The haze was smoke from dung fires burning to protect both the herd and the boys from mosquitoes and tsetse flies, and the boys were dusted head to toe in ash. The camp was unusual in one respect: The boys didn't appear to be armed. There was nothing more precious than cattle. Raids were common, and deadly. The boys stood by the water and watched us pass; they didn't return our waves.

Soon we reached Bor. The barge passed a rusted half-sunken steamer and a waterfront strip where women washed clothes and men slaughtered livestock. We moored at Moses's camp on Bor's northern outskirts and the crew mustered on the covered deck. Moses came down from the bridge in crisp fatigues and shined boots, a John Garang button pinned over his heart, and addressed them in Dinka for several minutes. He turned to the chief engineer, said a few more words, and the chief gave him an elaborate salute—marching in place, his right hand moving slowly to his brow—before dismissing the crewmen. "You come," Moses told us, and we followed him across the gangplank and into his camp: ten fenced-in acres, with a vegetable garden where giant green pumpkins basked in the sun, a half dozen tukuls, scores of fifty-gallon oil drums, and, sitting in the swept dirt near a circle of benches and lawn chairs, a green wooden ammunition crate bearing the stenciled label "PARTS OF TYPEWRITER."

I pointed to the clearing and asked Moses if I could pitch my tent there. "No," he said. "You are my special guests. You will stay in the new hotel, Freedom Camp."

"We're good to camp out here," Matthew said. "Dan's got a tent, I've got a tent."

"We don't need a hotel," I added. "We'll really be fine here. Happy, really."

Moses was unmoved. "Come."

We followed him past the armed guards and through the gate and walked a half mile south to a fenced-in camp modeled on Juba's ritzy expatriate villages. They charged forty dollars a night, enough to set us grumbling, but we had no choice. Moses was captain, and this was where he wanted us. Freedom Camp had thirty army-style tents, each with a single bed, a lawn chair and a small card table. There were two outhouses, each home to its own resident plague of toads, and a bathing enclosure for private bucket showers. A big metal barn served as the cafeteria and bar, with a diesel generator to keep the beer cold and the satellite TV running. We registered and crashed after a buffet dinner of goat, potatoes, cabbage, rice and beer.

In the morning we walked down a sandy path through patches of tall yellow grass into Bor town. A major Dinka capital, Bor had the feel of a prosperous frontier burg. The market district was full

of shoppers, women in ankle-length dresses, young men in Western T-shirts and slacks and the male elders strolling the muddy
streets in leather cowboy hats and long robes. They carried small
clubs or swagger sticks—no two the same—and smoked pipes
fashioned from hammered steel and brass. Bor was their town.
Where Juba struggled with the tension of its refugees, the SPLA,
the local Equatorians, the foreign peacekeepers and a growing
population of aid workers, Bor's identity was straightforwardly
and unmistakably Dinka and had been for centuries. John Garang
was a Bor Dinka and the SPLA had been dominated by them and
by the Dinka from Bahr al Ghazal to the west. It was here that the
first shots of the civil war were fired, and it was here that raiders
from the rival Nuer tribe struck in 1991 after the rebel movement
split along tribal lines. More than two thousand people were killed
and thousands of cattle stolen before the city was retaken by the
SPLA.

"Nobody believed Bor would fall," Matthew said, as we wove
through the stalls selling Goodwill clothes, detergent, pangas and
framed prints of Garang and Salva Kiir. "People were traumatized
by the symbolism as much as by the actual destruction." It took
more than a decade for the rift between the rebel factions to be
even partially repaired.

Moses met us at the hotel during lunch with news and an edict.
He would be leaving to visit his four wives, each of whom lived on
a separate homestead in the interior, and he had to see the local
JIU commander about acquiring a detachment of troops for the
Sobat. We were not to enter Bor without Moses as an escort, he
said before leaving. We were trapped. "Anybody want to take bets
on when he's coming back?" I asked.

Diversion came in the American form of Lola Dee Toloba, a
social worker from Washington State who had come to Bor with
a group of Episcopalians looking to link development projects in
south Sudan with donors and volunteers in the United States.

Matthew and Alexandre had been bent over sheets of drawing paper designing an amphibious Land Cruiser that we would one day pilot up the Nile and the Atbara River into Ethiopia. They were calculating water displacement and propeller gear ratios when Lola asked to join us. A large woman with sensibly short blonde hair, her flesh running from pale to pink in the southern heat, she continued fanning herself as she turned away from CNN and walked over to our table.

Lola wasn't a professional aid worker, nor was she a proselytizer. She was a uniquely self-motivated Samaritan. "I was sitting at my computer at work one day at the old St. Helen's Hospital in Chehalis," she said. "It was October of 2000. I was looking up the *Post-Intelligencer* about the Department of Social and Health Services, because we had been getting a lot of negative press, and there was an article which included a picture of three or four young men. I can still see that picture—these long-legged, very dark-complexioned young men. The story was about their journey to the United States, and as I read the story it was as if God were speaking to me through the screen of the computer. Like a lightning bolt the decision was very clear. The article said there were agencies looking for homes to host the young people coming in from south Sudan. I knew my husband would not agree with the idea God had for me, but I have always had a strong connection to people of African descent. I just knew it: Here was my duty and responsibility to care for these children. I felt the farm I had would be a good place. I had a sister and my parents nearby, so the kids would have a ready-made family. The five children had lived together and now they would stay together. My husband was not happy about three, let alone all five, so I found a family to place the two older boys in our community, but they were with us nearly every weekend."

I had been nodding along at Lola's story, with its familiar contours of recognition of a distant emergency and the moment of clarity that says *Do Something.* But to Do Something five times in a single stroke? "You adopted five children?" I asked. "At once?"

"Well," she said, holding up her fingers to help me keep track. "I adopted just the three—Rachel, Michael and Rabecca—and then there are my two birth children, but my kids are all equal. My husband wasn't around much longer after that, and so pretty soon I was a single mother of five. Then, in 2003, another young man came to live with us. He, Elijah, was uncharacteristically short, just five-five. He was a childhood friend of my other children. Well, Elijah is now over six-five. My mother claims that he grew so tall from my food and my love. Mary came in 2003 also; she's a cousin of my kids. So that makes seven."

She looked at Matthew, who was nodding off, and at his sweat-conditioned Newfoundland cap and said, "I can wash that for you if you want."

He opened his eyes. "Um, that won't be necessary, thanks."

Lola and her group were waiting for a meeting with the governor. In the meantime, they planned a trip to a nearby leper colony. Would we like to come along? Indeed we would. The next morning Lola and the other Episcopalians squeezed into a Land Cruiser while Matthew, Alexandre and I rode in the back of a pickup truck to a spot half an hour south of town. We got out and walked down a squishy path, past the bombed remains of a school, past a pond created by a giant bomb crater, to a ragged village surrounded by trees and thick bush. The residents greeted us with cheers and Dinka-language hymns. We shook hands all around, including with men who had no hands. "Good morning," I said, pumping the wrist of a cloudy-eyed elder, my palms tingling with psychosomatic infection. Matthew, the social scientist, set to interviewing the local chief, who showed him a log noting ninety-five households in the village.

Soon it was time to distribute the booty. Lola and her comrades had bags of donated castoffs: slacks, children's dresses, a leopard-print skirt, flip-flops (which drew applause) and a Frisbee (which was greeted with puzzled silence). The chief parceled out the goods, and there was angry talk over how the spoils were divided. Almost everyone's head was shaved. Women without hands were jostling to try on dresses while the children wailed and the chief took the aspirin and ibuprofen out of the donated first aid kit and gave them to a woman I assumed was his wife. I began to feel repelled.

"I don't get it," I told Matthew. "It looks like less than a quarter of the people actually have leprosy. Why do they live out here? Why not live in town, where there's a clinic?"

"I'm getting the impression they think it's an inherited disease, incurable," he said. "I asked the young guys what they need and they told me fishing equipment and building materials. Nobody mentioned medicine. They don't know how easy it is to treat leprosy." I left the village and sat at the edge of the bomb crater pond and looked out over the Nile marsh framed by a pair of tall palms, the low clouds all wide and flat, running from black to cotton and black again. I could hear singing from the new church school down the path. The original, built in 1981, was bombed after Garang's 1983 mutiny; there was little left of it besides the cornerstone.

Moses was gone for five long days. When he returned, dressed in a denim and leopard-print combo topped with a hat extolling the American rapper 50 Cent, he took us on a tour of Bor town that wound up at a dirt-floored snack shop in which he was a partner. There we sat on plastic chairs as three of Moses's children—two boys and, later, a reed-thin eleven-year-old girl, the very image of her father—joined us. We chatted a bit with the children before they were dismissed, and then Moses set down his Coke and leaned forward with his elbows on his knees. "Alex!" he commanded. "What do you think of my children?"

Alexandre pursed his lips and gave a sage nod, as if he had just tasted an unusually fine Bordeaux, and said, "Yes, Captain. They are very good children. You are very lucky."

"And my daughter," Moses said, "she is also good. Strong."

"Yes," Alexandre said, nodding, a sheen of moisture on his stubbled cheek. "A quite good child."

"So you and this girl, you like her, you can be married," Moses said. "You can be in my family."

Alexandre paled and swallowed hard, his Adam's apple scraping up and down the length of his throat, and said apologetically, "Thank you, Moses. That is a very kind way to think of me, but I cannot get married now. My work is too much."

Moses turned to his next victim. "Matthew! What about you? You should have a Dinka wife. You are practically Sudanese."

Matthew was now wide awake, his eyes twinkling. "I'm not opposed to the idea of marrying a Dinka," he said genially. "But I'm afraid my father wouldn't allow it—he prefers for me to concentrate on my studies, and I have years to go. A lot of years."

"Good. That's fine," Moses countered. "By the time you finish she will be ready. Then you come back and take her to London."

An engaging silence fell over the unlit shack. Moses had apparently noticed my battered wedding band and, hep to the Western horror of polygamy, spared me the invitation. After a slightly uncomfortable interval, in which he appeared to be formulating a new approach, he asked if we had finished our drinks, and we resumed the tour.

The four of us meandered toward the Nile, Moses exchanging greetings and handshakes along the way. At the riverside a crowd was gathered around a man and two boys busy hacking away at the carcasses of two Nile crocodiles with rusted machetes. The crowd wasn't gawking—it was buying. The animals were laid out on flattened cardboard boxes. Their meat was weighed on a blue metal scale; the shoppers took it away in thin black plastic bags after paying the lead butcher, whose face ran with sweat but whose tan chinos and red Snoop Dogg T-shirt had avoided even a stray splattering drop of reptile blood. With little left to sell—all but the waxy heads and some loose cuts remained—he threw the feet into the river, wiped his hands on a rag and pulled us aside.

He was a croc hunter, a member of a Dinka subtribe that lived in the marshes and had developed an intimacy with the water even as their cousins ranged the land with their armies of cows. The governor had hired them to kill crocodiles outside Bor. Women and especially babies were being taken from the banks, and it wasn't hard to see why. Not twenty feet away goat's blood was running into the river; animals were being slaughtered just yards from where women brought their children to bathe and wash laundry.

"You are from America?" the crocodile hunter asked.

"Well, he's from Canada," I said. "And he's from France."

"Good. America," the hunter said. "I want to ask you this question: I am always looking for new techniques. What are the methods for capturing crocodile in your country?"

"Dynamite," Matthew said.

"Dynamite." The hunter's brow furrowed. "That is difficult to come by in Sudan."

We were just a couple days away from regaining the river. Moses had completed his conjugal visits. He had also been to see the local JIU commander, and a platoon of soldiers would soon be joining us. The crew had begun prepping the barge for launch, moving barrels of fuel to the engine room, swabbing the deck and cleaning their weapons and ammunition—hundreds of 7.64-millimeter and .50-caliber rounds—with copious amounts of diesel. But this progress was too slow for Matthew. After a month in Juba and a week in Bor, he had decisively run out of time and would soon be leaving on a World Food Program plane to Juba, with onward passage to Lokichoggio, Nairobi and London. I bought his Kata-dyn filter pump (mine had cracked) and his high-tech sleeping pad and stood him an afternoon beer at the Freedom Camp cafeteria. "What kind of name is LeRiche, anyway?" I asked. "It sounds like a cartoon villain. You know, LeRiche versus the Mounties."

"It's actually the name of a pirate," he said as he dropped his waterproof duffel into the back of the pickup that would take him to the airport. "Something my grandfather was always saying, that we're descended from a fugitive pirate. I'd been hearing this my whole life, so I figured, why not put it to the test? I went into the archives in Greenwich and London, and I found it: In the 1700s one James LeRiche was arrested by a Royal Navy vessel and charged with piracy. But he never made it to court in London. The other prisoners did, but his name isn't on the docket. So it looks like my grandfather wasn't just telling stories. And we've been lodged in Newfoundland ever since. My grandfather wouldn't even give up his Newfoundland passport after we were forced to join Canada in 1949. He knew where he came from, and it sure wasn't Ottawa."

In the morning Alexandre and I boarded the barge and were joined by a dozen new faces, members of the JIU. They were ten Equatorians—smaller than the Dinka crew though just as hard, some wearing mustaches and even trim beards—and two Nuer sol-diers. They were on the barge as security, yes, but also to demon-strate to the Nuer tribesmen who lived along the Sobat that the barge was a southern vessel, and not just a Dinka one. It was an important and potentially lifesaving distinction.

The Nuer and the Dinka—competing tribes of cattle herders—had been at odds since the late 1800s, a rivalry that found full bloody flower during the civil war, when large tracts of the Upper Nile region were controlled by Nuer militias loyal to Khartoum. Most of those forces had been absorbed into the SPLA in 2006, but hundreds of holdouts in the pay of recalcitrant warlords remained in the northern reaches of the Sudd, on the Sobat and in the oil

areas north of there. Among most observers, the Nuer were considered superior warriors to the Dinka. Some Nuer clans even used
mortars and rocket-propelled grenades during their cattle raids.
"It's basically the most militarized society I've ever come across,"
Matthew had said of the Nuer. "Everyone has a gun, and there's
no central authority." (Number one in the badass sweepstakes
were the Muerle, who, though numerically small, were the most
feared warriors. "They will walk for days without water to raid
cattle," a United Nations political officer once told me. "They will
eat dirt.")

Alexandre and I watched the JIU men muster on deck for an
address by Moses. They saluted smartly when it was finished, after
which they were drilled in Arabic on the art of the flotation device,
slipping on and off the newly purchased life vests at the chief engineer's command. The lesson was more than a formality. Just a
few weeks before, seventy-five SPLA men had drowned south of
Malakal when two boats transporting troops collided in the dark.
Finally, with a clean deck, clean guns and the buoyancy of its
armed guards assured, the barge was ready to go.

CHAPTER SIX

For the next five days our diesel-powered dormitory pushed through one of the world's biggest marshlands. We followed the main branch of the White Nile, known as the Bahr al Jabal, or mountain river, which curves to the west and northwest along the outer borders of the Sudd, and avoided the tighter channels of the Bahr al Jadid, or new river, formed by massive flooding in the 1980s, which takes a course down the middle of the swamp.

Each of the JIU men had been issued a mosquito net and a new foam mattress with a colorful floral cover. While Moses's crewmen and two Sudanese passengers slept on beds at the rear of the boat, the JIU men colonized the front, some in hammocks, others taking places inside and on top of the stripped white Land Cruiser. Alexandre and I resumed our spot on the pilothouse roof.

Alexandre and I quickly fell into a routine of sleeping, eating, reading and sleeping some more. I was well into one of those summer afternoon naps that sends you deep into the muck, dead still and sweating, when James, a student en route to collect a scholarship from the Anglican bishop of Malakal, woke me and said it was time to eat. "Thanks, man," I mumbled. "I'll get some later." A few minutes later he was back.

"They won't eat until you and your friend have eaten." Nor would they serve James. I sat up, cracked my knuckles and stumbled to the front of the boat, where one of the Equatorians was using a stick to stir five gallons of overcooked rice and beans around an aluminum cauldron sitting on a pile of coals. He handed me a metal plate and I thanked him in Arabic. It was a heaping serving, with traces of onion and no salt that I could discern. I ate it all, rinsed my plate from a jug of river water and sat next to James on the repair platform.

"James," I said, "can you help me a second?"

"What is it?"

"I can't tell a Dinka from a Nuer. I've been looking and looking and I just can't figure it out. You're a Dinka, and you have these vertical marks on your forehead, like an eagle clawed you—don't get me wrong, it's handsome, it looks good. But I've met Dinka who have those horizontal scars across the forehead. And these taller guys in the JIU, they have horizontal lines, but they're Nuer. I can't figure it out."

"Oh," he said jovially. "That's easy. This"—he pointed to the ritual scar on his forehead, a vertical stalk with shoots coming out the sides like a series of stacked Vs—"is Bor Dinka. The lines you are seeing that go across, those are for the Nuer, and also for the Dinka from Bahr al Ghazal. They do it the same as the Nuer."

The horizontal scarring, usually five or six raised lines or creases running along the forehead, gives the brow a permanently furrowed appearance and makes the bearer seem wise and noble beyond his years or standing. These long cuts were apparently filled with ash, which made the ripples stand up in bold relief. Some people, however, had weak and less impressive scars, created in haste or by an unskilled cut-man. These were shorter, perfunctory, not as deep.

Still, I was confused. "How do the Nuer and the Dinka from

Bahr al Ghazal set themselves apart from each other if they wear the same scars? Isn't the point of the scars to show who you are and who you aren't?"

"The point of the scars is to show you are an adult," James said. "Traditionally, you cannot be treated as an adult and cannot take part in important decisions unless you have the scar. This is not as true today as it was in the past, as many educated people do not take part. But there is another way that Dinka and Nuer look different from each other, and this is the teeth. We take out these"—he raised his upper lip to reveal gaps where two canine teeth used to be—"while the Nuer take out these teeth on the bottom. So you see it is really simple: If it is up here, Dinka, and if it is down there, it is Nuer."

I am not infrequently beset by dreams in which I find myself ripping out my own teeth, and while these dreams are marked by manic determination, copious blood and, finally, extraordinary regret, they are never accompanied by actual pain. I doubted this was the case in real life. "Doesn't that hurt, when they knock out your teeth?"

"It does hurt," James said. "But you must not make a sound. That is a great humiliation. Not just the boys. The girls too. You suffer it in silence, and then you are an adult."

Later that afternoon the barge slowed to meet two fishermen in a dugout canoe, each of them naked save for black Hugo Boss briefs that covered their genitals and not very much of their posteriors. "That is some kind of fashion, eh?" Alexandre said as they haggled with the crew.

"America should ship its obese to Sudan, teach them how to live," I said. "Those dudes are fit."

"It is not a regime I would like to follow," he said.

The crewmen bought four or five lungfish and a catfish from the canoers. The catch was hacked into four-inch sections with a machete and thrown into the empty cauldron with water and salt.

That night, two plates appeared on the roof, each with a hunk of fish in broth and a small jerrican of water. We washed our hands, passed the can back to the man at the ladder and ate the strong-tasting fish with our fingers, tossing overboard the skin, bones and black bowel. Around nine that evening the boat slowed and stopped. The spotlight came on as a crewman dragged the mooring pike through a patch of papyrus and onto shore. "Are we stopping?" I asked.

"The crew maybe cannot go all night," Alexandre said. "They would be tired in the morning, I guess."

There was a *thok-thok-thok* as thumb-sized waterbugs assailed the spotlight, the barge and us. I smoked my tenth cigarette of the night, and went to sleep with a new coating of DEET smeared on my sleeping bag and on the brim of my hat, only to wake at three o'clock with the barge again in motion and raindrops pelting us in the dark. We got our things together and made for the ladder.

We paused on the landing, where the door to the pilothouse was open. I peered into the dark bridge and it was a moment before I realized Moses was standing just a foot away from me, his mouth open, eyes deep in the river, his hands jerking the wheel every few seconds as he chased hidden channels we couldn't and never would see. Finally, still looking forward, he said loudly, "This is a place for work now. You go down to sleep."

I descended the wet steel ladder and walked past the thrumming engine room toward the left-side railing to watch the river and the rain and was promptly pulled back by my collar and prodded into the rear of the barge by a crewman. "You sleep, there," he said, pointing to a sagging foam mattress supported by two benches. Michael's bed was on the left, a proper string bed with a metal frame, and he pushed it against ours to share some of his space.

We woke up to a radio playing Sudanese pop, loud conversation and clanging metal tools. The barge had been in motion the rest of the night, steering down channels marked by drifting colonies of hyacinth and loose islands of dense vegetation—the *sudd*, or obstructions, for which the marsh was named. Alexandre and I were served too-sweet tea in red plastic mugs and a pack of gluco-biscuits to share. At the front of the barge, the JIU men were stripping down their own .50-caliber gun, meticulously washing each part in diesel. Individual soldiers were doing the same with their Kalashnikovs. Their AKs were a motley arsenal. Some showed a lifetime of careful maintenance, while others appeared cobbled together from a variety of cannibalized and ill-treated weapons. The barge now had two heavy guns at the ready, one on the roof and one on deck.

I was sitting with Michael on the roof that afternoon when he pointed to a spot in the reeds, a patch no different to me from any other, and said, "There. Mayen. That's where we made the ambush. March 1992." There were two boats, he said, the barge and a smaller craft, hidden away on the western side of the Nile. They opened up on a government troop barge with heavy machine guns and small arms in the dead of night, cursing and taunting the northerners as they gunned them into the crocodile waters. "In what language?" I asked.

"In Arabic," he said. "It's the language we all know."

"Were any of your men killed?"

"No. Many of theirs died. I don't know the number." The long war had been a decades-long series of such engagements—skirmishes, ambushes and full-scale battles, all of them unknown to anyone besides the combatants, the civilian victims and a tiny number of aid workers, journalists and academics. There was so much unseen waste—and so much hidden valor.

Now Moses and his crew feared they would be the ones falling prey to an ambush on the water. In a day or two we would reach the northern edge of the Sudd and the confluence of four Nile tributaries—the Bahr al Ghazal from the west, the Sobat from the

east and the Bahr al Jabal and Bahr al Zeraf from the south. It was
a region of overlapping hot zones. A barge of Indian peacekeepers had taken fire there months earlier. Canadian helicopter pilots
working for an oil company had been kidnapped nearby.

"Khor Fulus and Atar," Michael said. "They're at war."

"Those are people?" I asked. "Warlords?"

Michael shook his head. "They are places. Counties. Well, they
are one county, but Atar wants to be separate. So they are fighting." I took my Sudan map from the raid pack and spread it out on
the roof. "Very nice," he murmured, running his finger down the
river from Bor, stopping a quarter inch short of Malakal. "Here
is Khor Fulus. Here is Atar. And here, more important," he said,
pointing to the northern bank of the Nile as it bent to the east, "is
Phom Zeraf, where is Tang, Gabriel Tang. He is a SAF general with
his own militia. He refuses to join SPLA. He still wants to fight. It
is a matter of time."

Moses and the gray-haired chief engineer joined us and I stepped
back so the three of them could delve into the map, matching its
written features against their decades of experience. When they
finished, Michael and the chief folded and refolded the map in a
vain effort at returning it to its original form. I reached in and
accordioned it back into shape. The chief said something in Arabic
and everyone laughed.

"What was that?" I asked.

Michael wiped his brow. "*Kull rajul ya'rif kayf yujami' zaw-
jatuh*," he said. "Every man knows how to fuck his wife."

I found my Thuraya satellite phone in the raid pack and brought
it to the front of the barge. An aid official in Juba had suggested
I call a friend of his in Malakal for help in finding lodging. I had
been trying for days to reach Jeremiah, and was surprised when he
finally picked up on his mobile. "Ben told me you are coming," he
said after I introduced myself. "There is not much available in the

way of guesthouses, but I think I have something. It will be ready when you get here."

"But I don't know when that will be," I said. "Are they holding the room? Do I have to pay for the days they're holding it? What's the rate?"

"Not to worry," he replied tartly. "The room will be ready. There is no charge. I have to go now. Call when you arrive." Then he hung up, with no time for my thanks. I always feel better about taking kindness from strangers when they give me that extra thirty seconds for obsequious gratitude. Jeremiah apparently didn't care about my needs. I returned to the roof and stared for an hour at the unending vista of languid water and waving papyrus before the first smoke appeared. It was miles away, a cone of black rising from some spot deep in the swamp grass. It wasn't the smoke of a smoldering dung fire, like we'd seen at the cattle camp. Something was burning, with no sign of what might have caused it.

"What do you make of that?" I asked Alexandre.

"It is more than one place," he said. "Look, behind that one, there is another part burning." The Sudd, or part of it, was on fire, the flat horizon billowing ash every half mile or so. For an hour we motored through thick smoke and at times passed near enough to feel the flames on our arms and faces and to hear their solid insistent roar as fire consumed miles of papyrus, leaving behind charred white stalks topped with crisp blackened poms. The fires had to be man-made, but they were spread over such a wide area that I couldn't see how that was possible. Michael suggested someone had tried to burn down a patch for cultivation and things had gotten out of hand, but there was no way of knowing. I counted three crocodile snouts moving from east bank to west to escape the flames, but these were the only signs of life, human or animal, that I could see. Alexandre and I shot roll after roll of the strange inferno.

The barge had been running almost twenty-four hours a day for the first three days. Now as we neared Phom Zeraf, where some of Gabriel Tang's forces were based, Moses and his crew traded speed for caution. We started dropping anchor for the night, making us prey to the mosquitoes. I slept under a pink bug net I'd purchased in Bor, the top supported by my pack, the bottom anchored by my boots.

With Malakal approaching, the crew and the soldiers prepared for shore leave by taking bucket baths off the open back of the engine room and scrubbing their civilian clothes on the repair platform. I leaned on the railing and watched a JIU man apply more vigor to cleaning a white pair of low-top sneakers than I would apply to the cleaning of a wound. For a platoon stationed on the outskirts of Bor, Malakal was the big time. We now shared the river with a growing number of boats, long steel launches porting people and animals and sugarcane and flour up and down the river. We passed groups of SPLA men bathing in the Nile outside a base south of town, followed by the colonial-era promenade with its tall trees and its World War I memorial and the stately buildings where the administrators from London and Cairo once sat. Dozens of steamers, two- and three-story passenger boats that had plied the route between Juba and the northern city of Kosti, now sat low in the water, rotting through rusted hulls. Civil war had ended the age of steamers and economics would ensure it never came back.

We berthed at Malakal's long river port and waited on the barge for an hour while Moses announced himself to the authorities. Then we were released. With little ceremony, I gave Moses my last bottle of Johnnie Walker and a box of doxycycline and took my leave. Alexandre planned to stay for the ride down the Sobat; I left him with one of the Nalgene bottles, some packets of mosquito repellent and Schon's foam sleeping mat. I shook hands with the crewmen and the soldiers from the JIU, left my business card

Dan Morrison. *(Photograph by Schon Bryan.)*

Schon Bryan, before the Nile rapids.

Seasick on Lake Victoria.
(Photograph by Schon Bryan.)

The boat,
ready at last.

Crossing Lake Kyoga.

Fellow passengers on the NPA barge.

A humanitarian vessel, crewed by soldiers.

From left: Michael, the engineer and a crewman.

Morning on the Nile, south of Bor.

Crocodile meat.

Below: Moses with some of his children.

Seeds and ammunition.

The Sudd burns.

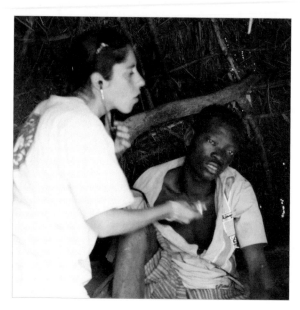

A sick soldier at Kaldak Camp.

John Malwit, the embattled
commissioner of Phom
Zeraf.

John Ivo Mounto.

Malakal port.

Malakal: Mary and Jesus watch over a Shilluk house.

Malakal from the air.

Jailed in Paloich.

The bus to Renk.

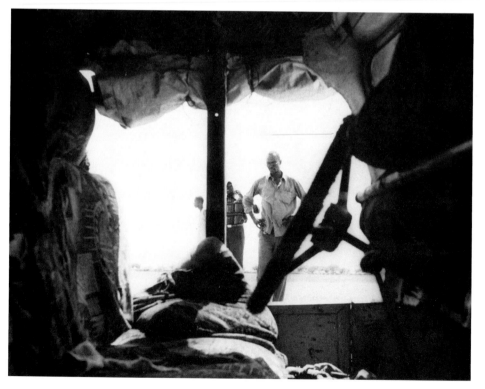

Antiquities guard and son near Meroe, Sudan.

"He's an absolute mystery."

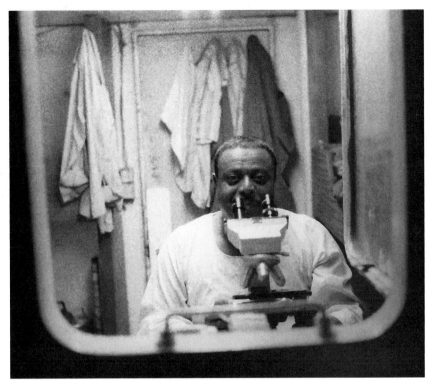

Medical technician, the Aswan ferry.

Cairo: Saad El Soghayar in action.

End of the line: sunset in Rosetta.

with Michael, strapped on my bags and walked down the wooden gangplank.

For the first time in many weeks, I felt I was on something like familiar ground. Malakal was just four hundred miles from Khartoum and I breathed easy at the sight of the traders and shopkeepers in their *jallabiyas,* and at the Ottoman mosque and the dusty town square behind it. The city's Arab character meant development; it meant consumer products; it meant the possibility of comfort. The old historians and geographers say that Africa begins at Malakal, but that's only if you're traveling upriver, from Cairo and Khartoum. I, coming downriver, in the opposite direction, felt the waning of Africa and the beginning of Arabia. "To the north lie the Sahel and the desert, Arab and Muslim," the historian Robert Collins wrote. "To the south sprawl the Sudd, the Nilotic plain, and the Lake Plateau of Africans with different cultures, languages and religions. Like any border town, Malakal belongs to neither world, absorbing some of the best and most of the worst of each." In addition to the Dinka and the Nuer, another tribe was prominent in Malakal: the Shilluk. The Shilluk nation had been a major force on the Nile for four hundred years before its borders were pared by Turkish-Egyptian and then British forces until it was finally absorbed into colonial Sudan. Where the Nuer lacked a centralized political authority and the Dinka's traditional power structures were almost equally horizontal, the Shilluk had long possessed their own kingdom; they still had a nominal king, known as the *reth,* who continued to carry symbolic weight.

Like Juba, Malakal had been squarely in northern hands during the war. It was now part of the autonomous south, but Khartoum's influence remained strong. Thanks to a power-sharing provision in the Comprehensive Peace Agreement, the governor was a member of the Islamist-led National Congress Party, who ruled the north with an iron fist. (The SPLM, in turn, had received several governorships in the north, part of the peace treaty's emphasis on unity and power-sharing.) A strong Sudanese Armed Forces garrison remained in Malakal, as well as military intelligence units that operated out of sight.

Malakal straddled many lines—between Africa and Arabia, between the competing tribes of the Upper Nile region—in all kinds of interesting and dangerous ways, but in those first hours, as I walked through the port gates onto the main drag to wait for Jeremiah, I allowed myself to believe that I had left an area of potential chaos and bloodshed and was entering one of order. In Malakal, I was sure, it wouldn't take a .50-caliber machine gun to make me feel safe.

I sat on the steps under one of Shilluk Avenue's covered sidewalks and watched the mashup of north and south: the Arab merchants in their *jallabiyas* moving among the old Shilluk men with their customary pink tunics tied at the shoulder over collared shirts and cotton slacks, their brows dotted with a row of black pill-sized ritual scars, the local women in their gauzy, multihued wraps. This was the old town's financial hub—just far enough from the Nile to escape flooding, but sufficiently close to the river port and the customs house for businessmen to keep an eye on their stock. Two- and three-story cement buildings lined the avenue for fifty yards, the upper stories jutting out and shading the street below. Arab and a smattering of Darfuri traders—black Muslims from Darfur—sat fanning themselves in the dim recesses of the dry goods stores, while younger African shopboys worked the wooden counters, weighing out portions of dried lentils, garlic and beans and wrapping bundles of tomatoes and onions in faded Arabic newsprint.

Farther inland, past the mosque, came the homes of the well-to-do, where many of the aid groups kept their offices. These were stucco and concrete-block homes with corrugated steel roofs, sporadic municipal water, barred windows and high walls. After that came the poorer suburbs, where Malakal's different tribes clustered in segregated districts fronted by muddy yards, stray chickens, rooting children and blowing trash.

Bor had hummed to the local, Malakal sang the cosmopolitan. I bought a bottle of water and scanned the window of a pharmacist's shop, taking in the old-fashioned safety razors, the teething ointment and the skin-whitening creams—Fair & Lovely, Skin Success, Bio Claire.

A slim man of middle height approached and presented his hand without smiling: "Jeremiah. I hope your trip was comfortable." His large serious eyes were framed by small ears, sharp cheekbones and a high unscarred forehead.

I suppressed the urge to effuse and said, soberly, "Very good to meet you. How is everything?"

"Things are good, thank God. Would you like to see your accommodation?"

We had a tug-of-war over the bags, which I barely won, and we set off with me carrying the rucksack and the tent and Jeremiah toting the raid pack, a small crucifix swinging on its chain as he walked. We took a broad side street past the mosque and moved deeper into the town to a white-walled compound. I followed him in through the gate, past the main residence and into a large outbuilding, where a screened-in porch led to two doors. Jeremiah opened one and pointed me into a ten-by-ten room with two beds, a small barred window and two yellow lightbulbs dangling from the ceiling.

"It's great," I said. "How much?"

"I told you," he replied. "There is no charge."

"You know the owner?"

"I am the owner."

Jeremiah had inherited the property, and it would have made a fine home for him and his wife and daughter. The compound was a fifteen-minute walk from his office at an international aid organization, and it was close to Malakal's shopping district and to the hospital. Instead, he chose to live outside town, a thirty-minute bicycle ride during the dry season, a ninety-minute walk during the wet. Why?

"When you live away from the city your relatives have to make an effort to visit," he said. "Therefore they don't. If I lived here you would not have room to walk for all my relations. They would want to be fed and they would never leave and I would be responsible to them. This is the African way. It's like quicksand." Instead, Jeremiah, a Christian, let an Islamic charity use the main house as its regional office, preferring their humble rent payments over those wealthier tenants who might be harder on the property. Jeremiah's uncle acted as a caretaker and took in boarders who slept in my room and in beds on the screened porch.

"Is anyone else staying here?" I asked, dropping my bags on one of the beds.

"He will sleep outside while you are here. He doesn't mind," Jeremiah said. "Let me show you where to eat."

"This is your first time in Sudan?" he asked as we sat down at a dirt-floored restaurant to lamb kebabs and rounds of bread served on greasy metal plates with hunks of raw onion on the side.

"It's my first time in the south," I said, crumbling a clump of salt over my kebab. "I spent about a month in Darfur in February."

"Darfur," he said, shaking his head. "Let me ask you. Where was all this attention when we were being killed? Three million died. Where was the uproar? And Palestine. What is it about Palestine? A chicken is stolen in Palestine and the whole world hears of it. That is why I'm helping you. So maybe people can hear about this place."

According to Jeremiah, the war wasn't quite over in these parts—the trouble in Phom Zeraf had actually taken up residence in Malakal. A main provision of the peace treaty stated that there would be only two armies in Sudan's new Government of National Unity. Fighters in the various southern militias, most of whom had been aligned with Khartoum, would have to either join the SPLA or move north to join the Sudanese Armed Forces. Most of Gabriel Tang's men had chosen the southern army, but he and a few hundred holdouts refused to go along. "He wants to be commissioner at Phom Zeraf and at the same time to remain a major general in the SAF," Jeremiah said. The southern government had rejected such a deal and instead named one of Tang's former lieutenants, John Malwit, as commissioner. Despite this appointment, Malwit, who had a reputation for corruption, couldn't actually set foot in his district under threat of death from Tang's forces.

So Malwit sat in exile in Malakal, protected by the SPLA, and Tang, his nemesis, also sat in Malakal, protected by the local Sudanese Armed Forces garrison. There were a dangerous number of armed groups bivouacked in the town: the SAF, which had yet to withdraw to the north, as per the peace treaty; units of the SPLA; a JIU, divided like most JIUs; and Nuer and Muerle tribal militias that had been ordered to assemble in and around the city to prevent them from terrorizing the countryside while the authorities figured out how they might be absorbed or peacefully disarmed. All these forces were monitored by a contingent of Indian peacekeepers, a corps of military observers from a dozen countries and by political officers at the local United Nations mission. It made for a potentially toxic brew. Aid workers were getting robbed at night, and minor barroom dustups threatened to become major battles because every aggrieved illiterate drunk had an army to back him up.

I walked to the town's four corners, rounding past the large SAF army base and then the SPLA camp on the Nile south of town and tried to make friends at the local United Nations office. I was alone for the first time in my journey, and Jeremiah, a hardworking family man, was seldom around.

There was much to see and learn in Malakal, but I could feel time was running out. My blue south Sudan travel pass was about to expire, and this preyed on my mind. The Sudanese visa in my passport, which was supposed to cover the entire country, still restricted me to Khartoum. I would be forced to make a choice once the travel pass ran out: attempt a run from Malakal to the capital and plead with the authorities to let me continue my journey (at the risk of being deported for violating the restriction in the first place), or withdraw to Cairo and try there for a new, clean, unrestricted visa. Both options were lousy. If I sprinted to Khartoum I would have to bypass the villages of Melut and Paloich in the contested oil areas of Upper Nile. Thousands of people in that region had been forced out of their villages at gunpoint during the civil war to make way for oil development, and there were rumors that such displacements were continuing. In February 2006, eight months before my arrival in Malakal, an acquaintance of mine was driving past a familiar village in the Thar Jath region of Unity state when she noticed something strange. "There was no village," she told me, "only a wellhead." Eight hundred people had been forced to move to a swamp without compensation. The order came from their governor, an SPLM appointee who nevertheless was apparently under the sway of oil interests. I needed to see the oil areas, but they weren't the place to be caught packing a bad visa. If I withdrew to directly Cairo, however, there was always the chance the Sudanese authorities wouldn't allow me back in.

I was mulling my predicament at the humanitarian community's weekly happy hour when I met Ana, a Portuguese doctor with a European aid group. They were trying to stanch a cholera outbreak at a militia camp an hour upriver. Would I like to join? The next morning I met the team—Ana, a French logistician, a French nurse and four Sudanese staff—at a spot on the river not far from the governor's mansion, where I helped transfer a hundred boxes of Ringer's lactate, an intravenous solution, from the back of a truck to a forty-foot metal launch. To this was added a big blue picnic cooler with a padlocked chain wrapped around it. "What's that, medication?" I asked.

"It's water," the logistician said. "They take it all if you don't lock it up." He pulled the rip cord on the Yamaha and we moved south on the Nile, weaving through the islands and channels, passing what appeared, in the tiny distance, to be a group of hippopotamuses wallowing in the weeds, the first I'd seen on the Nile.

"This outbreak has been going on for weeks," Ana said, ducking out of the wind to light a cigarette. "We arrive, we set up our treatment camp and the first days it's chaos. They want to be paid to bring water from the river. It's their own soldiers who are sick and they want money to carry water! We hire women to clean the tents and they complain and steal the mops. The supply cabinet is empty. Where did the supplies go? We tell them not to move from this place, but some of them do anyway—they think they can outrun an epidemic—so now there are two camps with cholera instead of one. At the end of the day I say to the colonel in charge, 'Here is what we have done today, here is what we wish to do, here are the problems. Do you have any questions?' And he says yes, he has a question: 'Are you married?' I say to him that I am a doctor and I am here in a professional capacity and does he have any other questions. And he does: 'Are you Christian? What are the Christians of Europe doing to help us fight the Muslims?'" She rolled her eyes.

"What's your specialization?" I asked. "Infectious disease?"

"No," she said, flicking her cigarette into the Nile, "I'm a pulmonologist. I study lung cancer."

We tied up to a small dock at Kaldak and unloaded the boxes of IV fluid. The camp was home to more than a thousand soldiers, the bulk of Gabriel Tang's forces, now loyal to the SPLA. The base and the men had been his for at least a decade, but there was no evidence the place had been settled for months, much less years. The soldiers lived on a sandy plain in base shelters of branches and castoff plastic sheeting, and they seemed to possess nothing save weaponry and a few foam mattresses. They all bathed in, shat near and drank from the river. There was a single pit latrine at Kaldak and the French logistician had dug that one himself. The camp commanders spent their days playing cards and drinking tea by the water, sunglasses perched on their noses and swagger sticks at their sides.

The treatment center was made up of four rubbery white tents surrounded by an orange plastic fence. There was a single entrance, marked by a red plastic basin of bleach solution. You walked through the bleach on your way in and again on the way out. Similar basins sat at the entrance to the individual tents. Inside, impossibly tall men lay naked or seminude atop canvas cots, each cot with a hole cut out near the middle. The men took liquid by IV and they voided liquid through those holes into plastic buckets that were then emptied into the bleach-treated latrine. They were gaunt and wasted, their skin gray and cracking—far too exhausted to object when I began shooting pictures.

"They're really not ready," Ana said during a cigarette break.

"Ready for what?"

"Anything," she replied. "It's like they have power now but they never prepared for it. We were in a meeting with the health minister and we said, you know, the rainy season is coming and so cholera is coming. And he said, 'Yes, who is going to take the lead on that?' And we say, it's you. You are taking the lead. Cholera comes every year."

The medics spent the afternoon treating their two dozen patients and when it was time to go an officer appeared and asked if Ana would have a look at a soldier who didn't have cholera but was in a bad way. She draped a stethoscope over her neck and followed him. The boy—he could not have been eighteen—sat lolling alone on the sandy floor of a woven-branch shelter, his face a puffy mask of misery. His flesh was swollen, and it hurt him to move; he hadn't walked in days. Ana checked his vitals and told the officer she would take him to the hospital in Malakal.

I took one side and a soldier took the other and we walked him to the boat. He was surprisingly heavy and he seemed to be struggling to remain silent as we carried him over the gunwale and set him down on the metal floor. We motored back to Malakal and when I held his arm too tightly on the way to the truck he gave a desolate cry for rescue—rescue from me, rescue from pain—and that was the last I saw of him. Later, during dinner, Ana said he was suffering from edema. "Probably his kidneys have failed," she said. "Kidney failure here means he will die."

Malakal owed its largesse to the Nile. The city's location on a high bank ten miles below the river's confluence with the Sobat made it an ideal spot for British (and later Egyptian) engineers to track the river's volume. On the north end of town a complex of weathered buildings marked the Egyptian measuring station, once the city's true center of power. Its bureaucratic offices and other buildings had dwarfed the British governor's home during the colonial era. I wanted to see the grandeur for myself, so the next morning I walked through the compound's rusting gate to what was still, despite the weedy neglect, an elegant old house with a broad front porch. Inside, I introduced myself to one of the surprised engineers and was passed to Mohammed Abdelaziz, the director of the station. I asked if he might give me a tour of the compound and he shook his head. "It is forbidden to speak of the Nile."

Egypt has for millennia viewed the Nile as its property, and Egyptians have been tracking and manipulating the river since the dawn of civilization. Business cards at the Egyptian ministry of irrigation and water resources sport the motto, "Since 4241 BC," and they aren't kidding. The Nile was, truly, a matter of national security.

But forbidden?

"It's right there," I said, pointing out the window. A hundred feet away, down a grassy slope and past a vegetable garden tended by a shy-looking Shilluk woman, the Nile was shining like gunmetal. Green patches of hyacinth coasted on its surface.

Abdelaziz, a big meaty man in shirtsleeves and dark slacks, had devoted his life to the Nile; as a member of the world's oldest bureaucracy, he just wasn't authorized to share. "I cannot help you," he said. "You must send fax to Cairo for permission."

"I've been to Cairo. The director promised they'd help and hasn't returned my calls since."

Abdelaziz seemed unsurprised. "I am sorry."

"It's right there," I said again.

He made a polite gesture toward the door with his hand. Seething, I followed it out.

Egypt's long shadow over the Nile dated as far back as its business cards boasted. Egyptian forces had followed it deep into present-day Uganda before the British established their colonies in East Africa, and Cairo's nineteenth-century wealth was derived in large part on the extraction of slaves and ivory from Sudan. Egyptians still looked at the darker-skinned tribes to their south—Arab and African alike—as their little brothers, rightful subjects to be civilized and exploited. It's a sentiment that persists in Cairo today: Sudan was Egypt's property and patrimony, stolen away by British colonialists. Sudan's independence from Britain was opposed by Egypt on the grounds that Sudan was rightfully hers. The Sudanese civil war had been sparked in part by an Egyptian-backed project, the Jonglei Canal, which would have drained the Sudd marshlands, adding an additional sixteen billion cubic meters of water—enough to irrigate two and a half million acres of Egyptian farmland—to the White Nile's flow, while draining traditional cattle watering grounds. John Garang's PhD thesis had argued against the project; the canal was three-quarters completed when he bombed it. The canal remains unfinished, an enduring dream in Cairo and an enduring source of anger in the south.

The next day I sought out one of the main players in another, more immediate controversy. John Malwit, the exiled commissioner of Phom Zeraf, wasn't home at his compound on the south end of Malakal, so I waited outside with a few of his guards. The young Nuer gunmen received me with suspicion and not a little scorn. "You should get rid of that beard," one said. "You look like a Muslim. I tell you, whoever puts his head on the floor to pray, that man is a terrorist. He should lose that head."

"What about the Bor massacre? Wasn't that terror?" I said. "Who's killed more south Sudanese, the Arabs or other southerners?"

"That's tribal," he said, as his friends nodded. "It's different. We will handle our tribes. You whites should help us kill the Muslims." I was about to remind him that his salary, and certainly that of his boss, had been paid by radical Islamists for almost fifteen years. Just then two Land Cruisers rolled up and Malwit himself hustled past, hidden in a cloud of bodyguards carrying AK-47s and rocket-propelled grenade launchers. A half hour later I was invited in. He was seated in a plastic lawn chair, a tired man in a gray two-piece suit, the pants unhemmed, sandals on his cracked feet, his brow a ripple of scars. A servant brought me a bottle of Sprite.

The dispute with his former commander, Malwit said, was about law and order. "We don't want the forces of bandits to be in Phom Zeraf. If Gabriel Tang wants to threaten the people with the force of the gun then the law should take its course. He should withdraw his forces to the north or face the consequences."

Oil companies, including a firm with close ties to a New York businessman, were trying to prospect near Phom Zeraf, using their connections with Tang in an effort to bolster their credibility. "They think Tang can give them the right," Malwit said. "They want to take out the tusks of the elephant and leave nothing for the people."

Why, I asked, did Malwit think his nemesis was holding on against the SPLA's superior numbers? What made it worth Tang's while? And hadn't Malwit himself been accused of corruption? He responded by insulting Tang's manhood. "My brother Tang, he doesn't know the benefit of a child. So he doesn't care about the future. Gabriel Tang is a criminal. I am a man of peace. My forces are in Kaldak. I left them to the SPLA. I am not a soldier anymore. I am a commissioner, *khalas*."

Khalas: It's finished, end of story.

But the story of John Malwit and his rival Gabriel Tang was far from over. I met Jeremiah the next day for a lunch of fish soup at a restaurant near my residence. "There was some noise at John Malwit's home last night," he said.

"Noise?"

"Thirty men attacked with rifles and RPGs," Jeremiah said. "Some people were killed, two, I think."

I pulled a fish bone from my gums and set it on the plastic tablecloth. "Last night?"

"Last night."

"Tang's guys?"

"Who else? It is going to become very difficult for us all if he does not leave. Trouble is really in the air."

I still didn't see it. If Malakal was in peril, I thought, the threat lay in its deadly torpor, not the raft of gunmen who called it home. Microbes and parasites dogged the place. Nearly every family had someone laid low by malaria. Even the internationals, with their superior drugs, were going down with it. Cholera would return in force with the rainy season, and if the government's response to the outbreak at Kaldak Camp was any indication, the city would soon be on its knees.

And yet. The south's dim prospects made the bright spots shine all the more. A dedicated group of energized young comers were waiting their turn to lead. Rebecca Malual was one. "She was a child soldier in the SPLA, lost her husband in the war, founded a women's NGO and now she's been appointed to the state legislature representing a district northeast of here," an acquaintance said. "She's a little more . . . facile than the average politician."

Malual was in town and was rumored to be dropping by the United Nations offices. I lurked around the UN complex, a colonial administrative building whose giant yard had been filled with office trailers. Inside the trailers, international civil servants worked to monitor the nutritional intake, medical care, human rights, gender rights, protection of children disarmament of combatants, agricultural challenges and emergency humanitarian needs of several million southern Sudanese. There were the riverine police unit, manned by the Bangladeshi army, and the international police monitors, whose job was to watch and nudge toward justice the local constabulary, and the headquarters of the Indian army protection force.

I was leaning in a doorway outside the human rights office when I spotted a tall, dark-skinned woman, conservatively dressed in a long black skirt and a patterned short-sleeved shirt, her hair pulled back and held by pins. I said, "Excuse me, are you Rebecca?" and she smiled, revealing white teeth with a friendly gap in the front. We agreed to meet in a few hours, after she finished a day of meetings.

We met up in late afternoon and walked about eighty yards from the UN offices to a back alley that opened to a fenced compound. It was made up of several stone-walled buildings with tall straw roofs, the first I had seen. "I just need to stop for a moment. My uncle lives here," she said, adding, "Not my uncle in the sense of whites. It's my elders' house." She chatted for a few minutes in Arabic and Nuer with some relatives who were sitting outside. As we left the compound I mentioned the impressive stone houses.

"Thank you," a male cousin said. "They are from the British."

We walked to Shilluk Avenue, jumping one at a time over a patch of sodden grass, and she flagged down an autorickshaw, a three-wheeled taxi common in South Asia. We banged down the road past the state assembly building, made a right or two at the northern end of town near the airport and continued past the cantonment where the Indian peacekeepers stayed, the road increasingly choppy, the rickshaw pitching and lurching over the ruts. "Now you will see how a member of parliament lives," she said. We came to a wide field dotted with mud-walled tukuls and turned down a path to a rectangular mud house, about thirty by ten feet. "My aunt stays on that side and this is mine," she said. "Come in." It was a tidy little room with a bed, a few chairs and a small wooden table holding books, papers and a Scrabble board.

"Maladroit," I said, studying the board. "That's got to be worth some points."

She laughed and set down her purse. "There's not much to do in Malakal. I am playing Scrabble with myself." We carried the chairs outside and Rebecca's aunt served us warm *posho*, a cassava porridge with sweetened milk, and then withdrew to her side of the house.

"So," I asked, as we sat down with a view of the sun setting over the muddy plain, "how do you like politics?"

She blinked, and leaned forward in her chair. "I find it a little bit complicated," she said at last. "I joined the SPLA in 1985, when I was fourteen years old. I was trained in Cuba for three years. I've been in the world of the military and I've been in the world of the NGO. The military, it is focused. The NGO is focused. The world of government is broad and vague. With the government, it seems not a lot is accomplished. They want a lot of achievement with less commitment. Each finger points to the other. The attitude is that 'I am the authority, I am the bull.' It is not the way to evaluate and focus priorities.

"There are so many things that have gone wrong since the peace agreement was signed," she continued. "We had high hopes, but it seems like nothing gets done—here and on the national level. The SPLM was supposed to receive the governorship of Upper Nile, but the governor today is from the National Congress. We were to have the mining and oil ministry, but they have that as well. For people like me, of my generation, we are very saddened and confused. We don't know how these things happened."

We talked about oil, and the rumors that militias and corrupt local officials were still displacing villagers to make way for oil exploration. There were also reports that county registrars were forging land transfers to help the oil companies. "These cases are difficult to confirm," she said, "and I myself cannot confirm them. But one thing is clear: The peace agreement will not survive if the theft of our resources continues."

"Isn't it a giant step to go back to war? You yourself are a widow," I said. "Your children are in Nairobi?" She nodded. "It must be hard being away from them."

"It is," she said. "My mother cares for them, but it's difficult. My youngest is still a baby."

"Ah!" I said. "So you've remarried, that's great."

She set down her bowl of *posho* and smoothed her skirt. "I did not remarry," she said. "He said he was leaving his wife and he didn't, and I resolved I would not be his second wife, his other wife. So I had the child alone."

"Jesus," I said. "Do you know another woman anywhere in your community who has had a child out of wedlock?"

"I am the only one, as far as I know." It was dark now, and the rickshaw had returned to take me back into town. She seemed relieved at its arrival.

I ignored the driver's honking. "I mean." I hesitated. "It's got to be a scandal—both from the tribal and the Christian perspective."

"My mother is very unhappy about it," she said with a small smile. "But you mention the Christian perspective and this is a perspective that I think south Sudan needs. Not in my personal case, but as a society. We have been fighting a Muslim state for so many years. I think we need to be a Christian state. Our constitution should say it."

I was stunned. "But isn't that the root of the problem? You put God in government and sooner or later infidels are getting shot. Right? And aren't Christians outnumbered by followers of traditional religions? Most southerners don't worship Jesus. Besides," I said, as she walked me to the rickshaw, "what's the church going to say about polygamy?"

"That," she said, laughing, "we will never give up. Even my mother, a strong churchwoman, would never turn against polygamy. It is our culture. You won't get rid of it in a thousand years."

The day after I spoke with Rebecca Malual, two SPLA soldiers were killed in a firefight with Gabriel Tang's gunmen not far from John Malwit's house, a second attack in just a few days. For the SPLA, after a year of provocations, it was the last straw. Tang had to go. But I wouldn't be there to see it. I had decided against an illegal run to Khartoum. With my southern Sudan travel pass about to expire, I reluctantly cobbled together a series of flights from Malakal to Juba to Addis Ababa in Ethiopia, and then to Cairo, where I hoped to obtain a new visa. Twenty-four hours after I left Malakal, the SPLA attacked Gabriel Tang's home, killing several of his men and taking control of the residence. Tang took refuge at the Sudanese Armed Forces base, and the city exploded. Nuer militiamen aligned with the SPLA—including some of Tang's former soldiers from Kaldak—overran the SAF garrison. Hundreds of people were killed during two days of fighting, and the city was terrorized and looted by fighters from both sides before a cease-fire was established more than a week later. Jeremiah fled to safety across the river with his wife and baby. Rebecca Malual spent the battle taking cover. Her elderly aunt was among the many hundreds wounded. Bullets, not microbes, had undone the town after all.

PART TWO

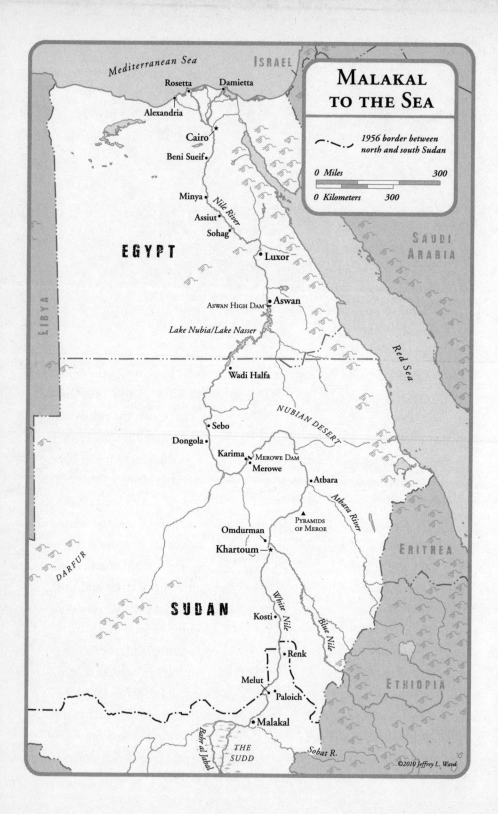

Mediterranean Sea

ISRAEL

Rosetta • • Damietta
Alexandria •

Cairo ★
Beni Sueif •

Nile River

Minya •
Assiut •
Sohag •

EGYPT

• Luxor

Aswan High Dam • • Aswan

Lake Nubia/Lake Nasser

• Wadi Halfa

NUBIAN DESERT

LIBYA

• Sebo
Dongola •
Karima •
Merowe Dam
• Merowe

• Atbara

Atbara River

PYRAMIDS
OF MEROE ▲

Omdurman •
Khartoum — ★

SUDAN

White Nile
Kosti •

Blue Nile

SAUDI
ARABIA

Red Sea

ERITREA

DARFUR

• Renk

Melut •
• Paloich

• Malakal

Bahr al Jabal

THE
SUDD

Sobat R.

ETHIOPIA

©2010 Jeffrey L. Ward

MALAKAL
TO THE SEA

— · — · 1956 border between
north and south Sudan

0 Miles   300

0 Kilometers   300

CHAPTER SEVEN

After several months and uncountable visits to the Sudanese embassy in Cairo, I was blessed with a new visa, one that would allow me to travel in both the north and south without restrictions. I was uneasy as I packed for my return. I would be alone for the second half of my journey. Schon was back in the piney woods of North Carolina serving drinks. Matthew was in London, grinding out his PhD thesis. And Alexandre was in Cuba shooting photographs. My flight reached the Sudanese capital in time for the biggest *khamseen* in a decade. A dense static of orange grit came screaming from the desert; it filled the sky and trapped Khartoum's eight million souls in a suffocating and radiant silica heat. Fine sand infiltrated under the metal balcony door of my room at the tatty Badr Hotel, leaving six-inch dunes at the foot of the bed. Still more blasted in through the plastic vents of the broken wall-mounted air cooler, scourging my eyes, ears, armpits and lungs. I had just finished duct-taping a black Hefty bag over the unit when the power went out, killing the fluorescent bulb, the creaky brown ceiling fan and the television. I filled my water bottle from the hot brass bathroom tap and sprinkled it onto the floor to suppress the dust. I dumped another bottle onto my greasy scalp, felt my way to the bed and tried to sleep with a wet undershirt molded over my face.

When the dust cleared in the morning, my new hacking cough and I caught a United Nations flight to Malakal. At last, I was back. I hitched a ride from the airport and jumped off at the outskirts of Shilluk Avenue, the city's long main street. This sprawling malarial town of mud huts and walled compounds had somehow become my favorite in all Sudan. I wanted to reacquaint myself with it on foot.

A mile into this triumphant march I had sweated dark bands through my tan travel shirt and green construction pants and was lurching with every step under two packs. Cutting three bags down to two was an achievement if you were flying coach to Phoenix, but it didn't mean dick while trekking in the Sudan. Despite all the lessons of my first three months on the Nile, I was still overweight and understrong. Were all those bungee cords necessary? Was Joan Didion's *Slouching Towards Bethlehem* really crying out to come along?

Four flip-flopped boys in rough sweatshirts and wide, frayed dungarees shouted from the road as they bobbed past on a wooden flatbed cart. I took two heavy bounds and jumped on, landing almost neatly on my hip. The gray-patched donkey slowed for a couple paces and then adjusted without protest to its new cargo, yanking us along the slippery road and into Malakal's late-morning scrum of minibuses, camels, motorcycles, asses and Land Cruisers. "*Kef?*" I asked, shaking leathery hands all around. They indicated they were very well indeed, riding through the sun in the biggest town for miles, punchy cigarettes cradled in their ebony fingers and gripped in chalk-white teeth. We approached the Ottoman-era mosque and the mudded square of the Jallaba district, Malakal's merchant center. I mounted the sidewalk with a high step, made way for three tall, gray-haired Shilluk men and ordered a mint tea from the shai lady squatting with her pots by the corner. The mild-mannered crone received my order without looking up, and continued her conversation with two pretty younger women as she poured water from a white plastic jerrican labeled "Carbolic Acid" into a squat tin kettle and fired up the kerosene stove with a piece of straw lit off her cheroot. I took a seat on a low metal stool strung with blue plastic cord and watched as she sprinkled bits of tea, like tiny curled beetles, into a three-inch glass. She reached into a rusted can for two dried sprigs of mint and had shoveled three scoops of sugar into the glass before I snapped out of my reverie and told her that was plenty, thank you. She poured the now boiling water, gave it all a swirl with a pinkie-sized spoon cut from a tin cooking oil container and handed me the drink on an engraved metal serving tray. I was puffing my lips and blowing on the thermonuclear refreshment when a white Nissan Patrol SUV— the kind with air-conditioning, cup-holders and seat belts—braked to a halt in front of me. The passenger-side window slid down with an efficient whirr, and in the shade of the cab I made out the Mongol features and striped Soviet-style commando shirt of the driver, a Kyrgyzstani military observer I'd met in the winter.

"Newsman! You're back! Where did you go? You missed all the fun."

I leaned on the passenger door and used the arctic blast inside to cool my tea.

"I told you to stay around," he said, drumming his hands on the steering wheel. (He hadn't.) "You missed some real fighting. Real action, SPLA, militia, the SAF, everything, and everyone had a piece of the mess. The Indians finally got to show their tanks! Let me tell you newsman, Upper Nile, south Sudan, these people are fucked. The town was looted, two, three times, by both sides—*both* sides. It is everyone for himself here. But it's better now. More stable. It was a necessary evil, even with three hundred people dead. Yes, you heard two hundred, but I am telling you—it was at least three hundred. This government can't count money, much less their dead. They only count cows."

Now, the military observer said, Gabriel Tang and Malakal's other warlords were out of the picture. Their forces—those that survived the November rout—were still in town but would be absorbed into one of the Joint Integrated Units in a confected demonstration of the new southern unity. ("Unity!" he barked, turning up the AC.) The northern garrisons were preparing to leave and had already begun barging heavy equipment and ammunition north to Khartoum, signs of a historic withdrawal. Soon Malakal would be without Arab troops for the first time since its founding in the nineteenth century. The town was still thick with soldiers, police and militiamen, but the rowdiest elements were now confined to the Sudanese Armed Forces base, and they were no longer allowed to carry their weapons in public. "There you have it," he said, his blue eyes shifting to the two-way radio as it squawked out an inquiry. "You missed a real party. Who knows? Maybe they party again." I stepped back from the clean white ride and he raised the window and was gone. I finished my tea and stepped down to the street.

I walked past the mosque and saw that thousands of rough bricks were piled along the north side of the boggy town square. Maybe the struggling city administrators would get the field paved before the rainy season hit its stride in a few weeks. This, I nodded, approving and proprietary, is just the kind of visible public works project Malakal needs. Turning south, I pushed my way into the packed Nile Commercial Bank and waited two hours with thirty other men to change money. It was payday at the United Nations mission and local employees were trying to convert their dollar salaries into new Sudanese pounds. In the south, the Sudanese dinar had given way in my absence to a new model currency. Where the dinar was seen by southerners as an Arab currency, another face of northern oppression (the dinar's Latin origin, *dinare*, notwithstanding), the new pound was yet another symbol of the new, peaceful Sudan. These notes were printed in both English and Arabic, and they featured beautiful engravings of flora and fauna from both regions. The ten-pound note was printed in shades of violet and blue, and it paired a Bedouin camel with a longhorned cow; two clasped hands were superimposed over a gnarled but thriving baobab tree. Today, however, the bank was running low on notes of all kinds and the men I'd wedged myself among were beginning to fear they wouldn't get the cash they needed for rent, medicine, school fees and the dozens of dependent (or freeloading) relatives that each was obligated to support. "Relations are like locusts," a driver for UNICEF muttered as we rode out the sweaty scrum.

I changed just a hundred dollars, unwilling to dig into my groin pouch for more in front of so many witnesses, and tromped outside. The room I'd mooched from Jeremiah before was now unavailable, but at his recommendation I tried ADRA, the Adventist Development & Relief Agency, headquartered nearby in a walled office compound. Ter Majok, the local head of office, greeted me there with a Thuraya satellite phone on his ear and two Motorola VHF radios at his side. His local mobile phone lay on his desk, struggling for a signal. He was one of hundreds of young rebel fighters who'd migrated from combat duties to relief work during the war, a small elite of educated soldiers. ADRA's guesthouse across town had a spare bed, Ter confirmed. It was twenty-five dollars a day. There was a kitchen if I wished to cook. He couldn't guarantee privacy.

South Sudan's rainy season hadn't officially begun, but the preseason was in full swing. An overnight downpour had turned much of Malakal into a slush bowl. The wide roads behind Shilluk Avenue had been reduced to a viscous jellied earth. The ditches bloomed an intense green algae and the smaller side lanes hosted fevered schools of minnows. We roared through these streets in

Ter's stripped-down Land Cruiser, racing past family compounds clad in tall reed fencing, riding invisible currents of wet paste. Ter jerked the wheel like a bargeman negotiating a villainous stretch of river while I braced my knees against the peeling dash and squelched the urge to cry out. He charged up one street, only to find a mud sea—complete with a family of Muscovy ducks—blocking the way, and doubled back with a horrible spin, fishtailing 180 degrees to the left and then back to the right to propel us forward across the slime. An old man and a boy crossing the street bounded out of our path, a leap from mud to mud to earth, landing safely on a patch of high ground, clothes and dignity intact. We whipped around another corner, clotted a pair of tethered cows with a coat of finely milled Upper Nile loam, cut across an empty field dotted with a few out-buildings and slurshed to a stop outside the ADRA guesthouse.

The guesthouse compound, one of three on this stretch of road, was fenced in sections of cement and corrugated steel. It was a modern setup: A long cinderblock house with steel roof and barred windows took up the right half of the plot; a cobwebbed kitchen hut sat in the rear left corner, near a shower stall and a black poly-urethane water tank. The remaining yard was crossed with clothes-line and decorated by a few small flowering bushes and a young papaya tree.

We crossed a ditch on an old plank, stepped through the metal gate and entered a broad main room lined with string beds. Several young ADRA men slept here, a rotating cast waiting for assign-ments in the hinterlands. (A picture of Christ hung from the wall, one of those compassionate Anglo Jesuses who look like they're about to kiss the female lead.) Next door were my quarters, a large room with two beds, two windows overlooking the yard and two more that opened into the hall. A ceiling fan was bracketed to a steel beam, and a single fluorescent light fixture was mounted high on the wall. The place looked clean and felt secure. It wasn't free, but I could cook my own supper and brew my own morning tea. "It's perfect," I told Ter Majok.

Crossing the wet road and the drying field to go shopping, I kicked up waves of spooked grasshoppers. Dozens of hawks hovered above in the warm medium blue, each waiting for that one right . . . there.

Everyone, I learned over the next few days, had a different version of the November battle: The SPLA brigadier, a Dinka, downplayed the role of his Nuer militia allies. The Middle Eastern UN security officer couldn't keep the tribal factions straight. An Indian peacekeeper took credit for the "peaceful resolution." I had to look hard for evidence of the fighting—scattershot pocks in the walls of some of the better compounds and an occasional crater in the unpaved streets. A damaged tukul could be rebuilt in a matter of days—all one needed was mud and straw. Politically, too, the city seemed well repaired. Gabriel Tang had been hustled onto a plane to Khartoum in the aftermath of the carnage and barred from returning to Malakal. John Malwit had decamped to Phom Zeraf to mismanage as he saw fit.

Still, nearly every aid worker I had known in Malakal, including the team that had taken me to the cholera-stricken militia camp, had been evacuated, and most hadn't returned. Projects worth hundreds of thousands of dollars—for clinics, roads and agricultural development across Upper Nile state—had been delayed for months or scrapped altogether. The hardy souls from the UN mission, however, had remained through the fighting.

Walking back to the guesthouse early one evening, I came across a broad plain of drying mud, its surface curling in a million places with thin, chipped layers of earth. I took a step and tested. Just as I hoped—a skimcoat of wet dirt hugging a slab of solid firmament. A track of shallow hoofprints seemed to confirm this. Eight confident paces later I plummeted calf-high into a crease of quickmud that filled my left boot and somehow my right shirtsleeve. I pivoted out of the stew, and as I pushed back to the guesthouse it occurred to me that surely the Nilotic tribes must have excelled at the daily challenge of reading mud, generation passing to generation the secret of how to tell an externally dry puddle from one that is truly dry or a genuinely shallow patch of muck from a hidden man-trap.

I knocked on the ADRA gate and saluted the old watchman, made a right into the house and a left into my room and found I had a roommate. He sat on the edge of the opposite bed, barechested in scarlet and cream sweatpants, reading a Bible opened onto his knees. He was smallish, moonfaced and just a bit thickset, with none of the long features of the Nuer, Dinka or Shilluks whose tribes converged on Malakal. The Bible pose gave the man the look of a ten-year-old Sunday schooler, despite the peppering of moles across his cheeks, brow and chest.

We shook hands. "Ah—so we are staying here together. I am John. John Ivo Mounto." His English was lightly accented, and delivered with a humbleness that verged on apology. "I am from Maban, to the east, near Ethiopia. That is my home place, but I am living now in Nebraska with my wife and my daughter. The government have asked me back to Maban to make an investigation of the conditions. There has been trouble. Babalala Marsell, the commissioner, was killed in Maban by unknown people, ambushed with panga at night. They asked me to report what is going on there."

The American Midwest was a popular destination for southern Sudanese refugees, thanks to the work of Lutheran missionaries. Tens of thousands of southerners had relocated there; very few ever returned. "You came all the way from Nebraska to investigate a murder?" I asked.

"Not that, no," he said. "It is the county, the villages— they wanted to know what is going on now with the present

commissioner, the man who replaced Marsell. I am well known
there. I was the first man to rebel against government troops in
Maban, in 1984. I was a catechist. They arrested me more than
three times for teaching Christians. They wanted everyone to be
a Muslim, and I can't accept that, so I joined SPLA." With those
credentials—the first man in Maban to take up arms against the
Islamists—John Ivo had set his sights on taking control of his
hometown. "Now I am contesting for commissioner," he said.
"The present commissioner, Ali Kata Oshi, is not cooperating with
the community. He is not well known. He is a Muslim pretending
to be Christian. They are accusing him of cooperating with Dawa
Islamiya."

I had been advised by a contact of mine to see Ali Kata Oshi if
I made it into the oil areas north of Malakal. Now John Ivo was
linking him to Dawa Islamiya, a radical Islamic charity that had
a reputation during the war for abducting African boys from the
streets of government-held towns and forcing them to adopt Muslim identities.

"It is an Islamic program for non-Muslims," John Ivo said of
the charity. "In Maban they give the people basic assistance, while
there is a political program underground. They are giving clothing,
giving food money and then opening Koranic schools."

In Maban, he said, "there are no services or facilities. They live
off tree roots for medicine. In some areas people have to go seven
or eight hours to find water. Since the peace treaty, nothing has
changed. The Arab army is still there. Everything is controlled by
those in Khartoum. They took the shingles off the school and used
them to cover their bunkers. They left land mines everywhere. People
don't know if there is peace because they have seen no changes."

I'd heard these complaints since I first crossed into Sudan in
the fall. The people—largely uneducated tribesmen, bludgeoned
by thirty years of war and dislocation—wanted a peace dividend,
and they wanted it now. They knew there was oil, and they knew

someone was selling it. Their leaders, most of them uneducated rebel officers, were struggling to govern. "Can it be true that nothing's different?" I asked. "The peace treaty may have taken people from zero to one, but that's still something, isn't it? You're telling me that one year into this, there are no schools, nothing?"

He listened with patience. "There is a small primary school near Jamam," he said. "It has two teachers, both Koran teachers, not qualified teachers. I asked why. They said, 'It is not a government school. If the government wants English, it should build its own.' This school is Arabic and Koran. It had almost fifty students. It is true what you say—times have changed, and they cannot force you now in the way they used to. Now, they will come to you as a father—'We will bring you this and this. We can give you this and we want your kids to enroll in a religious school.' They teach them just the basics of Koran. Then those kids are to bring the others."

Still, he said, "In some ways it seems like it's better than before. Before, we couldn't have evening prayers. Because the Christian prayers start with a drum and they said, 'We don't want to hear your drums.'"

We'd been standing for fifteen minutes, just inches apart—my interrogation had started the moment we shook hands—and realizing this, I slipped off my canvas tote bag and sat on my bed. The power was still on and the metal ceiling fan pushed the moist air around like it was a new element. John Ivo said he'd been in Malakal for six months waiting to see if the authorities in Juba would name him commissioner of Maban county.

"John," I said, "is oil an issue in Maban? I'm heading to Melut and Paloich after I leave Malakal." Thar Jath wasn't the only southern locality to fall in the name of petroleum. The region between Malakal and Renk, on the north-south border, was full of such stories. Maban and Melut counties alone had lost more than fifteen thousand people during the war. The oil fields where they once lived were controlled by Petrodar, a consortium dominated by the state oil companies of Malaysia and China.

John Ivo looked down at the bed and closed the Bible. "The population knows nothing about oil. They don't allow people to enter the oil areas. I went to the oil management in Maban. I sat in the manager's office. He said, 'We are ready to help. We are ready to do some schools.' He was just talking. In the oil areas, people are arrested and never seen again. Their Arabic is poor, so the local people don't get jobs. The companies hire people from the north— they are trusted. You say you want to go to Paloich. That is not my place, but let me tell you this: Paloich is now called Falluja—that is the name the Arabs gave it."

I asked John to tell me what it was like flying into a peaceful Sudan, one where southerners held high offices in Khartoum. Had he reunited with long-lost relatives after twenty years away? But he avoided the personal and pulled the conversation back to his fact-finding mission. With some seed money from the U.S. Agency for International Development, he'd organized a conference in Maban of local legislators and tribal elders to assess the community's needs and priorities. It was the kind of grassroots work that was just now beginning in much of the south, remarkable only because it hadn't ever happened before. Still, he said, Ali Kata had tried to shut it down.

"The commissioner heard about this conference and came back from Khartoum and Renk. He said, 'On whose authority are you here?' He said, 'This conference is not going to take place.' He left, went to Renk and sent a deputy down to declare the conference canceled. I said, 'If you want to cancel it, call Juba or call the governor of Upper Nile.' Instead, he sent a colonel from the SAF, Khartoum's army, to cancel us. He came at night, before it was to begin. I told this colonel, 'I cannot cancel this conference. Tell the commissioner I am holding this conference.'

"So the conference began and the commissioner appeared on its second day with fifty militia. The leader had a rank of captain. The SPLA stopped them at the gate and told them to lay down arms. They refused. It got heated. I am back in Maban, and again I am facing these guns. Finally the elders spoke to the commissioner and he agreed and came to join the conference. He came in and he's just sitting there, uncomfortable. I said to him, 'I'm not coming here to create a problem, I am coming here for peace, to tell people about the peace agreement and what the peace agreement wants us to do.' I have a right to do this. I am not a foreigner—everyone knows me. I am the first man to fire a bullet in this town."

The next afternoon I was sipping tea on the sidewalk in the Jallaba district when a white Toyota pickup stopped in front of me. I was on my third cup, waiting for a man who had said he could get me an appointment with the Shilluk *reth*, the king of the Shilluk tribe. It was a lark, but an interesting one. The *reth*'s influence had eroded during the civil war, but it wasn't every day one had the chance to meet a king. Only I didn't get to meet the king. The three men piled out of the pickup and stood around me and asked for my passport. "Who are you?" I asked. They were intelligence, they said, and they wanted me to come with them. All three were Arabs. None were armed.

"But how do I know you are intelligence?"

Because we are. You are to come with us.

"I will show you my identification," I said, "but I'm not going anywhere until you show me yours." I handed them my passport and my Sudanese press card, issued the week before in Khartoum. They seemed relieved to see that. Still they insisted I join them. I insisted I would not. I'd been bantering with a pair of men on the sidewalk; they had faded away. The small crowd of onlookers stayed small. Some grew bored and left as newcomers lingered to watch the standoff between the hairy *khawaja* and the Man.

"Are you Christian? I am Christian too," the mustached operative said. "It is all right. You can come with us. It is just two minutes." None had an ID card. None had ever been asked for an ID card. They were perturbed by the request. "We are not police," one pointed out.

I tried to stay breezy in my tone, but adrenaline was seeping into my blood along with, just maybe, a little white American dudgeon. "Come on," I said. "Be professional." Then I ordered another tea. They conferred in Arabic and one left on foot while the other two stayed with me and their Toyota. I told them about my Nile trip. This pleased them as much as my refusal vexed them.

In time their supervisor appeared, hot and angry. He shoved his Arabic-language ID into my face, like a cop when you demand his badge number, and jerked it back when I tried to hold and actually read the plastic card. He was shaking as he ordered me into the pickup. Just a year ago, no one would have dared mock the orders of a security man. I acquiesced and stepped into the bed of the Toyota. The mustached one said, "No, Daniel, you ride in the front with me."

"I'm happy in the back," I said.

He gave me a look that said, Cut the shit, and I got into the front and we drove off. The others were left to walk back to headquarters, or maybe to graft a free taxi ride. We made two right turns behind the mosque and stopped outside a butcher shop, where coarse cuts of goat and cow hung by steel hooks in a haze of blackfly. "Daniel, I'll be right back," he said. "One minute."

I leaned out the window and looked at the donkey carts and the shoppers and considered stepping out and walking away. Two small boys approached, maybe ten or eleven years old, in thin white school shirts and tan shorts. They wanted money, they said, speaking something that wasn't Arabic and wasn't English. I told them I didn't have any. The taller of the boys tapped my platinum wedding band. This was his proof that I had money. He was himself wearing a gold necklace, and this I reached out and pinched between my thumb and forefinger to show that he too had money. It dissolved like a dry leaf and the remainder slid down his small chest into the dirt. He looked at me, his eyes wide. I was mute. Money! I thought. I must give him money. As I reached into my pocket for a small bill, the operative returned, dropped a side of lamb into the back, jumped into the cab and roared us away. Wait! I said. Wait! I pointed dumbly at the boys, growing smaller. He drove on and they disappeared.

We regained Shilluk Avenue on the south end of town and turned onto a wooded brick drive that led to a large colonial bungalow that overlooked the Nile. Tall antennae waved in the breeze. I was led to a chair on the porch, where two older men joined us and began gently to ask just what I was doing in their town. A tall, neat-looking man with a Glock on his hip stood farther back. They all nodded abstractly as I described my journey but sharpened when I mentioned the *reth*. "What is your interest in the Shilluk nation?" one said, wary of outsiders meddling in Malakal's delicate tribal balance.

I don't know anything about the Shilluk, I admitted. I just thought it would be interesting to meet their leader. They were satisfied in less time than it took to finish the chilled mango juice one of the underlings had brought me. Did I wish to stay for tea? Very kind of you, I said, but I must be going. But let me ask: Do you arrest many people in Malakal? The gentler of the men, cool in his gray safari suit, gave a small smile. "Not anymore," he said. "But in the old days—that was something different." We shook hands, and I slowly walked down the porch steps, across the brick driveway and back into daylight. An hour later I found my contact. The *reth* wasn't even in Malakal. He was downriver in Pachodo, his traditional seat of power, on the western bank, out of my reach.

That night, back at the ADRA guesthouse, I asked John Ivo to tell me more about his journey from Maban to Nebraska.

"I joined the SPLA in 1984. I was a government wildlife officer. I recruited some young men. After nine months of training in Ethiopia, we came back as the Maban Battalion. We attacked Maban for two days from south of the Yarbus River, our first battle. We fired mortars into the town, 100-millimeter. We fought until 1989, when I was transferred to Torit in the south for military and civil administration training. Then Lam Akol and Riek split the SPLA. Then I was arrested."

In 1991 Lam Akol, a Shilluk, and Riek Machar, a Nuer, tried to unseat John Garang as leader of the SPLA, igniting a civil war within Sudan's civil war. Backed by arms and air power cynically provided by Khartoum, they pounded John Garang's Dinka-dominated forces and sacked Bor in the Dinka heartland. As a native of Upper Nile, where the breakaway faction was strongest, John Ivo's Dinka superiors would have viewed him, a member of the tiny Maban tribe, with paranoid suspicion during those years of panic and retreat. "For eighteen months they kept me in an underground jail. First, they tortured me. They put us in the generator building of a Catholic school in Torit. We were nine officers. They took us out one by one, kicking, beating—they tie your back, asking why you did this, have you been sent on a mission? One day they took me as a ringleader because I speak different dialects, more than five languages. They accused me of coming to recruit people against SPLA. I said I cannot do that—it is my cause also. Then I was transferred to the Nimule jail. There were fifty-one in the jail there, under the ground, with no light, almost no water to drink or for washing. Nine died from disease. The humanitarians knew there was a jail, but they didn't know where. The guards would put a tarp over the door and play dominos during the day.

Finally someone escaped to Adjumani when they brought him up
for interrogation. He told the humanitarians, 'Look for where the
soldiers are playing dominos.' After three days of negotiations with
the Red Cross, the jail was opened at nine-thirty in the morning.
When you come out, it makes you dizzy. It's like the trees are moving. You have to sit down. It was December 1992, before Christmas. I spent three months in Kampala for treatment. Some of us,
they lost their minds. The SPLA asked me to come back and fight
in Blue Nile, but I said no, and I went to United States as a refugee. I lost a lot. I had three wives, but they were married to my
uncle and to my brothers after the funeral rites. Everyone thought
I was dead. I had six children—they are with those other families
now. In Kampala I met a woman from Equatoria, from the Bari
tribe, and we started a relationship. We got married in America
and attended the college at University of South Dakota at Vermil-
lion. She is a registered nurse." I tried imagining John Ivo's first
exposure to the Great Plains winter, to the bleak flatness of Ver-
million. To fat healthy cows that nobody fought over. To Kroger.
"What did you study there?" I asked.

"I took up military science," he said.

My mouth, jaw and eyebrows had begun to ache from grimac-
ing through his story. This last bit liberated my face—it slackened
in disbelief. "Wait a minute," I said. "You're held in an underground jail, accused as a traitor, tortured by your own guys, you
lose your wives and children, you see men go mad and die in the
dark, and the first college classes you take in America are military,
what, military science? Did you really still want to return to fight
for these same people?"

He looked at the window and the cooling light. "I dismissed
this in my heart," he said. "They did not know what they were
doing. It was a tribalistic thing. It was the way of our leader, the
late Dr. John Garang. The first priority was Dinka Bor, then Dinka
Bahr al Ghazal. They dominated the promotions and training. It

was a time of communist ideas and all the young Dinka were being sent to Cuba. They didn't know."

This ability to let bygones be bygones was, to me, one of the strangest features of Sudanese politics. Riek Machar was loathed by many Dinka for his role in the Bor massacre, but he was also at that moment vice president of the autonomous Government of South Sudan—Salva Kiir's number two and chief mediator of the peace talks between the Ugandan government and the Lord's Resistance Army. Lam Akol, meanwhile, was serving as Sudan's foreign minister, a plum job that he used to defend Khartoum's conduct in Darfur, even as his southern comrades condemned it. (The consensus among southern politicians was that it was better to have Lam shilling for the Arabs abroad than making trouble in the south.)

What chance did ideology have in this world of shifting alliances and situational ethics? Garang had been a Marxist when Marxist states like Ethiopia and Cuba were paying his freight. Later—or even simultaneously—he was a pro-Western reformer backed by a network of American church groups. "I've heard him argue persuasively for southern independence and I've heard him argue just as persuasively for the unity of Sudan, both within the space of a year," a United Nations relief official in Malakal told me. Whatever worked.

I spent most of the next day waiting out the rain when John arrived and lit up the room with a bottle of Ethiopian ouzo. "You are a man of influence," I cheered, and seized the bottle while he left to rescue two glasses from the kitchen. The label had Amharic script running along the top, white on blue, over an engraving of a tall stag with long barnacled antlers. The bottom read, "Distilled and bottled by Sylvana Testa & Sons Liquor and Soft Drinks Factory, Addis Ababa." It was the coolest thing I'd seen since sipping tea in northern Uganda from red Coca-Cola mugs that read "Vladivostok Bottling Co."

We each drank a healthy glassful, John sitting at the edge of his bed, me sitting cross-legged against the wall in mine. He was hunched slightly forward, his body sinking into the mattress. I didn't know how he dressed in Omaha, but in Malakal there was nothing in his bearing or possessions to suggest someone who had spent ten years in the United States. His primary piece of luggage was a knee-high polyfiber bag with a tin zipper and two narrow looped handles. A picture of the New York skyline, complete with Twin Towers, was screened on one side; the Paris skyline decorated the other. His briefcase was a hardshell Samsonite knock-off, his shirts and slacks and tracksuits all appeared to have been bought on the local market and his shortwave radio was a Chinese no-brand. The candle on my bedside table (mine because John insisted I take it) threw a small yellow light on his face and cast a large, lumpy shadow on the pale wall behind. The lumpy beast gestured with soft fins as John Ivo spoke of the gulf between Maban and Nebraska. "Little Telly—she doesn't understand where I am, or why I am here," he said. "I try to tell her I am helping our people."

Late that night, well into sleep, came real reason to celebrate. John's mobile phone rang—a special occasion in itself, considering the overwhelmed network—with word that a political caucus in Juba had named him the new commissioner of Maban county. Hours earlier we'd been talking about what it would mean for him, leaving his family, his seven-year-old daughter, struggling to bring up his native place. He would visit the United States but twice a year. There was no chance that his wife would relocate to Nairobi, much less Maban. The commissioner's pay was about $3,000 a month, much more than he made as a hospital translator in Omaha—and tax-free, I noted, which got a rare laugh out of him. Now it was all real. He asked his friend to double-check and the man called back, confirming it. John spent the night pacing the compound, listening to the radio and drinking ouzo. Twenty-three years after leaving Maban and joining the rebels, he would return as head man. As I drifted off, I thought I heard him breaking the news to his wife. The celebration had left his voice.

That morning, I asked if as commissioner he would get a swagger stick like the generals carry. "All those who joined with me, they are major generals," he said. "For me, they said, 'You have been away.' So I will be a brigadier." It's all based on time served? "Yes," he said, "that and favors. If your friend is in power you get promoted. It is meaningless." I was pouring myself the dregs of the prior day's tea while John got dressed. No gaily patterned shirts today. It was a black African-style safari suit. "I will go to see the governor."

It threatened rain all that afternoon, low clouds in bands of dark and less dark, giving over to short spells of drizzle. The later sun burned hot, drying the roads a bit, before the sky opened up for real and the city reverted to muck. Maybe, I thought, I could salvage the evening by catching a ride to the UN mission's weekly happy hour at their camp near the airport.

I left the compound after an attempt at cleaning myself up, my old Nikon and a rain jacket stuffed in a tote bag. In the field directly across the road a European man in long denim cutoffs and a green T-shirt was walking casually toward a cement-block shed, a pail slung over his shoulder. I put two and two together and figured he was an aid worker and that I might get a ride with him. But two and two didn't equal beer; it equaled Jesus. Simon and his wife, from Holland, six Egyptians and a pair of Sudanese had come down from Cairo to celebrate the way of Christ. They had flown to Khartoum and traveled by bus to Renk, Melut and now Malakal, making their way south by the route I would soon be taking north. That very day, he said, they had visited Malakal's prison to lift the spirits of the detainees. They had sung songs.

"You sang hymns? In what language?"

"Not hymns," he said. "We are not evangelizing. Not at all." The prisoners, he said, sang in their own language and the visitors strummed along. I couldn't right then think of a more abject misery than life in a southern Sudanese prison. A group of foreign visitors strumming their guitars to my native tunes would at least break up the day. Simon introduced me around. There were two Egyptian girls named Dina, a southern Sudanese refugee who lived in Cairo, a young Egyptian man and Simon's wife. The rest were asleep in the metal-roofed shed. Simon was tall and very thin, with close-cropped hair and a spare goatee. The girls looked like upper-middle-class daughters of Egypt's Coptic Christian minority, with shiny black shoulder-length hair and snug blue jeans. Were they Copts? Simon eluded the question. The Dinas pretended they didn't know English and looked with suspicion at my hair and beard and the dirty cuffs on my slacks. It was curious. I had planned my trip for months—read books, purchased equipment, taken out insurance, struggled for visas and permits, and here this group had simply hitched themselves to the Spirit and cantered into town with nothing more in mind than making people feel good.

I chatted with Simon until the gorgeous dusk—cloudy, backlit by the low moon—switched itself off, and then picked my way west to the UN headquarters, where by now everyone had left for the night. I turned and walked back to the guesthouse, mudding my boots on the way.

The power was out at ADRA, the room quite warm. I lit the candle nub, drank the remains of my ouzo from the night before, polished off the last of my ginger cookies and sat listening to John's shortwave. Pushing the dial down into a valley between the otherworldly squeaks and whines, something truly exotic—an American Bible program—came into the clear. I leaned toward the sound, and in the dull planar tones of another universe, a midwestern woman was asking the host if the prophetic impulse wasn't an aspect of the Holy Ghost and, if so, how then could each person have it? How indeed? The journey so far had shown my prophetic gifts to be nil.

After several days of lumbering alone through Malakal I feared I was losing track.

No one in the United States cared about a months-old spell of terror and death in south Sudan. They barely cared about Darfur, and Darfur was the rage. I needed a thread that would take me from Malakal to the oil areas, a thread to connect this stop to the next and the one after that. I needed for something to happen and I feared I might plod through the next two thousand miles as I had plodded through Malakal that day, without luck and without connection. "You make your luck," I said to myself. It was a rebuke: Today I hadn't made any. Would I snap out of it? So far, the Holy Ghost hadn't given any sign. I switched off the radio, blew out the candle and fell to sleep.

John came back sometime in the night and in my slumber I could hear him laughing with others in the courtyard, their celebration punctuated by a series of pops and bangs. I could understand his joy, but this—fireworks, at this hour!—was too much. In my annoyed slumbering fog I in time noticed that the fireworks were happening in many places at once, not just in our courtyard. And they weren't fireworks.

Gunfire was popping outside our gate, near the Sudanese Armed Forces barracks up the road, and, it seemed, everywhere else.

I sat up on the edge of the bed. You should be on the floor, I said to myself, and sat there some more as my ears trained to bursts of automatic gunfire, some close and some very close, and to the creepy skin-crawling sound of ululating men running by. I got down and squatted on the cement floor and pulled my flashlight from under the mattress. Where was cover? To the left were windows into the courtyard. To the right, the bedroom door of thin sheet metal, followed by the wide hall and a steel door to the back walk. Safest, I thought, to take a piss. The outhouse at the end of the walk was windowless cinderblock and would give me full cover and time to clear my head. I dashed out, took a long one and tried to think. Would they come over the wall? They were coming over the wall. What would I do? They would kill me no matter what I did. I didn't want to die in the toilet, cowering over a shitty hole in the ground. I left the outhouse in a low crouch and against all sense I pressed my eye to a small hole low on the fence to see three shirtless men sprinting in the mud past the compound, rifles in hand. One appeared barefoot. All they had to do was leap over the drainage ditch that separated us from the road. One warrior, his spiderweb-scarred chest clear for a second in the moonlight, seemed to look directly at me. He made the sound, the same creepy war call, and I pulled my head away and duckwalked back into the house.

John, Ter Majok and the other ADRA boys were sitting in the dark living room. What the fuck is going on? "They are shooting," someone said. Who? "Militia. It was a shootout with police." Outside was well lit—a full moon and low clouds alive with horizontal tendrils of lightning.

"I saw it driving here," Majok said. "Two cars, a joint patrol, were heading to the SAF barracks when *paw-paw-paw-paw*! You see?" he said to James, another ADRA man. "I was right to change my route. We could have been in the middle. I came a different way." Apparently, a police patrol had come across some of Gabriel Tang's fighters walking armed outside the SAF base. The gunfight erupted when they refused to lay down arms. Even in his absence, Tang was toxic to the city's peace.

Everyone was reclined on lawn chairs or on string beds listening to the gunshots advance like a rippling breeze over the town. I sat on the floor in the corner, keeping my head below the windowsills. After fifteen or twenty minutes, Ter went outside to peek over the fence. "They are moving," he whispered. After more waiting they opened the gate a foot and he peered out into the street. He gave a quiet order and they threw the gate wide while he sprinted to his abandoned Land Cruiser, cut the machine a hard ninety degrees and drove it into the compound. I heard bursts of AK-47 fire. I heard the single *pop-pops* of handguns and I heard the *whooom* of rifle rounds passing close, very close by, parting the air and sound itself like they were flesh. I went back to my room and sat on the floor in the corner. I ran my thumb along my sternum and ribs and thought about how fragile this body is in the face of physics, of that single round during the November fighting that had passed through two metal fences, a trailer wall, and ended up in a friend's filing cabinet, a pristine pointed stray that just ran out of momentum.

John poured some ouzo and drank deep. Then he walked into the dark kitchen, probably the safest room save the toilet, and sat there on a lawn chair in gloomy darkness, surely thinking of Nebraska and seven-year-old Telly. He came back twenty minutes later, slumped into bed and was soon snoring. I pulled my sleeping mat from the rucksack and lay on the floor in my sweaty clothes. During a lull in the shooting the bullfrogs emerged, at first slowly and then with gusto, reclaiming their sonic territory. The birds joined in, followed by the pariah dogs and the asses in an evening chorus. It went on thusly past dawn. At least once an hour someone would start shooting and the toads of Malakal would go silent and wait the bums out. I heard the last shots sometime after 5 a.m. Along the way I dreamt I was looking through a pile of sensitive documents, maybe Somali, with a colleague who was a star reporter at a well-regarded newspaper, but I wasn't clear if the documents were mine or his or ours or just there for the taking. Was I glomming? Was he? The scene shifted. I was in New York, and Rudolph Giuliani was belittling me at a press conference. This had happened many times during my days reporting from City Hall, but on this occasion all the other journalists were joining in the ridicule. As if to salve that mental welt, I then dreamed I was on the precipice of seducing two long-limbed young women I had happened across at a backyard swimming pool. But the prospect of straying from marriage, even in slumber, only brought additional stress. I awoke aroused and with a migraine, stinking of panic.

I sat up at six, having slept no more than an hour, and most of that in ten-minute parcels. In the open field across the road a cluster of cows lay hobbled in a semicircle, each waiting to be milked by a man in a turban working the teats of a contented Sudanese Bessie. Women in long Shilluk tunics walked down the road in groups of three and four, and near the gate children poked at ticks in the dirt, comparing prizes. All appeared normal again after the passing storm of Kalashnikovs and testosterone. I crossed the road to check in on the foreign churchpeople. They were already stuffed into a minibus, their luggage piled high and strapped on top. The two Dinas were almost in each other's laps, pressed against a window on the van's left side, sorrow and fear and the memory of fear plain on their puffy faces. They would never again leave Egypt. Hell, they would never leave Cairo. "It was very close, and very bad," Simon said. "It could get worse today because tensions are very high." He said this with authority, but I was doubtful: He was even greener than I. "How are your spirits?" I asked. "It's not good," he said. "Some were very, very scared."

It was time to leave Malakal. Upper Nile's oil areas beckoned. I convinced the head of the UN mission to get me onto a helicopter bound for Melut, ninety miles to the north. The chopper would represent a break from my plan to use local transport, but it would drop me inside the UN peacekeeping base in Melut, where I hoped to find a place to sleep. There were no guesthouses for more than two hundred miles north of Malakal. It wasn't safe to camp, and in any case, I'd left behind Schon's tent to cut down on the weight I was carrying.

Packing up, I went looking for someone to hand an envelope with $225 in rent for Ter Majok. I heard voices in the back, from the strip of concrete that led to the latrine, and walked through the metal doorway to see Bern, an ADRA official, squatting over the pavement, head down, with tendrils of blood pouring from his clean scalp. Two men were crowded around him murmuring in Nuer.

"Are you all right?"

"Yes," he said. "It is a traditional treatment."

"He had a headache," one of the men said.

I brought out a couple alcohol swabs from my kit and daubed some of the blood off his face with a gauze pad. The incision by his right temple was a real bleeder. A smaller cut on his forehead had stopped on its own. A box of double-edged shaving razors, each wrapped in wax paper, sat on a deck chair. "Hold this on the cut," I said with false authority. "Don't move. And maybe sit where your head is up higher, not pointed down." He shifted to one of the chairs and leaned back, his tan loafers dotted with tiny mites of blood, his gray dress slacks untouched, his blue tartan polo shirt bundled up around his neck, blood pooling in his sternum and navel.

"I've had the same headache for twenty years," he said. "I have tried everything, just everything. I've had MRIs and CAT scans and they don't show anything. So I tried this, and maybe it's helping." A pile of deep red blood, wide as a hubcap, dried on the concrete. (The ants will be at that, I thought.) "Most people in Nebraska would not agree with this," he said, squinting through the blood and sweat. "But most people in Nebraska would not travel where I travel. It is always on one side—sometimes the left, the whole of the left side—and other times it will be the right. Maybe it is the change in weather, or the change in time. Everything that seems plausible is undone by something implausible."

This phrase piqued my spirits. Now, I thought, it's really morning. "So one hemisphere rages at a time, and never both," I said. "What if you had it the two sides at once?"

"Then I would die," he said gravely.

He was a refugee from Upper Nile, had spent some time in the United States and now worked in ADRA's Middle East office, based in Cyprus. "This man, he is a traditional doctor, a local doctor. People line up to see him. He fixes all kinds of problems—head injuries, pain, broken bones."

"Well, your blood looks very healthy," I said.

"I think you passed a liter," someone else added.

We walked through the house to the courtyard, where he sat down and prepared to wash his head with a pail of water. "Just leave it for now," I said. "You want the bleeding to stop." He doused his skull as I carried my backpack through the gate to the ADRA Land Cruiser. When I went back in for my second bag the blood was again running down his face. I went to the car, pulled more gauze from my kit and used his hand to press against it. "Just hold it there. For a long time." He nodded, maybe a little annoyed. "And give this to Ter, please," I said, pushing the envelope into his other hand. The ADRA driver gave a honk and I jogged back. We splished through the mud to the airport. On the way, I saw the big rough bricks behind the mosque being sold and trucked away by private buyers. They weren't for the public at all. It seemed nothing was.

CHAPTER EIGHT

I crowded into the white United Nations chopper with a platoon of Indian peacekeepers. The porthole windows sent wide shafts of light boring across the dim cabin, illuminating a metal floor piled with duffels, the sides lined with narrow benches. I sat at the back, stretched out my legs, then stood up and grabbed a set of acoustic earmuffs from a thin cord stretched across the cabin. The engine kicked on and thrummed for a moment, sending up nimbuses of dust before the chopper beetled on fat tires down the runway and hauled us off the ground.

The soldiers were tall and wiry, the fruit of India's northern Hindu belt, most of them mustached, wearing pressed green camouflage uniforms. When I worked as a reporter in South Asia, I was often asked by Indian airport security officers: Where are you from? From America. But where were you from before that? The beard and black *Easy Rider* hair convinced the airport bulls I was some kind of Afghan or Arab. Now my interrogators' army cousins were trapped in a metal can several hundred feet above the Nile, waiting, I imagined, for the unkempt stranger to scream *"Allahu*

Akbar!" and light them up with an explosive satchel. The Hindu jawans would die in black Africa, and vultures would feed on their charred guts, something that would never happen in India—vultures there being nearly extinct.

From the air the river appeared swollen and slow, the sum of the Bahr al Ghazal and the Bahr al Zeraf and the Sobat and its other tributaries, all of them pushed together into a single White Nile that would descend from central to northern Africa over two thousand miles. At Khartoum it would meet its energetic sister, the Ethiopian-born Blue Nile, and forge its way north to Egypt. There, at the dry lip of the Sahara, the Nile was *everything*—the sole source of life for the more than seventy million people clinging to its banks. As I hovered over Malakal, it was plain that life here went on well beyond the river's grasp. Clusters of tukuls sat in clearings amid the trees as small herds of cows ambled through the scrub. I pulled out my old Nikon, unbolted the latch on my porthole and, while my cabinmates pretended not to notice, shot a roll of black and white out the open window.

We landed thirty minutes later at the UN team site in Melut, an arid base for the foreign military officers whose job it was to track armed groups the peace treaty had officially made idle. The military observers and a team of police monitors were backed by a protection force of several hundred Indian soldiers. As in Malakal, they had brought everything they needed direct from home. Their jeeps were Mahindra & Mahindra; the bottled water was Bisleri. (I allowed myself a moment's hope that I might cadge a plate of channa saag from the mess hall.) The landing zone was hot, graveled, dusty. I grabbed my rucksack and walked with what I hoped looked like confidence through the fence and onto the base proper in search of a friendly face. My UN press card hung from my neck on a chain, though it only applied to the UNMIS headquarters in Khartoum and had no official currency here. I'd had my boots shined on Shilluk Avenue in Malakal the day before, but they were already the color of the dun earth.

The team site looked like a proper military camp—ready for the worst. The perimeter was dug out with machine-gun nests and sandbags and razor-wire fencing, and I saw at least two pieces of light artillery. I walked past long lines of small modular housing containers—all of them empty, their windows dark and their white walls coated with grit—and came to a row of office trailers alive with the hum of air-conditioning and clomping feet, behind which sprawled big canvas tents where the Indian forces bunked, trained and stored their equipment. The five trailers were bolted together side to side—five doors, each holding a potential accomplice or a possible spoiler.

Where to knock? Nowhere, I decided. One bad interaction could get me put off the base a mile out of town without a single contact. Surveillance was the better course. I leaned on a Land Cruiser and pretended to talk on the Thuraya whenever a man in uniform walked past. After fifteen minutes of babbling words like "payam," "Sector Three" and "duty station" into my phone, I saw a dark-skinned Arab in street clothes leaving one of the trailers. At last, a civilian. My quarry, Bilal, was a Sudanese employed as a civil affairs officer. The first nonmilitary person permanently assigned to Melut, he was alone there and would make, I hoped, a valuable ally.

Bilal gave me a ride north into the town. On the Nile side of the road, under a stand of baobab and doum trees, sat the new village hall, a brick-and-concrete complex of half a dozen offices, the seat of the county commissioner. There were no hotels in Melut, but perhaps, my new friend said, the commissioner could place me with a local family. The official guesthouses were already filled with military observers, he explained, while the housing containers I'd passed on base still lacked furniture and electricity. We peered into the commissioner's dim office, but the boss was away at Malakal, a staffer said, reclining with an orange Fanta on a red velvety couch. Tomorrow the executive director—Melut's number two—would be in, and I could speak with him.

Bilal brought me across the road to the small souk, where we took tea and coffee in the pleasing shade of a sun-bleached tarpaulin canopy. "I am new to this post but I can tell you the situation is very difficult," he said, picking a cardamom seed from his cup.

"You think I won't find a place to sleep?" I asked. Already I was imagining a night spent on the steps of the commissioner's office, or in the bed of my new friend's pickup. It would be difficult planning a foray into Paloich without a base to work from.

"It's not that," he said. "I can ask after your lodgings with the military observers. Some of them are on long-range patrol and won't be back for days. Maybe you can take a bed from among them, the commander permitting. Your true difficulty is in Paloich. Everyone from the international community—the military observers, myself, even the chief of mission in Malakal—is kept away from the very subject of oil. No one from outside, no NGO or humanitarian, will bring you there. And if they cannot take you there, they cannot take you out if things become unmanageable. The oil is too important to allow a journalist. You are not safe there. There is a bus to Renk that passes through Paloich. You can view the town from the bus. But you are in danger were you to step off."

We returned to the base, the both of us now standing watch outside the office trailers, until he spied our man. Bernard was Belgian, with brown eyes that carried the tint of suffering so often found in Western soldiers serving under senior officers from the Third World. He didn't hesitate when approached. "Of course," he said, looking up at me. "You can stay in my bunk. It is not a proper hotel, but it is comfortable enough."

"Look, Commander," I said, "I don't want to take your bed. I mean, I'd rather sleep outside. I heard there might be empty bunks. Isn't that an option?"

His mustache gave an impatient twitch. "I can offer it precisely because it is my bed. I will sleep here in the office. Two nights of air-conditioning and privacy would be a change—a pleasant change."

At that Bilal, the trim Sudanese, faded diffidently out of frame; my mark, it seemed, had found his own. I killed the rest of the day at the team site while Bernard waited for his commanding officer, a Tanzanian colonel, to okay the arrangement. He let me check my email on his Dell—"A very good computer, from Belgian intelligence"—and then drove me to his quarters at the guesthouse. The observers occupied three cement bungalows overlooking the Nile on a plain behind the commissioner's office. A walk of sorts, lined with sandbags, led from the gate to steps and a narrow porch hovering four feet off the ground—you never knew when the river might jump its banks. Like most towns in Sudan, Melut didn't have a municipal water system. The observers washed and cooked from giant plastic bottles provided by the Indian protection force and they showered at the UN base. Each of the three bedrooms, one no more than a deep hallway, held two sets of bunk beds, a toddler-sized desk and an assortment of foot lockers, towels and dirty socks. Bernard had a bottom bunk in one of the bigger rooms.

The observers appeared to come in pairs so that no man would spend his tour trapped alone among a babel of alien officers. Bernard's fellow Belgian was on long-range patrol; so was the counterpart of his roommate, a Panamanian army captain. Neither would be back for days.

We dined that night on canned tuna (Bernard's), Emirati Ritz crackers (mine) and the last of his jibneh, a Sudanese feta, all of it washed down with tumblers of Tang from a jar I'd bought in Malakal. Then he took his bedroll and left for the quiet and cool of the office. I smoked a Sherman's on the porch, said good night to a

Cameroonian major resting in green bikini undershorts in the hallway and to two Peruvians in the other room and lay down to read
a few pages of Michela Wrong's *In the Footsteps of Mr. Kurtz.*
"You must be tired," someone tells a boy soldier, part of the long
column of juvenile fighters that has just taken Kinshasa. "Yes," he
says. "I've walked all the way from Kampala."

I dreamt I was swimming to Khartoum through hot black
water and woke up gasping, cocooned in heat, the mosquito net
trapping the air, my hair wet with perspiration. Bernard's roommate was already up and dressed. I groaned hello and went down
for another hour, which only drained me further. It was 9 a.m.
and already Melut was irresponsibly hot. I dressed, walked to the
porch and washed my face from one of the giant bottles. "Don't get
it in your mouth," one of the Peruvians warned. Returning to the
souk, I took tea and cookies and a single spotted yellow banana.
Nothing was happening here. Melut seemed as much a township
as a town. It grew away from the road in three or four patches
of mud homes and shops, but the long view was dotted with tiny
homesteads and camps and herds. A single-story brick schoolhouse
hugged the road, but it appeared empty—no children in the windows or playing in the clods outside. I wiped my eyeglasses with
a handkerchief, smoothed my pants as best they would allow and
walked back across the road. The darkened commissioner's office
was hopping today, the couches and sectionals thick with men in
uniforms, safari suits and street clothes.

Acwil Abwek Ayiik, Melut's second in command, was a
broad man behind a broad desk. Over the next ninety minutes he
addressed visitors in a mixture of Dinka and Arabic while a tiny
moonfaced woman in an orange wrap floated in and out on quiet
feet to serve tea and soda. When the flow of supplicants and subor-
dinates had finally dried up, he turned to me.

"I am hoping to learn about oil," I said, introducing myself.
"I've heard rumors that people are being forced from their

homes to make way for oil exploration. Is that still taking place today?"

"This oil, it is a resource we need for the new Sudan," Abwek said by way of a nonanswer. "We are stuck with these oil companies—the CPA says oil contracts can be revised but cannot be abrogated. They came during the war, when all the people had been removed from the land. The companies are not willing to compensate or even to provide services to those who have been removed. But still it is different now." The difference was consent: Under the Comprehensive Peace Agreement, local communities had to give their approval before exploration and extraction could begin, and permission was not forthcoming. Abwek and the entire southern leadership knew of the blood that had been spilled and the lives ruined over oil exploration. They also knew the south couldn't live without it. If the fledgling state was to survive it needed companies like Petronas and Total to drill, pump and sell. Just the week before, the community of Khor Adar had rejected a drilling request.

"We are trying to persuade people to take this chance, to let them go," he went on. "But the whole process was derailed. They did not let them. It is the only source of revenue we have at this juncture. The people have not organized and determined what they want. There is no organized list of conditions. There is just opposition. The local people want their share of the oil revenue. I too want my share—the state government receives a portion, but no part of that is sent to the counties. Just yesterday there was a riot in Paloich."

"A riot?"

"Two hundred people rampaged, smashing cars in the night." He sighed. "They want jobs and there aren't any. We have a legal system now; it isn't for them to go smashing. There is a government labor officer in Paloich. If you are aggrieved you can take your grievance to the court. We have been trying to represent them. To the oil company we say, 'Know your limitations. The CPA is fragile.' We enrolled 560 people for jobs, but they hired none. They just bring people from the outside. So last night one group went to the company there. They went to make a fight and advanced on the refinery. The Petrodar security and the JIU met them and arrested many people, maybe four hundred. I am sending someone to Paloich today to make an investigation. If you come tomorrow I can tell you more."

"What if I went with him? I could see for myself."

He glanced at the Fanta bottle on his desk, and rose. "Just a moment." He left me with my tea and appeared in the doorway fifteen minutes later. "Come with this man here. He is going to Paloich to make inquiry. He can take you."

"He" was Pancien Acwiel, the SPLM chief in Melut county. He looked thinner than me (which is saying a lot), but, like all Sudanese I had met, was stronger than his size implied. I learned this as we walked down the front patio steps to his green Land Cruiser and I headed straight for the back. He gave a short wordless push that redirected me with professional wrestler force against the front passenger door, paused for my rebound, pulled the door open and shoved me inside with a nudge to the small of my back. Smiling, and a little sore, I looked over my shoulder and saw the car was packed with three silent women, two unsilent babies, an old man in a brown woolen watch cap and enough bundles and packages to fill a subway car. I was glad to be up front, sitting between Pancien and his driver, with plenty of room for my tote bag filled with notebooks and the Nikon on my lap. The wheelman gunned the engine and blasted us forward atop a plume of dust. No one spoke.

Melut, Paloich and points north were a jurisdictional gray area—officially controlled by Juba and Malakal, but dominated by northern military intelligence, northern-aligned militias and private security forces of the oil companies. They kept the juice flowing to Khartoum and they kept the details secret. Local officials walked a fine line between asserting legal authority and bowing to the hydrocarbon imperative.

We raced south on the asphalt road past the SPLA compound, the UN team site and garrisons belonging to the SAF and their militias before hooking a left inland on a dusty track that dipped and twisted over dry creek beds and patches of stubby brown grass. In time this track was shadowed by a newer road of dense orange laterite stone, its base transected by arrays of narrow steel culverts. The new road, the only one that existed in the rainy season, had been built by Chinese workers to ensure access to the oil fields. These roads were notorious in the south for their lousy drainage. They dammed the landscape, soaking part of the floodplain while depriving farms and herds on the other side of their seasonal lifeline. Satellite photographs compiled by the European Coalition on Oil in Sudan show how between 1999 and 2005, significant acreage of agricultural land was ruined by this particular road. We left the dirt track and crossed over to the new road and soon its surface grew smoother and straighter. Small white signs printed in English and Chinese began to crop up—Adar 4; Heglig 2—pointing to different side roads and the wells they serviced.

We drove through oil concessions that stretched from the Sobat River north to Renk, all of it controlled by Petrodar. Hundreds of villages had been cleared by armed militiamen and Russian-made bombers to make way for the wells, and thousands of people killed. Still, this stretch of Upper Nile hadn't seen the worst of the oil displacement. During the 1990s tens of thousands of southerners were slain in Unity and other states to the west to clear the land for oil concessions now controlled by companies from China, Malaysia and India.

The ride to Paloich now took us past the Kotolok refinery, which looked impressive, but what did I know of refineries? It rose from the dirt, an industrial mirage, a metal-stacked complex of silos and pipes, a bit of the Meadowlands or Bhopal dropped in the scrub waste of Upper Nile. Distance and speed made it impossible to discern any people behind its tall fence—the engineers from China and Malaysia and from the north, the skilled workmen, the laborers, the cooks and drivers and sweepers, all of them vetted for their jobs by Khartoum's military intelligence directorate. I leaned past Pancien, bracing my left arm on the peeling dash, and shot frame after frame of the filthy Oz. More than one hundred thousand barrels a day moved through a pipeline from Kotolok to the Al Salam port on the Red Sea for shipment to China, Japan, South Korea, Indonesia and India. There had been a village on the site of the oil facility, but it was overrun by militiamen in 2005, a month after the signing of the Comprehensive Peace Agreement.

When we reached Paloich itself—a wide cast of tukuls and markets and nothing else really—we pulled into a complex of mud huts. Some had metal roofs, some grass; some were fully enclosed in reed fencing and others were open or partly open. Pancien and I stepped out to the dense sunshine and then ducked into the hot shade of one of the grass-roofed tukuls. Inside, eight men in plainclothes and two policemen sat on plastic chairs and wooden benches. Pancien pushed me into a plastic armchair and sat on my left and explained in Dinka who I was. Conversation resumed, and then the room went momentarily dark as an SPLA major squeezed his bulk through the doorway and sat at my right. He was a grizzly of a man, with a full beard and rough hands. His tan chocolate-chip camo uniform bore a JIU patch and he carried a two-and-a-half-foot swagger stick of carved teak with a three-inch slug of ivory at the tip. It was soon apparent that he'd led the JIU forces that had helped break the riot. He and the others discussed the incident for a very long time, the major's voice less conciliatory than those of the others, while I pulled at a bottle of water and tried not to doze off in the gelling heat. Just as I was closing my notebook to end the charade that I understood a word they were saying, a clean-cut young man in a Hawaiian-print shirt came in. With one hand

Pancien lifted me out of my chair and with the other he clamped the new entrant's wrist. "You go with him," Pancien said. "He is judge coroner, SPLA. He can tell you what you want to know." Judge coroner turned out, after some modifications to my ear, to mean lieutenant colonel. We stepped outside and walked thirty feet to a fenced-in dirt yard, where we sat in the shade of a giant banyan while a few other men lolled and took water from a jerrican draped in wet burlap to keep it cool.

He gave me the basics. In the early evening or late afternoon, some boys had started throwing stones at cars in Paloich. They made a run for the refinery, where they were beaten back by the JIU and arrested. More had been arrested today, by the JIU, the police and new soldiers who had been sent from Malakal. Malakal? Additional prodding revealed these were the same fighters, including Gabriel Tang's rump forces, who had rampaged in Malakal the other night. They had been shipped out of town and put to use breaking heads in Paloich and Melut. "And the prisoners?" I asked. "Where are they?" Some are right here, he said. "May I see?" He stood and left the enclosure.

We crossed the dirt patch, past the tukul where Pancien was meeting with the others, to a gray shipping container sitting on concrete blocks at the top of a tiny hillock. The lieutenant colonel gave an authoritative-looking wave to two guards lampreyed to the shade nearby. We stepped up to the container and talked to the prisoners through a barred window of welded rebar. They were all local men in their twenties except for a forty-six-year-old schoolteacher from Malakal who had come months before looking for work. The boys had spontaneously started throwing rocks at Petrodar vehicles around 5 p.m., they said. The teacher too picked up a stone but was arrested before he could hurl it. Others had been seized that morning; security officers had swept the streets for young African men, grabbing whomever they found. The dozen prisoners sat on the clean metal floor and crouched against the hot metal walls and asked for water. I handed my bottle through the bars (I regretted drinking from it inside the tukul) and they somehow divided it with dignity and without haste though most hadn't seen a drop for more than eighteen hours. "I have been here seven months," said Paul Thomas, the teacher. "Life in Paloich is very terrible. There is nothing for the local people. The young generation is fed up and I am fed up also." He wore a stained T-shirt with a pen stuck into the right breast pocket; the pen struck me as a totem of his higher education. "This is for China," a young man, Manny Kuak, called out. "And the Arabs in Khartoum. Everyone is being beaten—all those who are black." I felt a silent urgency ripple off the lieutenant colonel and quickly turned my attention to the one and a half English speakers in the container, teased out a quick just-the-facts narrative, stepped back, and got off a single shot from my Nikon before running out of film, when a man in uniform came bitching at us in Arabic. The lieutenant colonel quickly steered me away, clockwise around the container and down the hillock, briefly out of the angry man's line of sight, and back toward the tukul where Pancien was debriefing the JIU major, an apparently safer zone. I reloaded the Nikon and asked the colonel to take me around town, but what I really wanted was another pass near the rear of the jail, where a few pairs of arms now stuck out of another barred window. I was looping in that direction when a dozen men barreled at me from a gate in a tall fence at the far side of the yard.

"*Put-it-away*," the colonel said evenly. I put it away, too late.

"What are you doing here? This is not your business," barked a man in dark green uniform, advancing double-quick-march. "Who gave you permission?" he shouted. My field of vision narrowed to the man's furious eyes, his brow speckled with new sweat. I could see he was breathing as hard as I was. He was afraid and angry and I was afraid and not, and that, for a second, gave me traction. "Good afternoon," I said, smiling and extending my right hand.

"My name is Dan Morrison and I am a journalist visiting Upper Nile." He took the hand without enthusiasm, but the civil introduction slowed his fury. "And you are . . . ?"

"I am Captain Michael, and you have no business here. This is not your concern. Not your concern." The other men had spread into a circle around me. The lieutenant colonel had disappeared. Twenty yards to the rear, hovering near the gate, two Arab men in street clothes, one wearing a pistol in his waistband, watched the encounter. The circle tightened and so did my chest. I would be arrested, deported, my film and notes confiscated and destroyed. The military observers would catch hell for sheltering me. I was wondering how I would get another visa after this one was revoked when Pancien pierced the ring in long power strides and said in Arabic—though my translation here may be rough— "Fuck you, boys. New sheriff in town." He gripped my arm and yanked me away, smiling for the first time in our short acquaintanceship.

"I'm really sorry about this," I said.

"You are with us," he replied. "They cannot touch you." Then he bade me wait in the colonel's shady enclosure until the Land Cruiser returned from dropping off the other passengers. From behind the fence I heard them argue for a few minutes and then each side, north and south, went back to its own patch of sovereignty. After a half hour of sweating in the shade I heard more commotion outside and, standing on my toes, watched from over the top of the fence as seven more young men were taken from the back of a truck and locked in the shipping container. Pancien didn't seem bothered by the confrontation when he finally summoned me for the ride back to Melut on the Petrodar highway. "What kind of trees are those?" I asked, pointing to the scores of succulents that rose across the floodplain.

"Wells," he said. "The roads lead to wells."

———

Back in Melut, I walked the mile from the commissioner's office to the UN team site, narrowly missing opportunities to hitch a ride on a passing pickup and two donkey carts. I was lightheaded and sweating when I reached the front checkpoint and the two Indian guards there asked me into their fortified tent. They were friendly, professional, happy to talk and to use the conversation to probe my background and intentions. Though they had seen me arrive on a UN chopper and watched me drive in and out of the base with colonels and majors and civilian administrators, they now needed to check me out. I was, after all, on foot. "You don't mind if I call my commanding officer to verify your status?" I didn't. The call to the Tanzanian colonel was swift and the junior of the two Indians wrote me into the visitors' log and apologized thrice for the inconvenience. We said goodbye and I walked onto the team site, the gravel road lined with inverted plastic bottles filled with water and buried halfway in the berm for use as nighttime reflectors. They kicked back a greenish glow when headlamps passed over.

It looked like Bernard and the other military observers were having a meeting, so I went into the office trailer next door and cooled my body to the sound of the air conditioner and their muffled voices until Bernard's exasperated howls crashed through the wall: "This person is a *guest* of the *United Nations*! They brought him here! It is only *natural*, and courteous—common courtesy—that I offer him a place to sleep." I sat very still and pretended they weren't talking about me and then bolted outside when I heard a car door open. One of the Peruvians had left the meeting and was driving back to their quarters. "Don't worry," he said as we pulled up to the guesthouse. "Everything here is politics." The Tanzanian colonel, it seemed, was having second thoughts about my presence.

Across the Nile a deep curtain of black cloud was coming our way like an advancing army. "It's a *khamseen*," the Peruvian said. Narrow dust devils, tall as town houses, swirled in and out of the approaching sandstorm. Overhead a checkerboard of black-and-white clouds moved with speed from the east toward the river. Heavy rain pelted us, dimpling the earth, and stopped the sandstorm's march at the west bank. On our bank, cool rain and breeze prevailed. On the other, hot wind and dust. In between, the Nile moved, black and silky under the late-afternoon light.

That night, as Bernard made Belgian frites, "the best in all Sudan," I walked through a way-camp on the riverside to buy fried fish from the traders and migrants waiting for a boat downriver. We ate bony breaded perch on the porch with fries and a mash of round cucumber, onions and garlic that was a valiant if failed experiment in making the most of what was around. Over bottles of Tusker, Bernard told me harrowing tales of Internet love, Euro-style, that boiled down to this one lesson: It is not an expression of carnal desire when a twenty-two-year-old Russian ballerina asks for your bank information. It really isn't.

In the morning I carried my bags across the road to the souk and bought a ticket for the bus to Renk, the last city in southern Sudan. Through the window of a small wooden shack the ticketmaster took my money and printed D-A-N on the narrow-ruled lines of a desiccated ledger. He tore a square printed receipt from a tissue-thin sheet and handed me the chit in his open palm. "Can I sit in the front?" I asked. "With the driver?" He nodded. "With the driver, I mean. Up front?" He nodded again, slowly this time, as if to a moron, and scribbled a word or two more in Arabic next to my name. "*Shukran, ya hadritak*," I said—Thank you, O Sir. I loaded up on bottled water and mango juiceboxes and bought a chrome flashlight at a nearby stall: Tiger Head brand, made in China. It had an LED bulb and ran on D-size batteries that so closely bordered the artisanal I could almost make out the impressions of the prepubescent fingers that had rolled the bare lead cells into their shiny paper sheaths.

The bus was facing south on a slight incline near the roadside. Painted a happy blue, it was a hybrid creature, with a fifty-foot wooden-slatted passenger compartment bolted onto the back of an old Smith's diesel lorry—a truck so antique that the grille boasted a vestigial slot, like an inverted keyhole, for an old-fashioned crank starter. To say the truck was a Smith's was but to guess based on the faint lettering on two dials embedded in the dashboard, one of them upside down. These gauges indicated nothing besides the possibility that someone had once aspired to measure the truck's amperage and oil pressure. Outside, I stepped onto the bumper and peered into the engine compartment while a crew of boys topped off the water and oil. The motor was clean, and had the simple look that old motors do—a radiator the size of a *Times* atlas, a battery the size of a milk carton and the valve cover with a cream enameled look to it, like an old crock pot. There were no markings on the engine, not even faint ones, that could whisper its original make or model.

Bernard drove by as I was hoisting my rucksack to the roof to tell me that more prisoners from Paloich were being kept at the nearby school. "You didn't have to risk yourself going to the place of the riot," he said. "The rioters have come to you." But it was too late for new interviews with these new wretches—my bus was about to leave and I had become a liability to Bernard. The passengers were gently pushing onto the bus. Some of the men wore *jallabiyas*, others shirts and slacks and a half dozen were in fatigues and carried AKs. The women, wearing batik-style wraps of violet, brown and blue, mixed easily with the men. I climbed into the front seat, followed by two of the bus's five-man crew. With passengers on, the cargo loaded and the engine at the ready, the driver now got in and said hello with a quick jut of his chin. He had short graying hair and wore oversized aviator sunglasses that set off the faint horizontal scarring on his brow. He gave the impression of one who had been plying the roads of Upper Nile since before there were roads. He pulled the choke knob and then reached under the dash to a jumble of faded red wires and thumbed their exposed ends into a ball. Then he let out the clutch and we rolled forward a few

feet before he popped it into low gear and the engine growled to steady if geriatric life. I wanted to laugh as I squinted through the smoky windshield at the road ahead.

The driver eased it into second and then third gear and after a moment I realized he wasn't going to turn around and take us north along the Nile—his route, I now realized, pointed twenty miles inland, past the refinery to Paloich, before turning north to Renk. He ground on for an hour through the dust track Pancien and I had followed the previous day before switching to the murram road, slowing to ease the bus past potholes and jagged patches of broken roadway with the same deftness my friends on the barge had displayed dodging sandbars in the Sudd. After another forty-five minutes we pulled to the side and idled while two of the crew leapt down from the roof and popped the hood. One of the boys wrapped his hand in a faded red rag and twisted off the radiator cap. His colleague fetched a jug that had been resting at the driver's feet, just under his seat, and poured in a thin stream of water until it overflowed. The first boy, his white tunic somehow both filthy and shining, replaced the cap and gently secured the hood, and then together they climbed in their sandals back to the roof, using the open window as a foothold, even as the driver put the bus in gear and steered us back onto the road.

I slouched low as we approached the refinery and lower still when we entered the town. The blue bus made several slow dusty circuits around Paloich in search of passengers. The place seemed deserted, a square mile of flat and dry and empty markets— weathered wooden stalls and bare tables under thatch or plastic covers. I hadn't seen much of the town the day before. It seemed more a location than a settlement, a place with enough importance that the locals had given it a name, but it appeared the markets had come with the new road and the oil. It was quiet—there was no radio in the bus, of course, and no one spoke. We passed two checkpoints, slowing at each while the driver traded niceties with the cops there and I tried to look away without appearing to be looking away. Finally at a metal barricade on the main road we came to a complete stop and two soldiers approached from the side and started chattering at me. They pointed to the police shack across the road, this view blocked now by another bus pulling into town from the opposite direction. "I'm going to Renk. Is this the bus to Renk?" I said with exaggerated volume, playing it stupid, but they weren't deterred. After a couple minutes of my stalling, they ordered the two boys on my right out of the cab and the smaller of the two soldiers reached in for my arm. I pulled a copy of my passport from the raid pack and turned to the driver. "*Do not* leave without me," I begged, pointing to the floor. In my shitty Arabic I said, "*Inta hinna*," You here, and I repeated it. "*Quais?*"

"*Quais*," he said, and I slid toward the waiting goons. The soldier took my arm and yanked me out, all without prejudice, really, and I walked with the two of them across the road; the driver got out and reassuringly followed. Had word gotten around about the foreigner at the jail yesterday? Was I fucked? Or merely inconvenienced? The dim shack appeared to be a sort of interagency node for traffic coming in and out of Paloich. A policeman in a light blue uniform sat at an old metal office desk. Sitting on stools and a bench were three men in well-pressed military fatigues. There were also two men in plainclothes with trim mustaches and pistols tucked in their waistbands, clones of the pair I'd spotted observing my confrontation at the jail, and of the angry security officer who'd rousted me in Malakal. Trouble, when it came, would come from them. Everyone looked on in the quiet as I handed the police officer a photocopy of my passport and my press card from Khartoum. He looked briefly at the passport copy and stared at the press card before handing it around the room. "What is your name?" he said.

"Ah, Dan," I replied, shaking his hand.

"*Adan?* You Muslim?" I looked around the room with a mien

of sincere regret. "I'm sorry, no," I said, compulsively placing my hand over my heart, "not Muslim." Someone said something in Arabic and they all laughed, and one of the mustachioed men said from the back, "No Muslim, okay. How you like Sudan?" Sudan was beautiful, I said, *jamila*, and they laughed again. We shook hands all around while the policeman opened his side drawer and dropped my passport copy atop a pile of similar sheets (all of which appeared to be printed in Chinese). With that, I stepped outside into the bright desert wasteland, the nubs of grass and low bushes clotted with plastic shopping bags, and walked with the driver back to the bus.

About two hours outside Renk, the trusty Smithy cleared its throat, went quiet and coasted ten feet to a stop. We had run out of gas. The passengers filed off without complaint as the driver and his crew took turns peering into the empty tank under the chassis. They squatted on the road and didn't say much. The empty steel tank didn't say much either. After a while, many people crawled back inside to escape the sun. I squatted with several men and boys—Arab, Dinka, Shilluk, Nuer—in a two-feet-wide band of shade on the right side of the bus. From time to time someone got up and walked into the field to piss. They all did so sitting on their haunches. Was this practical or cultural? Were they squatting because it's the neater way to piss if you're wearing a *jallabiya*? (Not that most of them were wearing *jallabiyas*.) Or was it modesty? Keeping your thing well out of view, below sin's radar? The sun kept moving and our band of shade narrowed and this sun, today, really did burn.

New Austrian-made long-haul trucks passed in ones and twos carrying loads of steel and pipe on their flatbeds; none stopped. After about forty-five idle minutes a southbound bus pulled over and offered fuel. A search began for a hose to siphon diesel from its tank into a jerrican and after fifteen minutes of watching the crew rummaging under and behind the front seat in their various kit bags, I almost offered them a rubber tube from my water filter. (Sanity for once intervened to keep my mouth shut and I would like to thank it, again.) In time they found a hose and someone drew the short straw and was sent to suck a few liters from the other tank. They crossed the road and poured it into ours but still the engine wouldn't turn over when we tried a groaning push start. They popped the hood again and the driver removed six small bolts sitting under the cylinders until diesel bled from each. Then we all gathered around, me near the front, and pushed until the machine rolled, caught, sputtered and failed. Three more tries and we were back under the power of internal combustion. The driver put the truck in neutral, the gang added more water to the radiator, this time from a black goatskin, and we were away, slowing every now and again to dodge herds of goats and cattle being driven across the road.

The landscape was one of desert floor and low trees, many of which appeared to have been burned for charcoal. These small dead husks were set in the earth as far as I could see in either direction. I gathered we were about an hour away from Renk when, as the driver moved to shift from third to fourth, the unthinkable happened: The gearstick broke off in his hand with a quiet snap, right at its base. He looked at me through his plus-size aviators and I looked back and shrugged. "Wasn't me, man." He looked down at the top of the gearbox, over to my boots and back to my face, and I shrugged again. He gave a small shake to his head, corrected course like a schooner captain and stuck the gearshift out the window for the crew up top to gape at. Then he reached across me to his number two, asleep against the door, and tapped him awake.

Now when we encountered the herds, the driver would put in the clutch, rev the engine—both to keep the rpms up and to alarm the livestock—and pilot a course between the dumb and the not as dumb. (In addition to air bags and a Bose entertainment system, the bus also lacked a horn.) At the approach of the bus, the skinny herdsmen and herdsboys, wrapped in white muslin shawls and carrying long walking sticks, would turn toward us with hospitable smiles, as if welcoming friendly aliens, slowing the dolorous progress of their mute meat across the road. Our last such crossing of the animal shoals was, if not a display of artistry, at the very least one of professionalism. A pretty, russet-colored veal stopped dead center in the road and our man had to brake, keep the rpms high, cut hard to the right and again to the left, bring the clutch out slow and still keep us moving. I slapped the driver's arm in congratulation and he grinned, eyes fixed on the road.

The herds couldn't stop us, but the heat could. With Renk almost in sight the driver put in the clutch and coasted us to a stop so the mobile pit crew could refill the radiator. We'd been in third since the stick broke; it would be impossible to get moving again in so high a gear. I pointed at the four bolts that secured the top of the gearbox and the driver nodded. He called out to the crew and a quarter-inch wrench was handed down through the passenger-side window. The engine still idling, his foot still on the clutch, the driver pulled up two layers of thick black rubber mats and passed them to the roof, revealing a floor of ancient wood and steel. The nub of the broken gearshift stuck out of a square black metal cover, which he unbolted and removed. Inside, two opposing steel brackets sat almost floating in a tight pool of sputtering oil. The driver again called out and a ten-inch slotted screwdriver appeared at his window. Bending at the waist, foot still on the clutch, he pried the left-hand bracket forward to neutral. Then he took his foot off the clutch, wiped his face with a washcloth, depressed the pedal again and pried and ground us into first gear. And so we moved. After dropping the washcloth over the gearbox to suppress the hot oil splattering on our legs, he let out the clutch one last time and we rolled back onto the road, and slowly gained speed. Soon enough it was time for second gear, and he bent down again, brushed aside the washcloth and pushed and grunted us there while I held the bucking steering wheel close to steady.

He kept it in second the rest of the way, and the bus crawled along the jellied asphalt, dodging animals and their companions until, hours later, we coasted down into the sprawling bus depot outside Renk. Once my bags were freed from the roof I thanked the driver and grabbed an autorickshaw into town with the first mate, who was taking the broken gearshift to be welded back onto its stem. He jumped out in front of an open-air metal shop and I asked the rickshaw driver to help me find lodging. He stopped every few blocks to ask strangers if they knew of a hotel. None did. It was now past six o'clock and Renk was quickly growing dark. The town of grass huts was set back from the Nile, with a few neighborhoods of cement and brick shops and the compounds of the well-to-do, and not a flophouse among them. At last, during our second circuit through what passed for the commercial district, I spotted an UNMIS Nissan SUV making a cautious U-turn around a deep rut and nearly mounted the hood to keep it from pulling away. The SUV's driver was a West African army major, blessedly anglophone; his local translator was riding shotgun. Their team, he said, was on patrol in Renk, staying at the local commissioner's guesthouse. (I, meanwhile, had been staying at this major's permanent quarters in Melut, courtesy of Bernard.) He was reluctant to offer me a bed, and recommended I find Renk's commissioner and ask him myself. It was well past business hours now; the commissioner could maybe be found at home. The translator got out and spent a good minute explaining the route to my driver. I gave them my exhausted thanks and we revved on. The driver twice called out to passersby to refresh his directions, each time altering the three-wheeler's course by a good thirty or forty degrees until, half an hour later, we had motored across town to a sandy street of walled yards and a prominent brick compound with mounds of bricks, gravel and reed poles piled outside. It was a substantial home, built on a corner plot with two steel doors, one for cars and one for people. We got out and knocked. After a moment a metal bolt slid back and the door was opened by a golden-skinned young girl of maybe ten or eleven wearing a simple black cloak, her black hair piled on her head under a knotted rag. She looked at me and without a word closed and bolted the door. We listened to her bare feet as they ran away, and to the measured longer strides of another person approaching. The door opened again to reveal a woman wearing a floor-length bronze gown with veins of dark embroidery running down the middle: the lady of the house. She looked at us in polite curiosity. She really is lovely, I thought, and, despite myself, I wondered if she was Arab or African, when the answer was that she was both, all Sudanese being Africans. Her gaze was direct, from wide-set eyes over a narrow nose. Her hair was pulled back and covered. Gold earrings—little links of dangling gold— twinkled against her jawline.

The driver explained my situation and she stepped back from the doorway and gestured me inside with a brief turn of her palm. It was a nice spread, with a broad, swept-earth courtyard surrounded by five outbuildings. She left me and returned dialing a Samsung phone. After speaking for a moment, she handed it to me. It was her husband the commissioner on the line, currently in Khartoum on business. "How can I help you?" he asked in clear English. I told him how I had come to his door, the journey through Sudan, the bus ride from Melut and my now acute need to spend the night, on the floor if necessary, at his official guesthouse. "You are of course welcome," he said. "You can stay where you are, at my home, in my guestroom. My wife will cook for you. But there is something that puzzles me. I am not the commissioner at Renk. I am commissioner at Maban."

"You're the commissioner of Maban?"

"Maban, yes."

I looked up at his wife in shock. She looked back, almost interested. Was this a trick? I had somehow been delivered to the door of Ali Kata Oshi, the official John Ivo Mounto had described as a stooge of the north, and whom he had just been appointed to replace as commissioner of Maban. "Sir," I said, "I don't understand how I got here. The rickshaw was supposed to bring me to the commissioner of Renk. I don't want to trouble your family. Do you have a mobile number for the local commissioner? I can still try him, especially with your reference." He clucked. "It is no trouble. Do you like fish? She will cook you fish from the Nile. And halvah, do you like halvah? She will bring that too. You know how drivers are. I am sure he has been asking people for the way to the commissioner's house. People in that area know I am a commissioner. So they sent you to me."

It made sense, quick sense really, but still I waited for Rod Serling of *The Twilight Zone* to walk through the gate or emerge from the outhouse. I paid the driver and made an appointment for him to pick me up at six the next morning for a bus north. This would be my last night in southern Sudan and it was shaping stranger than the day. Mrs. Kata took up the heavier of my two bags and led me around into the brick guest cottage, the most solidly built structure in the compound. Inside were two twin beds with polished wooden headboards and thick foam mattresses, two long couches and a thirty-six-inch television that sat under a tall wedding portrait of the ex-commissioner and Mrs. Kata. The tiled floor was crowded with glass-topped coffee tables that held ashtrays and dark wooden coasters. This was clearly Papa's preserve, and I had to admit it was cozy. Still: How did this happen? John Ivo had said there was nothing in Maban, no development of any kind. It seemed reasonable that an official there might keep a residence in a proper town, just as officials in Juba maintained their families in the more comfortable precincts of Nairobi and Khartoum.

I showered and brushed under the corrugated steel roof of a clean bathing stall, and was smoking a cigarette on the guestroom's couch when the first two visitors arrived. They were friends of Ali Kata, one of them a cousin of Kata's wife, sent to check me out.

As with Mrs. Kata, I couldn't classify them within my extremely limited ethnic vocabulary. Here, literally at the border of northern and southern Sudan, the rigid tribal and religious identities of the "African" south had to a degree melded with those of the north. Over a giant tray of homemade halvah, with a bowl of thick pure honey in the middle, Kata's friends asked me about my journey, and of my strange trip to this compound. They wore light safari suits and sandals, and described themselves as traders, though one also worked as a teacher in an Arabic-language local school. They invited me outside for tea; some lawn chairs had been set up in front of the cottage.

As we chatted, the homestead was coming to life. A few teen-age boys arrived by bicycle, members of Ali Kata's extended family. A girl appeared at the far end of the compound and stayed there. The men explained the layout: The boys slept in the long-house opposite my brick cottage. The metal-roofed hut diagonally across from us—farthest from the gate—was where Kata's wife and the girls slept. The next building, with a grass roof, was storage, and then, continuing clockwise, came the kitchen. A young man—another cousin or nephew—stepped through the gate and sat quietly with us, and conversation trailed as the freshness of the shower wore off and fatigue started to weigh on my face and my responses. No amount of tea would keep me awake for long. The servant girl came with two tall plastic pitchers of water and handed them to two of my companions. They walked across the yard, to where the girl had laid out reed mats, and washed their faces, hands and feet. "They're praying?" I asked Mrs. Kata's cousin.

"Yes. It is prayer time." The call was now echoing across town.

"Aren't you Christian?"

"I am," he said. "But they are Muslim. The younger one, his mother is Christian. And some of his uncles are Christian. Families in Upper Nile are like that. It is very common. One family can have a brother who works in the church, and another who prays five times a day and fasts for Ramzan."

"And our host, Ali Kata?"

"Kata is a Christian man."

"With a Muslim name."

"Yes. It is very usual here. Many families took Muslim names before the war, during the war. It was easier. The government maybe would give you less trouble. Maybe you can easier get a job."

Prayers over, they returned and all three said goodbye to me and then to Mrs. Kata. I limped back into the cottage and was taking my shirt off when two of the boys walked in without speaking and absconded with the big television, carrying it to a waiting table outside. Chairs and string beds had been pulled from the storage hut and laid out in a line. Seven children, boys and girls who appeared to range from six to fifteen, were waiting for the night's entertainment. The older boys carefully walked the set to the table, pulling with it a controller box and plenty of cable. For the first time, I noticed their satellite dish. I had been taking tea just a few feet from it. I pulled the door shut and lay down in my slacks and undershirt and tried not to think. I had only just acquired a weak grip on the fluid political and military alliances that had marked so much of the south's recent history. Getting a handle on the deeper notions of identity here seemed impossible. Rebecca Malual had wanted the south to be a Christian state. What would that mean for families like this one? John Ivo—as true blue a man as I would ever meet—had portrayed Ali Kata as a quisling. In his absence at least, Kata seemed a pretty decent man.

I was close to sleep when someone knocked on the door and stepped inside without waiting for me to answer. He was a tall, thin, unambiguously black man, another inquisitive Kata cousin. I sat on the edge of the bed and again told my story. I asked him what people did for work in Renk. He said there wasn't much besides farming, though the farms, like the oil, were controlled from Khartoum, and many of the farmers were northern tribesmen. Ali Kata, he said, was trying to work with the state to market and sell acacia gum from Upper Nile through traders in Kenya, though the volume had so far been small.

"Oh," I said, "you mean gum Arabic," the sticky binding agent that puts the bubble in Bubblicious and helps soda go pop.

"It is gum African," he replied with speed. "Gum African."

CHAPTER NINE

At six the next morning I waved farewell to Mrs. Kata and opened the gate to find the rickshaw driver waiting. He dropped me at the bus depot, where I bought a cup of tea and tried to make sense of the prior twenty-four hours. Ali Kata Oshi had just been fired from his job as commissioner of Maban, but did that make him a bad guy? I imagined in John Ivo and Ali Kata two poles—those who left home to fight for change during the civil war and those who stayed to make their lives from the world as it existed. John Ivo looked to Juba, and to America, for support. Ali Kata, who had remained in Upper Nile and lived under military administration, naturally looked north to the stability and opportunity of Khartoum. Millions of southerners had done the same during that dark era, some living in the relative safety of squalid refugee camps in the capital, others getting by far from the gunfire and starvation as junior members of Sudanese society. Wouldn't it be natural for Ali Kata to take a more accommodating stance when dealing with northern influence? That's how he and so many others had sustained themselves and their families. John Ivo had gone against that grain and lost his wives, his children and his freedom. And, well before I met John Ivo, Ali Kata had been recommended to me by a trusted contact, someone with years of experience probing injustice in Sudan. Didn't that imply he was on the right side of things? But when John Ivo returned to Maban and tried to organize the local chiefs, it was Ali Kata, backed by gunmen, who had tried to stop him.

People who work with refugees will tell you that the stories of migrants and asylum seekers are often full of holes, that the most straightforward story is usually the one that's false. Life in extremity is difficult to explain—things happen and people don't know why they are happening. Some events were fortunate and others were disastrous and that's how it went. While I was nothing like a refugee, I felt a similar inability to understand the things I had just experienced. I was on a bus; I was on a rickshaw; I came to the home of a friend's enemy, and there I was treated with kindness. I couldn't explain it. I hoped to find out more when I reached Khartoum—Ali Kata had invited me for tea and I looked forward to our introduction.

I took a bus north to Kosti, a true city of 174,000 on the Nile's western bank, and set up house on the fourth floor of a worn-out hotel by the river. I had almost forgotten that buildings could have more than two stories. My room was big, with a chipped red vinyl floor, red-curtained windows that opened onto the hallway, two single beds and a sink. I washed the fear out of the prior day's clothes, strung a drying line across the room and took a walk down to the water. After crossing a muddy irrigation canal on a bridge of felled palms, I walked for half a mile through fields of arugula and green beans before coming to the flat Nile.

Here by the river the landscape was still green—this was Sudan's cane belt, the region dominated by the giant Kenana sugar plant, the linchpin of a failed 1970s plan to turn Sudan into the breadbasket of the Arab world. But I had clearly left behind the lushness of equatorial Africa. The air and soil were dry. Nobody's face was scarred, save a few old women. The Dinka, Nuer and Shilluk had all but melted away on the road from Renk; they'd faded almost from the moment I crossed the disputed north-south border. English had disappeared from the signs and storefronts.

But it was Kosti, not Renk, that was the end of the line for barges from Juba. A low highway bridge was erected over the Nile in the 1970s, turning the city, a steamship way station for more than a century, into a terminus. Now, barges upriver of the bridge ran south to Malakal and Juba, while traffic north between Kosti and Khartoum had all but dried up in favor of the highway. I picked my way through the sand and muck to a pair of barges moored in the shadows just north of the bridge. "Khartoum?" I shouted hopefully to a man standing at the deck rail of the first one. "I want to go to Khartoum." He laughed and waved me off. The next barge turned out to be a police post, its crew probably keeping an eye out for bridge saboteurs from the mud flats below, a precaution born of the civil war and Sudan's history of coups and attempted coups. The cops inside were genially unhelpful, so I turned and followed with rising hope the sound of a diesel motor a mile north, but it was only an irrigation pump surrounded by boys playing on the riverbank. I spat and turned back to town.

The city had been founded in the late 1800s by a Greek merchant, Constantini Kosti, who built a trading post at the traditional Nile crossing point for Sudanese pilgrims making their way to Mecca. The settlement caught both the east-west caravan route and the growing river traffic between north and south, and it grew accordingly. As I walked back into the Greek's namesake on streets of sand and crumbled asphalt it was clear that Kosti needed a new coat of paint. The only brightness to be found was in the snack food wrappers and the Arabic-scripted Coke cans. The place felt shut in. I had a sandwich at a low-ceilinged snack bar and turned in the dusk back to my hotel.

An elderly man sitting on a wooden chair outside a tailor shop waved me over to his perch in the sand. "*Bonjour,*" he said, and I replied, "Good evening." "British?" "Not quite." "Ah, American. Please sit." He pointed to a low stool at his side, clearing away a small white coffee cup. Hassan had that timeless look, the sense that he would have appeared the same had I been walking past his street in 1960 or 1930 or 1900. He wore a turban coiled around his head in two bands of rolled white cotton, a white ankle-length robe and black leather slippers. He had a neat white mustache and a short white beard that ran in a crescent along the crest of his chin and no farther. Wrinkles cascaded from his eyes in dark rings; more notched his forehead at quarter-inch intervals as if he had spent decades peaking his eyebrows in skepticism or surprise.

"You've come from the south?" he said. "How do you find it? Exciting? Are they still angry? You know, we are not so different from them. We have our complaints. Look around, there is no democracy here, no development. The government blames the war but the war never reached here." He took off his black plastic eyeglasses and wiped the lenses on his sleeve. An old man cleaning his glasses—it created in me an instant sympathy, an uncalled-for familiarity. He said he was a supporter of the Ummah Party of Sudan's last elected prime minister, Sadiq al-Mahdi. Sadiq was Sudanese royalty, a direct descendant of the Mahdi, the revolutionary terror who evicted the Egyptian and Turkish colonialists in the late nineteenth century. I'd briefly met Sadiq once after a press conference in Cairo. Speaking of Sudan as a "subcontinent" more than a country, he radiated intelligence and strength in his robe and turban, and looked a decade younger than his then seventy years. By most accounts, however, Sadiq had made a lousy prime minister, both during his first go-round in the 1960s and again two decades later, before the National Islamic Front deposed him in 1989. An Oxford-educated paragon of Arabism, he'd stoked many civil war atrocities but was on the verge of opening peace talks with the SPLA when the generals and the radical Muslim Brotherhood stepped in and ramped up the war, eventually declaring it a jihad. I was planning to visit Aba Island, the spiritual home of the al-Mahdi dynasty, the next morning.

"Oh, we like Imam Sadiq very much," Hassan said. "If we have a free election, Sadiq will win in the north, especially with Garang dead. But I don't think they will have a free election. The government would lose, so what would be the point? Do you drink alcohol?"

"I do. Yes. Do you?"

"I am meeting some of my friends later tonight to talk over arak. It would be my pleasure if you joined us." Nothing would have made me happier than to spend the night drinking homemade date brandy with Hassan and his cronies. Still, this was my first night in the north, where sharia was the law of the land. I pictured myself listing back to the hotel, high on White Nile bathtub hooch, nose bloodied from a fall on the jagged pavements, stumbling into the arms of bored and malevolent police officers. I passed. Hassan didn't seem to mind.

I walked back sober and didn't sleep much for the heat and the regret that I wasn't tipsy. In the morning I took two minibus taxis to Aba Island, a few miles north of Kosti. Today's Aba wasn't much more than an eight-mile-long strip connected to the mainland by a causeway over the slow-moving river. But for imperial Egypt, imperial Britain and the ghosts of the Ottoman Empire, it's where the trouble started. In the late 1800s, Muhammad Ahmad, the pious son of a Nubian boatbuilder, came to Aba for a period of reflection. He saw a Sudan under the control of Egyptian colonizers flying the flag of the Ottoman Turks. The Egyptians viewed the Sudanese with the same superior eye that North American settlers cast on the Sioux and Cherokee, the same eye that drives the Han Chinese in western China or that drove the British in India. (Or the northern Sudanese in the south.) The Sudanese were to be taxed, exploited and civilized, in that order. Egyptian administration was cruel and corrupt and very impious. Fired by anger, Muhammad Ahmad predicted the advent of a Muslim savior, the Mahdi, who would cleanse the land of the foreigners. In time Muhammad Ahmad's ardent supporters gave him the mantle and he ran with it, routing the occupying forces with a growing army of Arab tribesmen in the first jihad of the machine age.

After winning an escalating series of battles against the occupiers, in 1883 the Mahdi's forces smote an incompetent British-led force of eight thousand Egyptian soldiers (some of them outfitted in heavy chain mail for the desert engagement). In 1885, they hit the jackpot and took Khartoum after a 317-day siege, killing the famed governor-general Charles Gordon, a British war hero and darling of the antislavery movement. Sudan became a Taliban-like state of summary judgment, famine and perpetual war. The flow of slaves from Sudan to Egypt, Turkey and the Arabian Peninsula resumed from a trickle to a flood. And Britain readied its revenge. The Mahdi died five months after his conquest, possibly of typhus, but his state carried miserably on until 1899 when more than ten thousand Mahdists fell to British machine guns at the Battle of Omdurman. (Winston Churchill was there, taking part in the last cavalry charge of the modern age.) The Mahdi's descendants dealt shrewdly with London, backing the Allies against the Germans and Ottomans in World War I; his son received a knighthood. Sudan was Britain's, but Aba Island remained a stronghold of the al-Mahdi dynasty—even as its true center of power shifted to Khartoum where Sadiq's Ummah Party was the most prominent among the northern political parties. Today the island exudes none of the revolutionary fervor of the past. It is notable mainly as the home of the progressive Imam Mahdi University, located in the former mansion of the al-Mahdi family. It is also home to an attentive cadre of government security officers, as I learned when I stepped off the taxi and went looking for something to eat. The Bradt travel guide had recommended Aba's fried

fish and I was starved. I'd had my feet on the island for fifteen minutes and was peering into a dark restaurant, trying to make out if
the three or four inert figures sitting at the back of the unlit room
were customers or staff or just the proprietor's family, when a man
approached and said simply, "Come with me." By now I well recognized Sudan's version of the flat-topped G-man and I wasn't at
all happy to see him again. I turned with annoyance stoked by hunger. "Come with me please?"

"Yes," he replied. "You come with me."

"Can I get a sandwich first?"

"No. Come with me now."

I hoisted my two bags and trudged after him down the sandy
lane, past clusters of shops and small fenced-in bungalows. He
opened the old wrought-iron gate of one of these buildings and led
me past a tethered goat to a gray wooden door secured by a thin
padlock and hasp. This was his station: a shuttered room with a
single bed, a few shirts on hangers, an AK-47—minus its clip—
leaning against the wall. An old computer monitor dominated the
scuffed top of a desk, but I didn't see an actual computer anywhere. There was a CB radio that might have been connected to a
steel tower I'd seen in the backyard. A television and a VCR rested
on the floor at his feet. He sat there and looked at my papers, fin-
gering my visas and press card. "What else?" he said.

"What else?"

"Documents."

"You want more documents?"

"Yes."

I pulled out my wallet and gave him my New York driver's
license and my Egyptian press ID and my long-expired New York
City press card. He stared at each for a moment before setting
them aside and again opened my passport. He looked around for
a pen, found his to be dry and then borrowed my green Bic. Propping the passport open with the banana clip from his Kalashnikov,

the security man copied my information onto the ragged bottom margin of a yellowed Arabic newspaper. "Would you like this?" I asked, proffering a crisp passport Xerox. "I give one to the police wherever I go." Indeed, I had been called upon to do so at the outdoor bus depot in Renk and again at Kosti.

"I am not police," he snapped, still copying onto the newsprint. "I am intelligence."

"So you don't want this."

"No."

"Okay, then." He finished his scribe's work, shuffled the various ID cards into my passport and reached out for me to take them without getting out of his chair. I stood up from the bedside, dropped the passport and cards into my front shirt pocket and asked if there was anything else. He shook his head and looked at the door and I used it. This man, I decided, was very unsatisfied in his work.

I stumbled in hunger and heat to a snack shop, drank a Coke for lunch and a bottle of Stim, a Sudanese apple soda, for dessert and washed both down with some Safia bottled water. When I asked the people behind the counter for the garbage they both looked at me blankly. A voice behind me said, "I will take it." I turned around. "Excuse me?" The speaker was a smiling young man of mahogany complexion. Wedged on a bench next to an attractive girl—they very nearly were touching—he repeated himself. "I will take care of it." I nodded and left the bottles on the counter, picked up my bags from the floor near my table and shuffled into the noonday sun, toppling an abandoned Sprite on the way out.

Tired and hungry and hot, wishing for a slice of something familiar, anything really, I contemplated leaving Aba Island right then. There was no denying the place had a huge role in Sudanese history. The Mahdi had risen here and, as recently as 1970, Egyptian bombers had killed more than three thousand people when twentieth-century Mahdists threatened open rebellion against the military dictatorship of Jaffar Nimeiri. But I craved ease and saw the prospects here for none at all. I turned toward the main road and a taxi back over the causeway.

"Excuse me!" It was the man from inside the soda joint. He and the young woman had followed me out. "You are a visitor, from England, yes? I will show you around." Omar and his wife were students at the university. I shook his hand and then reached for hers, converting the attempt at physical contact into a chaste wave over my heart. "*Salaam aleikum,*" I said. She wore a clingy long-sleeved black gown that reached to her knees, with flare-legged blue jeans underneath, hip elevator-heeled sandals and a diaphanous neon pink headscarf that circled her face and fell to her shoulders. One corner of the scarf was pinned back to ensure her throat remained covered. The outfit, common to young women in the north, struck a neat balance between the opposing forces of modesty and style. The tight blouses and hip-hugging pants and dresses put the figures of these daughters of the Nile on happy womanly display. At the same time, they remained covered, and more than technically—barely a strand of hair or a patch of the young lady's skin was visible. (Their mothers tended to wear equally fetching wraps called thobes that also pleasantly described the female form.) Omar's wife returned my greeting, he said a few words to her in Arabic and she turned and walked away. "She has to go somewhere," he said. "Come with me."

I said, "You know, you're the second person to say that to me today," but he was already off and I followed, the rucksack secure on my back and the raid pack slipped over my right shoulder. We entered the grounds of the university, an old colonial-style mansion flanked by long buildings of classrooms and lecture halls. For the next hour Omar led me from room to room, explaining each one, introducing me to his schoolmates and to strangers. The Mahdi's heirs had transformed his jihad into a liberal Arabist movement that would have been heresy in the nineteenth century. Imam

Mahdi University had six thousand students and a one-to-one ratio of women to men; its female enrollment was second only to Ahfad University in Khartoum, a women's college. We peeked in on lectures in Islamic law, engineering classes and the chemistry lab. But not once during the long march did Omar let me ask a question or engage another student in conversation. He just talked without stopping, to me, to them, to himself, a geyser of long-suppressed English flowing with deaf enthusiasm. It was with dull joy that I finally crawled onto an outbound minibus a block from the university when his tour was finished. The Mahdists had repelled another invader.

The taxi dropped me at a depot a few miles away, where I boarded a big touring liner of a bus for the ride to Khartoum. I had left the undeveloped south. Northern Sudan was almost entirely untouched by the civil war and, despite the combined effects of mismanagement and international sanctions, its main roads were paved, electricity reached the major towns and there was always a hotel to be found. The seats of the Khartoum-bound bus were mostly filled with old men in white robes, many with wooden walking sticks, a few with polished metal canes. We rolled north over smooth two-lane blacktop, sharing the road with Toyota pickups, minibuses and the occasional Mercedes four-door. After an hour of travel two men came down the aisle with a small cart and handed out boxed lunches—sliced lamb on factory-made white bread with some kind of mayo, a bag of Qatari cheese doodles and a slice of pound cake sweating in plastic wrap, to be washed down with a bottle of orange drink. It made for a surreal sight after my bus ride from Melut to Renk. I ate the sandwich and the pound cake, popped a Mega Man multivitamin and settled back in my seat. Four video monitors hung from the ceiling over the center aisle and these began to play an Egyptian farce that the men on board watched with thin interest. Next up was an American wrestling program. A raven-maned nipple jockey named Diesel was battling several villains for possession of a championship belt. Various sidemen jumped into the ring and joined the fray during the hourlong match. The graybeards on the bus enjoyed every minute of their spandex and shouts and sweat. Some nodded and chuckled when the inevitable metal chair made its appearance in the ring, but it was the steroid aerobatics that brought out the ahhs, relaxed sighs proclaiming, "Now that's entertainment."

We shadowed the White Nile, fed with waters from Lake Victoria, the Sobat and dozens of other tributary creeks and rivers. Ahead, rumbling down from the volcanic highlands of Ethiopia, came the river's other half, its robust fraternal twin, the Blue Nile. White and Blue would collide and merge at Khartoum into the Nile proper.

Khartoum had always struck me as a place of mystery. My first hint of this came while watching *The Godfather* on VHS when I was in the fourth grade, during the scene where Jack Woltz, the vain movie studio boss, is showing off his fortune to the Godfather's adopted son, Tom Hagen. Woltz's wealth is represented by an imposing black Arabian stallion that Woltz has named Khartoum. "Khartoum," Woltz murmurs, transported, as he strokes the stud's nose. "Khartoum."

While things didn't end well for Khartoum the thoroughbred, its urban namesake was riding an oil boom, with new luxury hotels rising on the Nile and fancy villas multiplying in the suburbs. Sprawling north and east of the Nile confluence, the capital and its sister city, Omdurman, were home to eight million Sudanese, with more arriving every day. It was the country's center of gravity, the unchallenged seat of political, economic and military power, and it drew comers and survivors from across Sudan's impoverished peripheries—Equatorians, Dinkas and Nuer from the south, Darfurians from the west, Bejas from the east and Nubians from the north. While I was happy to be back, I now saw the city in a harsher light. The prosperity here had come in part at the expense of the people in Upper Nile. Khartoum, Omdurman and the surrounding states were the turf of the *awlad al balad*, or sons of the soil, the Arab elites who had controlled Sudan since its independence in 1956. The *awlad al balad* had ruled in times of military dictatorship and parliamentary democracy and they dominated the political spectrum from left to the farthest right with Khartoum as their privileged seat.

Razed and rebuilt by the British, Khartoum had a dust-caked colonial core surrounded by rings of suburbs and pockets of hydrocarbon prosperity. The new petro-cash largely ignored the historic city center, but that's where the charm was, and that's where I headed from the bus depot. Two things drew me downtown—a cheap guesthouse and Waleed Arafat, a member of that rarest of Sudanese brotherhoods, a professional tour guide. I'd met Waleed, a tall and feline man, with an air of determined goodness, more than a year before while passing through Khartoum on the way to a three-week reporting stint in Darfur. He'd struck up a conversation while I was waiting to meet a friend in the lobby of the Meridien Hotel, and we chatted for a long time even though it was clear I didn't need a tour guide and couldn't afford one anyway.

Now I was back in Khartoum, in circumstances just as stingy as when we'd first met, and Waleed had offered to assist. A minivan taxi brought me from the bus stand outside the city downtown to the Souk Araby, a dense and dusty crossroads packed with tiny shops, hole-in-the wall restaurants, stands selling music cassettes, pyramids of limes, Chinese flashlight batteries, dusty ranks of leather sandals and baskets of dried fava beans. The people came from every direction, men and boys mostly, running to make their buses or standing in groups chatting. They ignored me and I them. My mood had somehow changed in Upper Nile; the night of gunfire in Malakal and my brush with arrest in Paloich had left me ragged and with a lingering case of nerves. I felt jumpy, in a hurry and at the same time carried a fatigue the heat and dust could not account for. Undergirding it all was nagging lonesomeness that I refused to acknowledge and for which my lousy Arabic would be no help at all. I hoped I could straighten myself out in Khartoum and maybe make better sense of what I'd seen in the south.

I was lumbering with my bags down the street, sidewalks in Khartoum being a sometime thing, when a stranger leaning against an ancient blue-and-white Toyota taxicab turned to me and said in a genial, familiar way, "South Africa? Egypt? Cairo to Cape? Or is it the other way around?" I brushed past him, muttering, "No thanks."

"Whichever place you are going, you will want a guide."

I turned and, still walking, said, "I have a guide."

"I know. Your guide is Waleed Arafat. I am Moez. Waleed is my cousin."

I stopped in my dusty tracks and, hurling rude overboard, summoned charm to the deck. "That's right," I said with a grin. "How did you know that?"

"We are practically the only guides in Khartoum," he said, ignoring my poor manners. "And we are the best."

"And it's my pleasure to meet you."

We waited for Waleed in the cool little office Moez kept, a pleasing room that brightened further when Waleed arrived smiling. "Ah, Dan," he said. "I'm happy to see you again. It will be my pleasure to help you in your journey in this country, Sudan, where you will find many interesting things, especially, I hope, the Nubian culture, which is a treasure unknown by many in this country." One wall of Moez's office was covered from floor to ceiling with colorful expressionist paintings depicting subjects like Love, Nubia and Love of Nubia, the region that straddled the border of northern Sudan and southern Egypt. Waleed sat opposite these on a metal folding chair. "How can we help you?"

"I'm not sure what I need," I said. "I only know I will need something—mostly expertise, I guess. I'm hoping to follow the Nile from Khartoum, staying as close to the river as I can, to Wadi Halfa. I was thinking that I might find a boat to take me part of the way, but judging from what I saw in Kosti I don't think anyone is traveling on the river—I think I'm twenty years too late. I want to see the pyramids at Meroe, and then see Atbara, which seems simple enough, and then from there go on to Abu Hamed, at the top of the river's curve." I raised my right hand, tracing the Nile's northerly route past Atbara in the dry air of Moez's office. "But"—I sliced my hand downward, the river's southern turn— "I'm not sure how to get from Abu Hamed down to Karima and the Merowe Dam. There don't appear to be any solid roads there, at least not according to my map. Without a road, I doubt there will be many buses. And I don't have a clue how I'm going to get near the dam, and I need to get near the dam." Rising from the Nile about two hundred miles north of Khartoum, the Merowe Dam was arguably the biggest thing happening on the river. The 625-megawatt dam was the bane of environmentalists and human rights activists. At least fifty thousand people would be forced from their homes by the project, and some weren't going quietly. Sudan's government was trying to scour anti-dam activists from Khartoum and the dam-affected areas, but I still hoped to somehow pierce the security.

"The route from Abu Hamed seems like it might have fewer police watching than the route from Atbara," I told Waleed, "but that's just an ignorant guess. I've been trying to contact the people fighting the dam to see if they can sneak me in, but they keep getting arrested, and I can't afford to be arrested. I think what I need more than anything is a sense of what's realistic and what isn't. To make things more complicated, I don't really have any money for private transport. And I can't afford a guide."

Waleed and Moez nodded. "Don't worry about money," Waleed said. "We will try to give you our best advices and advices are always free. I am glad for your interest in the Merowe Dam. It is a very important subject for investigation by an American journalist. But there is another dam that is very little known, called Kajbar, that I hope you will examine too, because it will be a very big disaster for the Nubian people. Last month the police were firing on the people there when they tried to make a protest. It is north of Dongola directly on your route. We will make you a plan so you can make a good accomplishment there. Moez's brother, Midhat, will help." At that, we left Moez's cubby and crossed the street, entering a long commercial building fronted by small shops and a corner juice stand. We passed three headscarved schoolgirls drinking from small stainless steel bowls and walked up a couple flights of stairs to Midhat's office. If, as I suspected, Moez was the dreamer of this group, his older sibling Midhat was the guy who got it done. Burly in his pressed white oxford over a crewneck T-shirt, he watched us enter with a focus bordering on glower, then rose and rasped, "Good meeting you."

Midhat's tourist office had in a prior life been a home interior showroom. The sky blue walls were lined with dozens of sample lengths of molding and wainscoting; two impressive plaster medallions, each two feet across, dominated the foyer. A professional road-racing bicycle with skinny tires and clamping pedals leaned against a wall. Waleed and Midhat spoke for a few minutes in Arabic and turned to me. "You're a cyclist?" I asked. "Yes!" Midhat said. "I have ridden across the country, from Ethiopia to Egypt. I have followed the Blue Nile from the mountains down to Khartoum. When cycle groups ride through Sudan on Africa tours, I organize the routes and ride with them. Some of the riders are very good. Very good."

"And you?"

"I am average," he said, confirming his skills with ironclad modesty. "Let me see your passport. You will need a visa extension. We will take care of it. Come here anytime—to talk, to rest.

Be careful of the sun. We will help you in any way. Waleed, Moez and me." We agreed to meet again later in the week.

The next day I took a taxi to the suburb of Khartoum Two for a sorely needed tutorial on Sudan's oil economy. My instructor, an East African diplomat, specialized in the hard numbers that lay behind the burned villages of Upper Nile and the hostile reaction I'd received in Paloich.

The Ozone café was an affluent enclave of chat and flirting. Sudanese ladies with designer handbags drank coffee and ate ice cream at umbrella-shaded metal tables. Young men and women sat relaxed in their chairs and talked without fear. Sudanese and European children played on the trim green lawn while their parents sipped fresh-squeezed orange juice from wax-paper cups. The air was cooled by a system of water misters—a network of black plastic tubes that periodically released a light spray. Industrial fans on cast iron stands circulated the newly refreshed air, giving the outdoor patisserie a relative humidity much higher than the rest of Khartoum, and a temperature just a bit lower. Short, thick palm trees stood sentry every fifty feet.

My contact was waiting at a table drinking a cappuccino. "It's good coffee," she said, "but not as good as the stuff we grow at home." With that, she dispensed with the personal, looked at her watch and began the lesson. Oil was the name of the game. The northern and southern governments were both hostage to oil revenues, she said, but while the north had agriculture as its traditional, pre-petro mainstay, the south would be completely lost without it. "There is a ninety percent oil dependence in the south," she said. "It's problematic. Eighty percent of the southern budget goes to salaries, and already they are over budget. So either the budget is not enough or they don't have the knowledge and capacity to use it properly."

"Which is it?" I asked.

"That's not for me to say," she replied, "but think of some of these ministers and administrators they have there. Soldiers. Brig-adiers. Straight from the bush and now you are responsible for a billion-dollar budget." She looked again at her watch. "It boggles the mind. The international agencies are just now starting to train state employees in simple basic bookkeeping. Meantime the money flows.

"Now, we know where that money comes from. It comes from oil. And how is that oil sold? The finance ministry says the oil revenue and the distribution of that revenue are completely trans-parent. Completely. Those numbers are posted on the ministry's website for anyone to see. All well and good, but the actual pro-duction statistics aren't public, and that means we have to take their word for it—not just the international community but the southern government and the citizens of Sudan as well. Now, an observer would look at this situation and conclude that there's an awful lot of opportunity for diversion between the extraction and sale of the oil and the posting of these limited figures. A person, a ruling party, an apparatus, could get rich."

"Do you think they're skimming?"

"That's not for me to say either. Now, all the oil contracts made before the CPA—no one knows under what terms those contracts were made. There are a lot of Chinese investments—in irriga-tion, dams, the chemical industries. How does Sudan pay for these investments when it has twenty billion dollars in foreign exter-nal debt? They're *highly* indebted. So how do you pay for all these improvements? You pay in kind. The price of oil is approaching seventy dollars a barrel, but they are giving it to the Chinese for as low as forty dollars, so I'm told. Sudan is desperate to invite investment. It will give in to the most ridiculous terms. And it's not just China. No one's looked at the Malaysian and Indian compa-nies. They are not doing any better than the Chinese on the human rights issue either. Logically, they could be criticized just as much.

"Now, besides infrastructure, how is this oil money spent?

Eighty-two percent of Sudan's federal budget goes to security—
military, the police, intelligence—and that doesn't count off-
budget funding. And it's not just in the north. Your friends in the
SPLA, they take more than half the southern budget. Do you think
some of that's not going into someone's pockets?"

"Is it?"

She stared. "Not for me to say. Now, when these refugees
return home to the south, they ask for three things: a dispensary
or clinic, schools and a church. No one is asking for new artillery.
They're not requesting an air force. Meantime, the Government of
National Unity has ended subsidies on sugar and petrol. The daily
life is growing progressively harder. Inflation has gone from five to
eight percent. The American sanctions are hurting the poor. The
medicines here are all from China. The prices are high and they
are of inconsistent variety and quality. This is the fruits of a closed
society. But look around. Money is being made by someone.

"Lastly, because, despite the pleasure of this monologue, I do
have to get back to work: The known oil reserves—the wells and
fields that are producing oil today—these are projected to start
depleting in ten years. So they've got to get what they can now,
because they don't know if there'll be anything to replace it. Most
of the untapped oil is deep in the south—not the ambiguous south
or the contested south like Abyei—it's in the true south. The government here won't be able to control it." She consulted her watch
again. "I have to go. And, of course, I wasn't here."

There was no love lost between the leaders of the north and
south, and probably even less lost between their constituents. There
was hardly a sentient being in the south who didn't wish to secede
once the referendum came in 2011. (A smaller group predicted
the south might leave by force—a new civil war—even before the
vote.) At the same time, the two sides, and their elites, needed each
other. Southern Sudan had the future oil reserves. Northern Sudan
had the refineries, the pipelines and the shipping facilities at Port

Sudan. Division could mean ruin, but many southerners were prepared for a few more years of ruin if it meant being rid of the Arabs.

Meanwhile, someone was getting rich. Who?

It wasn't the people on the street. Slums and squatter settlements thought to hold three and a half million people were scattered amid one of the most expensive cities I'd ever encountered. A cheapie lunch of a quarter chicken and a piece of bread, served with a hunk of raw onion, cost me more than a similar meal would at Kentucky Fried Chicken—though it did taste better. Rents in the city had skyrocketed thanks to the influx of foreign oil workers. A two-bedroom apartment that rented for $250 in 1999, before the oil boom, now went for more than $1,500.

It made for jarring contrasts. A newly widened asphalt road runs down the western border of the exclusive Khartoum suburb of Amarat, home to many foreign embassies and the offices of major humanitarian groups. Waiting for a taxi there early one 106-degree day, a medieval vision emerged from the waves of heat rising from the tarmac: An elderly Dinka man, nearly seven feet tall, naked but for a sackcloth shirt that reached above his knees, walked barefoot down the blacktop carrying a long steel beam on his right shoulder. He walked in short unwavering steps, his blued eyes set straight ahead, a slave in all but name. A few feet away Chinese construction workers were chatting with their families via webcam, the women holding the babies up to give papa a better look.

The key to it all were the sons of the soil. These Arab elites, members of three tribes hailing from the states just north of Khartoum, saw themselves as more educated, more Muslim, more Arab and, really, more Sudanese than the others. The country was their patrimony and other Sudanese—those from less sophisticated

Arab tribes, non-Arab Muslims like those in Darfur and Nubia and, of course, the blacks in the south—were all lucky to have their affairs run by these bluebloods. It was a fact of life that few were brave enough to discuss openly, until one Friday in May of 2000, eleven years into Sudan's Islamist dictatorship. As worshippers left afternoon prayers at mosques around Khartoum, stacks of booklets awaited them, each a photocopied indictment of the country's misrule by a powerful minority. The pamphlets, thousands of copies of them, appeared mysteriously, anonymously. It was rumored that President Omar al-Bashir himself found one on his desk at the Republican Palace.

The Black Book: Imbalance of Power and Wealth in the Sudan laid out in heated prose and cool statistics how Arab Sudanese from just two states—River Nile and Northern—had almost exclusively been running the country since independence. This region supplied just five percent of Sudan's population, but it dominated government, finance and the military. The effects were clear in Sudan's vital statistics. While more than eighty-five percent of births in River Nile and Northern states were attended by a doctor, nurse or midwife, more than half the births in Darfur went completely unattended by any kind of health professional. In the lands of the three tribes, infant mortality was lower and life expectancy was higher than in every other state. The *Black Book* showed how, for all the want in Sudan's western, eastern and southern provinces, the bulk of government spending and aid went to the same two states from which the elites hailed. There was no official reaction to the *Black Book*, but the speed and stealth with which it was distributed sent a shudder through the security services—as well it should have. The book's anonymous authors later revealed themselves as members of the Justice and Equality Movement, an Islamist-themed rebel group that three years later was one of two armed groups to declare war on the Sudanese military in Darfur. The ethnic cleansing, rape and pillage that followed were manifestations of tensions that had thwarted Sudan since the moment of its independence. While the civil war was typically reduced to the shorthand of "Muslims versus Christians" and the conflict in Darfur as one of "Arabs versus blacks," the deeper issue was that a few haves at the center maintained power by playing Sudan's myriad tribes of have-nots against each other.

Analyses of the *Black Book* by Western academics have supported its conclusions. What effect, I wondered, had the new oil riches had on that power dynamic?

Ali Kata Oshi might have had some insight, but the former commissioner of Maban was proving elusive. We played a game of missed calls, and I began to suspect Ali Kata didn't want to see me after all, that he had thought better of inviting a stranger's scrutiny, or that he had never meant to see me in the first place. While his disappearance may have been innocuous, it gave greater credence to John Ivo's description of Ali Kata's divided loyalties. Having his wife offer hospitality to a journalist was one thing. Meeting him face-to-face was maybe quite another. I gave up on Ali Kata and began marching from government office to government office hoping to speak with different presidential advisers and ministers for an establishment view of how power worked in Sudan.

I even entered into a flirtation with Hassan al-Turabi, the long-time Muslim Brother who was the spiritual and political leader of Sudan's ruling National Islamic Front during its Osama-friendly heyday. Turabi, educated at the Sorbonne (and married to Sadiq al-Mahdi's sister), had served as speaker of the parliament in the 1990s before he overreached and fell from power. The National Islamic Front split in 1999 after an assassination attempt against Egyptian president Hosni Mubarak was traced back to Turabi's wooly associates. Bashir had his former mentor jailed for a time, and Turabi's new Popular Congress Party lived in the shadows. Meanwhile, pushed by a growing cadre of moderates, Bashir's

National Congress Party negotiated the CPA, raked in the new oil dough and waited for its day in the international sun—until Darfur spoiled the party. Even out of power, Turabi was regarded as the evil genius of Sudanese politics, but he too declined to sit with me.

At last I was able to arrange a meeting with Fathi Khalil, a National Congress stalwart and the influential head of Sudan's bar association. Khalil's office was on the fifth floor of the grimy headquarters of the Tadamon Islamic Bank. The neglected exterior, broken elevators and dusty staircases gave way to a clean suite of offices, where Khalil sat at a substantial desk speaking on an Ericsson mobile phone.

As the president of the Sudanese bar, Khalil was one of thousands of members of Sudan's Muslim Brotherhood holding positions of civil and military power across the country. The Brotherhood, which advocated a merger of mosque and state, had been harassed in the republic's early days, but its influence over Sudan's institutions had steadily grown, culminating in the 1989 military coup by Islamist army officers led by Bashir. Khalil was a calm, honest face of a movement that legislated lashings for adultery and had tried to "Islamicize" the sciences. His party had never come close to winning a fair election and had banned music at weddings. I liked him instantly.

"There's a sense among the people I talk to here," I said, after settling into a cushioned chair and accepting a cup of tea, "that the leaders of the National Congress are amassing secret wealth. How is this seen within the movement?"

"There is more democracy in the NCP now than in 1989, and more than in the other parties," he said. "I don't see signs of corruption among the leading figures—the ostentatious houses, the cars. The old *Ikhwanis* [Brothers] are living much as they have since before the economy started growing." That may have been true for the party's rank and file. But after nearly twenty years at the helm of a country without a free press, trade unions or independent political parties, the leaders of the National Congress had done quite well for themselves. An NCP-owned trading company in China was reported to be taking a thirty-five percent commission on all trade between Sudan and China—a colossal skim worth hundreds of millions of dollars a year. Newspaper editors had in recent years been jailed for reporting corruption allegations involving the vice president and a presidential adviser.

"I don't know anything about that," Khalil said when I mentioned this. "It sounds like more of the lies this government has endured from our friends in the West."

How deep, I asked, were the connections between Sudan's *Ikhwanis* and the Egyptian Muslim Brotherhood? In Egypt, where the movement was born, the Brotherhood was officially banned, its members subject to arbitrary imprisonment and torture. Still, Muslim Brothers, running as independents, made up the biggest opposition bloc in Egypt's parliament. "Are you cooperating with them?"

"For years, the relationship with the Egyptian *Ikhwan* was not an easy one," Khalil said. "The point of contention is the relationship between Muslims and non-Muslims. The relationship between Muslims and non-Muslims is not the same in Egypt as in Sudan. In Upper Egypt, where the Egyptian *Ikhwan* is strongest, there is no interaction, no wish to interact. In Sudan you will find families where one is a Muslim, one is not, one is a Christian. In the same house."

"I've seen it," I said.

"So you agree it's true," he replied. "This is alien in Egypt. Tolerance in Sudan is greater than you will find anywhere else in the world."

"What about the 1962 missionary law?" I said. "It seems like the opposite of tolerance to ban the construction of churches, to nationalize church schools and force Arabic on people who don't want to speak it."

"That was repealed," he said quickly. "Christmas here is a national holiday. I encourage you to expand your view and see the real Sudan. Where are you going from here?"

"I'm following the Nile—Atbara, Karima, Dongola, Halfa. Then the ferry to Aswan."

He brightened. "Ah, Dongola! That's my home."

"You're Nubian?"

"Yes. I am Nubian."

Nubians, who make up only three or four percent of Sudan's population, were active across Sudan's political parties, but they had especially gravitated toward the Sudanese Communist Party. Fathi Khalil had landed at the other end of the spectrum. While he saw the Brotherhood as a paragon of tolerance, many Nubians viewed it as an instrument of Arabism, one that meant to destroy their millennia-old heritage.

Two days later I walked through the pale yellow heat to the office of Waleed's cousin Midhat to see if my visa extension had come through. "How is it?" I asked, walking into the cool, darkened room.

"Not very good," he said, almost in a whisper. He was slouched in his office chair, his head barely visible over the top of the desk. "America just sent seventy thousand army on Iran. Why? Why they did this?"

"Well, if they did, it's war," I said. "But really, that's impossible. They don't have seventy thousand troops to spare."

"I got it on my mobile," he said, "from SUNA"—Sudan's state news agency. "Why they attack Iran?"

"Look," I said, "even if our president were deluded enough to think he must invade Iran, the troops just don't exist. They're all bogged down in Iraq and Afghanistan." But Midhat wasn't moved. "Wait here," I said, and walked down the street to an Internet café, where I searched the web. Eventually I found it—seventeen thousand American personnel in naval maneuvers off the coast of Iran.

"No. Seventy thousand," Midhat insisted when I reported back.

"You're going to believe the government's news service? I'm telling you, it's seventeen thousand people in boats and planes playing games on the ocean. Nobody's attacked Iran."

He scowled. "Why they do this?" he said, low in his chair.

"They're trying to shake them up."

"But why?"

"This is what states do. Why does Iran do what it does? Why does Sudan do what it does?"

"I don't know." He sighed. "I don't follow politics. I don't read newspapers. Only these." He held up some tourism industry newsletters and a biking magazine.

"I don't think SUNA is the place to be getting your news," I said, but he was somewhere else.

"I don't understand politics," he said, looking past me, past the doorway and the molding samples on the wall. "Like ten years ago, Egypt closed the border. Completely closed. All because of something in Ethiopia."

"Dude, I think the something was that your government tried to kill Egypt's president."

"I don't know about these things," he groaned. "For more than one year you cannot see your family or visit your father's grave. There is no visitors, no trade. The people suffer. Why? They cut Nubia in half. They cut us in two." Years after the border was reopened, Midhat still felt that cut and deeper wounds as well. On his computer desktop he kept a photo of the flooding of old Wadi Halfa by the Aswan High Dam. It was a telling image for an ancient antagonism. The ancient Egyptians called the lands to their south "Kush," though it was usually referred to as "Wretched Kush." The region was at various times a colony, competitor and conqueror of ancient Egypt. In Midhat's symbolic screen photo, the last minaret of Halfa's last mosque is about to go underwater, its crest surrounded by a cloud of panicked birds—an Egyptian victory over the descendants of Kush.

"Last year we did a big tour, with an important group," Midhat said. "They came on boats—rafts—all the way from Ethiopia. I sent Moez with this group; he showed them all of Nubia, all the way to Halfa. He was supposed to go with them in Egypt also, to the end of the Nile. He had all his papers—his papers were perfect. Moez earned this. But the Egyptian police sent him back from the border. They wouldn't let him. Why they did that?" He looked at me and we sat in the quiet.

"Sudan is a very tolerant country," he murmured at last. "Everybody is getting along. In a Christian house they will have a sheet so that during prayer times the Muslim guest can pray. At the church, they let anyone come in. Moez, sometimes he went there . . . We used to be Christians before Islam came."

That evening, Waleed, Midhat and I took a series of taxis to visit the Nubian singer and opposition figure Mohammed Wardi. Wardi was a true Sudanese hero—as popular in the south as he was in the north, equal parts Frank Sinatra and Woody Guthrie, pushed through a syrupy Sudanese filter. His protest songs had made him one of the country's most prominent dissidents, and he'd spent two years in prison and fifteen years in exile under three different military regimes. Wardi's seminal hit "October al Akbar" chronicled the October 1964 uprising that overthrew the regime of General Abboud, and he later was one of the few northerners to align himself with the southern rebels of the Sudan People's Liberation Movement. In 1990 he brought his fifty-piece band to play for a quarter million southern refugees in Ethiopia, a Sudanese

Woodstock. Wardi was one of Sudan's few truly national figures, and, I thought, a man worth talking to.

As we walked to the taxi park down the middle of a side street, a trio of curvy young women passed us on the left. One, her lips lined with brown cosmetic pencil, looked over her shoulder, locked her amber eyes on mine and flared her nostrils before rejoining her friends in a cloud of giggles. "They're teasing me," I said. "Is it my imagination or were they teasing me?"

"I know," Waleed said, with bachelor's regret. "It's getting worse every year." I suppressed the urge to look back and we carried on past covered sidewalks where packs of men were gathering for the early evening prayer. They unfurled worn prayer rugs onto the sidewalk and removed their shoes and slippers, washing their hands, faces and feet from plastic pitchers. A few wore woolen business suits, others white cotton robes and others the thin slacks and cracked feet of the laboring class. The pedestrian traffic carried on around them while they prayed.

Mohammed Wardi awaited us in a private fenced-in garden in a suburban district of Khartoum. This oasis wasn't quite as technologically advanced as Ozone—a gardener was hand-watering the plants and trees backlit by small floodlights in shades of blue—but it was cooler and more inviting. Two fawns rested on the wet grass inside a steel cage. Wardi, in white robes and a turban, greeted us from a lawn chair where he was holding court with four others. He was a big man, slightly roly-poly. He liked to drink, it was said, and drink had taken a toll. Waleed and Midhat were starstruck, and gave their full names when introducing themselves so Wardi would know exactly where they were from and who their people were. A bottle of Chivas Regal appeared, and I joined Wardi and a couple of his cronies in drinking it, discreetly scooping the ice cubes from my glass and dropping them onto the grass.

I told Wardi that my friends in the south had insisted I meet him. Why was that?

"I am an observer of Sudan, of the entire Sudan," he said. "I've seen our entire political history. I've heard the first speech of every coup. Imagine how many first speeches I've heard—each one the death of democracy." One of Wardi's own nephews was executed in 1999, during his most recent exile, for allegedly planning a coup. But just a few years later, the crooner was welcomed back home. Wardi had been living in Los Angeles when, in 2002, his right kidney failed. When he couldn't find a donor in the United States, Osama Daoud Abdelatif, Sudan's leading industrialist, arranged for his safe return. By then the regime had mellowed. Peace talks were under way with the south, and some radical elements had been purged from the ruling clique.

Wardi arrived in Khartoum later that year to find hundreds of thousands of people in the streets, the biggest public gathering since independence. There was no shortage of would-be kidney donors. "The welcome I received was a clear message to the authorities," he said. "What I saw was a large crowd, unafraid to gather in such numbers." Later that year, he performed a series of concerts on the banks of the Blue Nile, breaking the capital's 11 p.m. curfew to lull and spark the audience with songs that hadn't been performed in Sudan for more than a decade. When the thirty-piece band played the last note of the final show, a fireworks display lit up the night and echoed across Khartoum. A shiver of fear was said to have run through the Republican Palace. Had the revolution begun?

After the CPA was signed, Wardi chaired Khartoum's welcome committee for John Garang. Garang's return to the capital attracted more than a million jubilant Sudanese. It seemed victory was finally complete, that a single Sudan—plural and intact— would emerge from the dismal era. Then came Garang's death and the war in Darfur, with its promises of continued misery. "You haven't asked me about Darfur," Wardi said, after an hour of scotch and reminiscence.

"What about it?" I asked.

"Rape," he said, holding out his glass for a refill. "There is no rape in Darfur. The Sudanese people don't rape. Muslims don't rape. Maybe the African Union are doing it. But not the Sudanese people.

"Darfur is something domestic. I know," he continued. "The United States and Europe are exaggerating it. The only way to solve it is through the Sudanese people and the Sudanese way. If the American people leave it, it will be solved easily." On this subject, he was a mainstream Sudanese: If the world was accusing Muslims of atrocities, then the world was wrong. Wardi had suffered personally at the hands of the Islamist regime; he was one of the few northerners to acknowledge the horrors the north had visited upon the south. But his response to Darfur was the defensive position that held across the Muslim world. Wardi's denials reminded me of something a Tunisian acquaintance of mine—a woman who worked with victims of sexual violence—once told me of visiting an Egyptian-funded field hospital for refugees in West Darfur state. She'd inquired about three preteen girls who had been violated in a nearby camp. "Cunt!" the Egyptian doctor there said to her. "This is a Muslim country. There is no rape."

Wardi's group, including a son-in-law who had only recently been permitted to return from political exile, looked at me politely, waiting for a fight, but I wasn't in the mood. I made a few boilerplate references to United Nations investigations, noted my own experience in Darfur and switched to a less contentious topic, the Kajbar Dam, which threatened to submerge twenty-six Nubian villages in Sudan's far north. What would it mean for Nubia? "We exist from antiquity," Wardi said. "We had our own identity, civilization and kings. We have our own ancient language, which we still use today. We once ruled over Egypt and all the way to Syria.

Those Arabs are just nomads. They came here—that's okay. They brought Islam—that's okay. But they can't Arabize us. The people who live along the Nile know this history, they know the crime of the Aswan Dam. It pushes us to take up the gun, like the people in the south—or in Darfur."

Wardi's visions of Nubian empire weren't an exaggeration, but that empire was long gone. In the fourth century AD the rulers of a kingdom called Meroe merged with two neighboring kingdoms to become Nubia, a Christian realm that stretched from present-day Aswan as far south as Khartoum. Nubia withstood a series of Arab invasions following the dawn of Islam in the seventh century, but was in time slowly converted through intermarriage and the efforts of wandering preachers. Over the centuries, many Nubian tribes took on an Arab identity, so that present-day Nubia extends only five hundred miles, from Aswan to Dongola. Today, the most renowned Nubian antiquities, like the pyramids of Meroe, north of Khartoum, lie well outside its current domain. In a week I would see Nubia for myself, and learn if Wardi's predictions of armed conflict were prophetic or the bluster of a pampered luminary.

On my last evening in Khartoum I paid a visit to the famous confluence of the White Nile and the Blue. In an upper-class amusement park on the water's edge, I was trying to photograph the marriage of the two rivers in the dying western light when a group of college girls stepped in front of me and demanded to know what I was doing and what I thought of Sudan. They weren't flirting; they were defending the republic. "It's beautiful," I said, hoping they would let me get a shot framed, but they weren't satisfied. What, they wanted to know, did I think of race relations in Sudan? Straightening my posture, I said with an almost true smile, "It seems like a family." They nodded with satisfaction. Was it similar in America? "You might say that."

"No," a young woman said hotly. "I don't think so. America is not tolerant like Sudan. There are many problems there. Many problems." Her friends nodded. By now two older men, dressed like bureaucrats, had joined us, and they berated me for shooting pictures and demanded to know who had authorized it, as if the river itself were a secret strategic asset. I was running out of light—the sun was down, and the golden hour was just about over. The air went from dim to dark while they bickered at me. I stalked away, cursing them all, and walked a mile upriver, until, just past a riverside tea shack, I came to a crumbling stone stairway leading down to the water's edge. There, in the twilight, a blue-uniformed inspector from the river police was tying his launch to a tree branch hanging low over the water. He agreed to take me to the black and shining confluence, motioning for me to duck beneath the gunwales when another police boat passed. We reached the confluence and he cut the engine and let us drift awhile in the coolness. We made a slow quiet circle, and I craned my neck to take in the yellow haze of Omdurman, the motionless Ferris wheel at the amusement park and the faded aluminum Pepsi-Cola billboard on Tuti Island. "*Quais?*" the inspector said, and I nodded. He rip-started the Yamaha and raced us back to shore with the stern lancing up out of the water, showing off for his guest. Then he tied the boat to the low-hanging branch and, asking nothing for his trouble, wished me good night. It was a fine last evening in Khartoum.

The next morning, after a breakfast of fried eggs, puffy Sudanese bread and salty cheese and olives, I loaded my bags into a waiting pickup truck, shook hands with Midhat, who had arranged the ride, and left for the pyramids of Meroe. In a low-budget plan to get from Khartoum to the Egyptian border, this was my one indulgence—a hired car to take me directly to the Lion Temple of Naqa, which lay in the desert off the main road, and then to the pyramids, where I would be left to fend for myself. There was a luxury tourist camp about a mile from the pyramid site. I doubted it

would be open at this, the opening blast of summer, but I felt sure
I could find some kind of co-op there. American sanctions meant
Sudan was without a single foreigner-friendly ATM, and credit
cards were not accepted anywhere. With a daily budget of 4,200
dinars, about $18, I wouldn't qualify as a paying guest anyway.

The driver and I used my GPS to find the exquisite Lion
Temple, with its wide-hipped queen etched in red stone relief—a
first-century AD throwback to the days, hailed by Wardi, when
the Nubian empire of Kush was a force to be reckoned with. We
returned to the road to find the tourist resort. I pointed the driver
to what appeared to be a trail heading east into the desert but we
bottomed out in the sand after five hundred yards. As we stood
outside the truck staring at the sunken tires, sweat blotting our
shirts, a barefoot boy of eight or nine came running. He must have
risen directly from the hot dunes—I couldn't see any nearby settlement. The boy was carrying the thoroughly rusted head of a
shovel, its thin blade chipped and uneven. He immediately dropped
to his knees when he reached us and began digging under the truck.
Soon other boys appeared, one with an intact shovel, some holding sticks, still others with nothing to scoop the sand but their bare
hands. They surrounded the truck and dug with abandon, pausing
from time to time to look up at me and shout, *"Foolus!"* Money.
After a short time the operation was hijacked by two older boys,
maybe seventeen years old, who intimidated the younger diggers
into following their direction. It worked.

They dug; the driver abused the gas petal; I pushed. Tires spun,
blasting filthy sand into my nose, mouth and ears and down my
chest. The truck was freed. A dozen barefoot boys in dirty white
tunics clamored at me for payment, each pushing the other to get
closer to me with his outstretched hands and Gatling-gun argu-
ments. I looked at the driver. "Just pay the older two and be done
with it," he said in Arabic, and somehow I understood him. I
gave five hundred dinars, about two dollars, to the two biggest,

broadcast a handful of change onto the sand for the youngsters to fight over and leapt into the pickup, locking my door. We made our getaway back to the road under a hail of desert stones and pre-adolescent oaths and quickly found a correct trail to the camp. I tipped the driver, said goodbye and surveyed my new home. It was a complex of three buildings, including a locked main hall that looked downright cozy. As I'd expected, the place was empty, battened down for the season. A Land Cruiser sat on blocks under the eaves of the main house, its windows covered with sections of sheet metal to protect against sandstorms. I found a string bed half buried in a dune in the shade of an outbuilding, slipped off my boots and took a nap there in the wavy heat. An hour later I opened my eyes to see a tall camel approaching from the horizon at a slow metronomic gait, two riders clinging to its back, rocking up and down with each step. They meandered ever closer, the camel knelt and a young man jumped off, lean and wrapped in white cotton. I stood up to greet him. He said he worked at the camp during the tourist season and acted as caretaker in the off; he offered me the use of his room for the night. "I'm probably better off sleeping outside," I said, and he agreed. I followed the caretaker around the building as he attached a hose to the bathroom faucet and, dragging it around back, refilled a *zir*, a ceramic water urn, for any strangers that might pass this way. He then poured more water into a truck tire lying in the sand. It had been sawed in half lengthwise for use as a crude birdbath. "The birds are lucky to have you," I said.

"We are lucky to have them," he replied. He showed me the key to the bathroom and its vast supply of sun-boiled water, prepared me a cup of tea from the resort's kitchen and wished me luck. Then he changed from his desert robes into a clean shirt and pants, splashed on some cologne and set off on foot for a nearby village to see his fiancée and his kinfolk. Late that afternoon I walked over a long stretch of hard rippled sand to a field of nearly a hundred decapitated black-and-tan pyramids. They were built here over the course of twelve hundred years, into the fourth century AD, to mark the graves of the Nubian Kushite royalty, who saw themselves as heirs to the great dynasties of Egypt. If Egypt's pyramids were solitary greats, these made a dense community of local heroes. They were much smaller than their Egyptian counterparts—the tallest topped out at around ninety feet—and were built at sharper angles. They would have cut a fine silhouette with the sun at their back if not for one inescapable fact: The top of each stately isosceles had been dynamited off in the 1830s, many by a dogged Italian tomb robber named Giuseppe Ferlini. Ferlini had heard there was gold inside the pyramids. He and his fellow vandals found almost none.

After a clear night under the stars I carried my bags to the road and tried to flag down passing buses, but none stopped. Two hours later on the steadily warming roadside, I found mercy in a man driving a truck for the government's Dams Implementation Unit, which was responsible for raising the dam at Merowe and for the work at Kajbar that Waleed and other Nubians were concerned about. The driver spoke fair English—he was of the last generation to learn it in the public schools, before the 1989 coup. "*To Kill a Mockingbird*," he said, laughing at the memory. "John Wayne." Still, I didn't want to spook him by asking about the dams, and I didn't think his English and my Arabic were sufficient to have a coherent conversation about it. So we drove north, testing the limits of our language skills, when he stopped at an intersection to chat with a colleague in a white government sedan. The conversation seemed to turn to me, and the colleague's voice turned hard.

We drove on for another hour before coming to a big depot on the right side of the road. It was ringed by fencing and guardhouses and flew the flag of the Dams Implementation Unit. "I have to go inside for lunch but you are not allowed," the truck driver said. "Just five minutes, Daniel, and I will come back." An hour later I was still broiling on the roadside. The driver had been told to lose me and so he had; my eyeglasses burned my fingers when I took them off to wipe the sweat from my face; my hair—why was my hat off?—had become a radiant heat source. At last a northbound bus glided to a stop just a few feet from me and three men got out—two to carry my bags and the third to personally guide me up the stairs into their Daewoo luxury liner. The bus was half empty, the passengers all smiling. I took a seat, someone handed me a bottle of cold water and when I woke at Atbara the driver refused payment. Did I really look that bad?

Atbara was a sleepy stopover of a town. It was the headquarters of the all but ruined national railway, a junction where the line from Port Sudan on the Red Sea met the north-south traffic between Khartoum and Wadi Halfa. Situated just north of the confluence of the Nile and the Atbara River, it was divided into two districts. West of the railway, leading to the Nile, was the British town, laid out in 1889 by General Kitchener as he made his way south to defeat the Mahdi's forces at Omdurman. There were no British remaining, but the streets were broad and lined with trees, and every colonial bungalow was fronted by a generous yard. East of the tracks lay Sudan: a dozen miles of low-rise buildings the color of old grime, hordes of Toyota minibus taxis and, strangely, a fleet of Ford Falcon vans from the 1960s, the only American cars I'd seen in Sudan. How they got here, and why they existed only in Atbara, was a mystery. Despite its near-total absence of trees, this was the Atbara I preferred, and it was here, over kebabs and a plate of *tameyya*, a deep-fried falafel made from fava beans, that I met a Nubian archaeologist who I hoped might help me find my way along the Nile's S-shaped curve, from Atbara to Abu Hamed, a hundred miles to the north, and from Abu Hamed south again to the controversial Merowe Dam outside Karima.

The archaeologist said he might be able to arrange a jeep and driver for a budget-busting two hundred dollars a day. "But please—don't try," he said.

"You think I'll be arrested? I know they're serious about keeping reporters away from the dam."

"It's not the police, it's the people, the Manasir tribe. They're crazy. Their lands will be flooded by the dam's reservoir and they refuse to budge. People have been jailed. People have been killed. The authorities have delayed filling the reservoir, but everyone knows they will lose in the end. If the Manasir see a Westerner in their lands they'll think you work for the dam. They'll kill you. They've banned archaeologists as well—no one knows the ancient treasures that will disappear because of this—Kushite, Christian, Kerma culture. The Manasir say we're only there to make the government look good. The government has offered to resettle them on good agricultural land, a place near Khartoum with good access to markets. When you live in a poor country you want to be near the government center—your problems are taken care of. But the Manasir are a river tribe. They want to be on the water where they can catch fish. Fifty thousand people will be displaced, some willingly, but not the Manasir."

"Why doesn't the government just settle them on banks of the reservoir?" I said.

"Because that will be very valuable land, a lake two hundred kilometers long," he said. "They won't waste it on tribesmen. They will give it to their own people, the Shaygiya Arabs. That's the vice president's tribe. They take care of their own. You know, when you deliver a paper on ancient Nubia in Europe, you have to be perfect. They are very sharp there. They hear every word. When you give the same paper to a conference of Arab archaeologists, you can say whatever you want. No one is listening."

I had, years before, hiked for several days to reach a village in the Indian interior that was threatened by a massive dam project. Back then I was escorted to the spot by a pair of young activists and two boys from the local tribal community. They were my protectors, translators and informants. I could find no such pipeline to the Manasir lands. Activists working in Khartoum on behalf of the Manasir had been driven underground by arrests and torture, and the Manasir themselves would be anything but welcoming to a foreign stranger. Added to that was a state of near martial law that existed around the dam itself. To make the trip up to Abu Hamed and then down along the river would be to risk violence from the Manasir or detention and deportation by the security forces. I couldn't figure how to make it work.

Dejected, I dropped Abu Hamed from my plans. From Atbara I crossed the Nile by ferry and took a minibus taxi 150 miles west through the volcanic Bayuda desert to Karima. The Bayuda and the Nubian Desert just north of it make up the eastern flank of the great Sahara. In satellite photographs the Bayuda suggests a flat, veiny slab of amber, something you might see in an ignored corner of a provincial museum, but up close this beauty was lost. The desert threw off a broiler-like heat that befitted a former volcano field. As I stared out the window at the mesmerizing plain of sand, stones and small stands of acacia bushes, my sweat-burned eyes deceived me. Lakes and ponds would appear in the far distance, and animals too—gazelles and fine-boned storks—but they dissipated before we got near them. We traveled on a rugged track running alongside a four-lane highway that was under construction. The new highway sat high on the landscape, looming over the taxi, and was marked by giant steel power lines that would one day carry electricity from the Merowe Dam to Khartoum, doubling the country's electricity supply. In a region that saw but a small fraction of the precipitation that the south received, this new highway had giant culverts, some more than twenty feet wide, to ensure that the seasonal rains were allowed to flow across the landscape unimpeded, preserving ancient watering holes and seasonal creeks and the migrating Arab tribes who depended on them. It was just the sort of consideration the residents of Upper Nile in the south had been denied when the oil roads were built.

I found a small and pleasant room at the Hotel Nasser in Karima and spent the evening wondering if a more nervy reporter wouldn't have rolled the dice on a jeep from Abu Hamed into the Manasir lands. Now sneaking in the back way was no longer an option. What about the front? The next morning I hopped a ferry across the Nile to Merowe town and asked a rickshaw driver to take me to the local dam implementation headquarters. We puttered to a destination well outside town, in an area desolate of everything but low-rise concrete compounds. These were new buildings built off new roads, all related to the planning, construction or protection of the dam and its power plant. The driver stopped at an anonymous gated complex, where a custodian wordlessly walked me down a long air-conditioned hall to the local manager's office. I knocked and walked in, suddenly aware of my exceedingly informal attire: a wrinkled formerly black short-sleeved shirt, dirty green work pants, a dusty blue walking hat and boots that now bore no evidence of maintenance. Two men greeted me with expressions of mild professional curiosity.

I explained that I wanted to visit and take photographs of the dam and handed over my Sudanese press card, shifting eye contact from the manager to his assistant, who spoke better English. To my surprise, they didn't throw me out. While the boss checked the fax machine and took some calls on his mobile, the assistant, Idriss, phoned a security office somewhere to ask permission. He placed the receiver back in its cradle and poured some tea from a red thermos pitcher on the table at our feet. "They will make some calls to check on you, and in one or two hours we will know. How many are in your group?"

"It's just me."

"And how many others?"

"It's just me."

Idriss and his boss looked at one another for a moment. They asked about transport. I said I would rent a car once I received permission to visit the dam. How much would a taxi cost? The three of us stumbled over the numbers, and they smiled when my eyes widened at 10,000 dinars, about $50. We sat quietly for another ten minutes when an idea came. "Would you like to see my passport?" I asked. "Maybe that will help whoever is doing the checking." They liked the idea very much and Idriss made another call and gave them my passport number and mentioned my Nile itinerary—Malakal, Kosti, Khartoum, Atbara. Idriss put the phone down and smiled. "In half an hour our car and driver will take you to the dam, you will make photos and then he will drop you at the ferry to Karima. But first, please join us for breakfast."

We took turns washing our hands in the manager's pink-tiled bathroom and then walked into a conference room to a big white bowl of *ful*, a plate of fried eggs, cans of tuna, a plate of halvah, some jibneh and bread. I ate enough to give honest protest when they encouraged me to have more. Five other men hung back while Idriss, the boss and I ate. When we finished they took our places at the table and finished off the communal tray, as befitted their junior rank. I washed my hands again and sipped more tea on the couch in the manager's office, and then it was time to go. A driver, clean-shaven and impassive, escorted me to a double-cab Toyota Hiace, where my first act as esteemed guest was to turn the air-conditioning down by half, and we were off, passing armed check-points with a wave, the radio playing lyric-free Arabic Muzak, past the time-ruined Nubian pyramids of Nuri (much bigger, and more Egyptian, than the spiky crowd at Meroe), past mud dove-cotes and old mud-slab tombs, and after twenty minutes we were fast upon the dam. On a rise to the right of the road was what appeared to be a model village of white two-story condos with AC units outside each room and a new mosque raised in a modernist style—no cupolas or onion domes. The road curved quickly to the left and just like that we were crossing the base of the dam itself, its upper reaches bristling with row after row of bare steel rebar.

Welders linked them in showers of acrid sparks while other work-men moved across acres of scaffolding. I saw Chinese managers in khaki and shirtsleeves hiding from the sun behind dark glasses and wide-brimmed straw sombreros; Chinese workers in hard hats, each carrying a bulky plastic canteen; and the heavy labor, Sudanese workers, black and brown, some of whom appeared to be as young as fourteen or fifteen, in coveralls and hard hats. A billboard on the east bank showed a Sudanese, a Chinese and a European looking with satisfaction over a set of blueprints toward the dam itself. In addition to the China National Water Resources & Hydropower Engineering Corp., French and German companies had a major role in its construction. Cement trucks churned on the tarmac, men walked with hard-work swaggers, and—whatever the serious human rights issues, the forced displacement, the lack of environmental review, the destruction of farmland, the arrest and torture of opponents—I had to admit the thing was a sight, big and impressive and cool. We pulled left again, onto the Nile's west bank, and drove past a long low barracks for the Chinese workers, and then, on the left, another barracks, of coarser construction, for the Sudanese, and across the road from there, a line of shops that sold cool drinks and candy. We passed a last checkpoint and came to the headquarters, which resembled a small Silicon Valley office park. I followed the driver inside, and as he walked almost too fast down along the central hallway, it occurred to me that I had neglected to get a contact name from Idriss. The driver turned sharp and sudden into the office of the resident engineer and his face, both blank and direct, made clear he hadn't been warned of my arrival.

"Please wait here a moment," he said in perfect English.

"Sure. You mind if I gawk at these blueprints?" They were beau-tiful and they covered the wall, showing in precise graceful lines the turbines, penstocks and control gates that had slowed the Nile and destroyed the fields and date palms of the Manasir and other tribes.

"That's fine," the chief engineer replied. On the desk was a pile of papers, apparently an unbound report, by the "Reclamation" section discussing the delays and the "resettlement crisis." As a hydroelectric project, the Merowe Dam wasn't really taking water from Egypt, but this didn't stop the generals in Cairo from threatening to bomb the site when the topic was first bruited in the 1980s. They've since come to terms with the dam, and it isn't considered a threat to Egypt's age-old domination of the river—an ancient hegemony cemented in the modern era by the British-brokered Nile Waters Agreement of 1959. The treaty allocates 55.5 billion cubic meters of water each year to Egypt, 18.5 billion to Sudan and not a drop to anyone else—a source of increasing ire in Britain's former colonies in East Africa, where the rains have become unpredictable and irrigation is now seen as a necessity.

A young man sat at the desk busily mousing his way through something. "What is your diploma?" he asked without looking up from the screen.

"Political science," I lied.

"Science?"

"Political science and creative writing. I'm not an engineer."

"Technical qualification?"

"I have no technical qualification," I said, and he went back to ignoring me.

A minute or two later an agitated man in a Sudanese safari suit—small, balding, with a black mustache—came galloping down the hall and slid to a stop in the doorway of the resident engineer's office. "If-you-just-go-with-this-man-to-the-village-for-just-one-minute-there-are-some-forms-for-you-to-fill," he said in one panting breath, and for a full second I actually believed him. I would be taken back to the modern-looking management village we'd passed on the way in. I would sign the liability forms. And then I would walk freely among the workers and shoot the $2 billion hydroelectric dam in beautiful Kodak black and white.

We walked back down the long hallway, the driver ducked into a kitchenette for a couple bottles of Coke and moments later the Toyota double-cab surged back over the dam, past the workers, across the Nile, past the new village, past the checkpoints and dustmote villages and the mud-brick saints' tombs and the ruined pyramids of Nuri, all the way back to the administrative office in Merowe. And another cup of tea with Idriss and his boss.

"So, Daniel," Idriss said. "You have seen the dam."

"Briefly—and I couldn't take pictures."

"You have seen the dam," he said with gentle finality. "For today, let that be enough."

With that, Idriss's driver took me past farmers' fields and canals full of splashing naked boys to a ferry point, where I crossed the Nile back to Karima. My transport this time was a wide-beamed rowboat propelled by a skinny oarsman with two old women and a cow for company. It was an abrupt contrast—one minute I was zooming through the 112-degree sepia desert, and the next I was rolling down to the water, surrounded by wide irrigated patches of beans and arugula. An hour later I was inside the Karima post office—a charming colonial bungalow set under broad shade trees, beneath which most of the staff were lounging. I needed stamps, and among the wax-papered inventory I found a set commemorating the dam. One 400-dinar rectangle showed a township of modern white houses set in the desert. "Merowe Dam Project: Rehabilitation Projects," it said in English, celebrating the resettlement that the Manasir had so far thwarted. Another showed an ancient clay urn, boasting, "Merowe Dam Project, Safe of Archaeology."

I asked around town and on the waterfront about a boat to Dongola, but no one remembered the last time a passenger boat had made the trip. That night I walked to the riverbank a half mile from my hotel to gaze at a half dozen Nile steamers rusting in the sand. The steel-hulled triple-deckers were piled one against another, wasting away within arm's reach of the water. As recently as the

1980s these floating hostels plied the route between Karima and Dongola, carrying passengers and cargo. They had dining halls, private staterooms, even post offices, promising a slow, steady and civilized journey along this river in the desert. The steamers fell out of use as civil war and mismanagement turned Sudan's economy to dust and the state got out of the business of floating hostels. Now travelers willing to suffer through four hours of furnace and grit could pay 2,500 dinars to cut across the Nubian desert in the open bed of a pickup-truck taxi called a boksi. Roads kill river travel. One day an all-weather road will connect Juba to Malakal, and those barges too will fade away.

I opted for a different route, one that reduced the personal ingestion of sand by half and kept me close to the river as it completed its southern bend near Abu Dom and turned north toward Egypt. I rode through a sandstorm, huddled with ten other passengers, to a way station called Ad Dabbah, a low-rise settlement of string-bed flophouses, kebab joints and dry goods stores. There, under a lashingly hot wind, I hunted on foot for a ride north to Dongola, and struck gold forty minutes later in the form of a small bus idling by the road. Inside, ten men in white robes and turbans looked at me without emotion. Another slept. And a man at the back beckoned me over. They were a group of legislators from Northern state, and I'd caught them at the end of a prayer break. The bus was a government charter—they'd just come from an official tour of the dam, part of a public relations offensive to win support for Merowe and, implicitly, for Kajbar. In fact, they'd been to the dam just a day before my aborted visit.

"What do you think?" I asked my new friend, the sole local representative of the SPLM. "It doesn't matter what I think about this," he said. "It's already built. The dam in Kajbar isn't built, but I guarantee you it will be."

"What do your colleagues think?"

"They are from the National Congress," he said. "They are told what to think."

Three hours later we were in Dongola, the capital of Northern state and the southernmost city of present-day Nubia. After registering with the local security office, as foreigners are required to do, I checked into the cheapest hotel I could find and waited to hear from Haroun, a friend of a friend who said he would take me for a clandestine look at the villages near the Kajbar dam site. A bucket bath managed to remove the first couple layers of desert grime from my flesh, and I set off for a look at the town. I walked well past dark through Dongola's fields and date groves, the furies of mosquitoes made bearable by the cool air on the Nile banks and the company of a group of farm boys who stopped their donkey cart to chat and observe me with soft curiosity. Dongola's date palms had made the town of nineteen thousand prosperous by Sudanese standards. The brightly lit shops were stocked with expensive canned vegetables and packaged cookies and cakes from Egypt, Turkey and, curiously, Bosnia. The electricity ran all night.

Haroun called two days later and we arranged to meet at a village on the east side of the Nile a few miles north of Dongola. I obtained an exit permit, as foreigners are also required to do, took a passenger ferry across the river and caught a taxi to the meeting spot.

Haroun was reassuringly nondescript. He had been an English teacher before the Islamists had stricken it from the curriculum. Now he farmed his father's dates. We continued farther north in his Toyota pickup, following a thin road along the Nile's eastern bank to the hamlet of Sebo, just upriver of the Kajbar dam site.

"It is tense now, but okay, not as bad as right after the murders," he said of the April 24 protests and police shootings that Waleed had first told me about. "Since the recent trouble, now we have a stand-down. A standoff. On the surface, nothing is happening. Underneath, the problem is building."

Despite the tension between the local people and their government, the view from Haroun's pickup was as pleasant as any I'd seen in months. The Nubian landscape was a refreshing tonic to the cinderblock and cement houses of northern Sudan. We passed orchards of date palms, fields of onions, garlic and fava beans, and broad, smooth-walled mud-brick compounds, most marked by an oversize front gate decorated in bright colors and simple paintings. The villages were clean; there were no piles of refuse on the streets, and gone were the rashes of desiccating plastic shopping bags that marred so much of the landscape elsewhere.

We drove to the home of a village chief, who'd agreed to tell me about the struggle over the Kajbar Dam. Two boys dragged a string bed from the main house to the courtyard. The chief's greeting was cordial, but he asked that I not write down his name or take his photograph, adding, "There are special police here now." He sat on a walnut-stained high-backed armchair, almost a throne, in the spare surroundings of the earthen courtyard.

"It started about eight in the morning," he said of the April 24 incident. "The youth went to the dam to show their opposition. The police came and they shot the gas, but the youth from all the villages, the twenty-six villages, refused to leave. The police fired and two people were shot, not fatally. This brought more people, at least three thousand, and when more police were sent up from Dongola, they stopped them on the road between Jeddi and Sebo." Police reinforcements sent from Dongola were trapped by a roadblock of boulders and palm trunks several miles south of the site, where the route is pinched by the Nile on one side and a steep stone embankment on the other. Residents surrounded the dozens of police in a polite standoff, offering tea and water but keeping them away from the work site.

A local SPLM representative secured a promise from the

governor that police would leave the area and that work on the dam would stop. Instead, once the cops were freed, the work site was reinforced with sixty-five soldiers and the region was locked down. It was a predictable betrayal.

"In 1995 some Russian engineers came and made a study," the elder said, pausing to take a bubbly pull from a rose glass *nargileh* at his feet. He released a cloud of sweet tobacco smoke. "The government said it would be a small dam, with minor flooding. Later they said there would be more flooding, that it would take all the banks of the Nile and the date palms and the islands in the Nile. They said they would discuss compensation and then for years we heard nothing. Then, just this year, in January, we looked up one day and a helicopter was landing near the village. They were Chinese people and Sudanese. They said they were building a hotel—Chinese people, here to build a hotel. Then, out of nothing, fifty Chinese workers, geotechnicians, were taking samples of the rock, ten-centimeter cores, and no one was telling us anything. They say the new dam will provide electricity for the district, but there is enough electricity at Merowe. The real reason is to scatter the Nubian area, to finish the work of the Aswan Dam."

Haroun cut in: "Lake Nubia is filling with silt," he said, speaking of the Aswan High Dam's 350-mile-long reservoir. "It has hundreds of meters of dirt at the bottom and soon it will be full and the High Dam will be useless. These dams in Sudan are made for Egypt, so they will take the dirt before it reaches Aswan. They are planning another dam near here, at Dal, and this too is for Egypt."

"It's just miserable," the village elder said. "After Halfa, we are all facing a dim future. The same thing will happen to us. We expect nothing better. We are river people. How can we stay in the desert without trees? We are free in our village. We fear only God."

"Is anyone coming to your side?" I asked. "Have any of the political parties tried to help you?"

"This area voted for the communists in the last election, in '86," the elder said. "They have no influence these days and because of that vote the government suspects we are all atheists. Look at my home," he said, waving his hand over the courtyard. "This is my area, for me only. My wife and children stay over there." He pointed to a wall and a smaller yard behind it. The two realms were connected by the main house. "There is no way to re-create this once it is destroyed. This house, those palms, this river: This is our life."

On one level, the forces threatening Nubia were the same ones that threaten minority communities across the industrializing world. The perceived needs of the nation—in this case, electricity and irrigation—would have to be met at the expense of an unlucky few. While a large body of evidence suggests that the benefits of big dams are outweighed by the social and environmental costs they incur, it seemed to me that projects like those at Merowe and Kajbar were undertaken, however brutally, by people who truly believed they were working in the national interest. It wasn't a multibillion-dollar plot to destroy Nubia, it was an ambitious grasp at economic self-sufficiency.

But my family members had not been forced from their lands, and my native language wasn't banned from the public schools. Nor, like many Nubians, was I looked at with theological suspicion by the dominant culture because my distant ancestors had been Christians. And really, no one in the ruling party was shedding a tear for the destruction of Nubia. It wasn't hard to see why Nubians saw the Kajbar Dam as another piece in an Arab scheme to blot them out forever.

We drove to Haroun's home, a less expansive version of the village chief's house, also with a broad courtyard, though without a traditional *haram*, or formally segregated women's area. Haroun's wife simply stayed away while we talked. Then, to my surprise, she joined us for dinner, a tasty spread of stewed spicy meat, fish and beans that we ate from small bowls with round chewy flatbread. Haroun and I walked through the empty village paths, each family safe behind its painted walls, past clusters of compounds, a mud-brick community privy (For visitors like me? For unmarried men?) and down through a band of date palms to the Nile's edge. From there we walked north on the reed bank, pausing at a point where the satin water became agitated, the beginning of the Nile's third cataract. A thousand yards ahead I saw a small group of buildings and pieces of earthmoving machinery, tiny modules backlit by the receding sun. "We should stop here," Haroun said. I kept walking. The buildings were specks in the Nikon's viewfinder. "I can't get a shot," I said and pressed forward.

"We should stop here," he said again. It was the same diffident tone, but now ever so sharp. I stopped.

"Sorry."

We walked the trail back to town. "The problem is that the families get bigger, but the land doesn't," he said, changing the subject. "As a family grows, there isn't enough land for all the sons. Some go to Khartoum to work, or to the Gulf, and they lose their connection to the village. So when the government is offering compensation, even if it is too little money, they might sign. Some won't ask the brother who is actually on the land. Some will sign even if the father is alive. That is happening here now—a government officer is paying out the money. They split the families and take the land. And the court sides with the government, even if the seller had no right. Our palms can produce dates for more than a hundred years, but they are offering just two or three years' compensation for each tree. How is that fair?" We stopped at the roadside and waited for a flatbed semi to pass, a load of cement strapped to its back, a man in uniform riding shotgun next to the driver.

I slept under the stars at Haroun's house and wondered if I wasn't romanticizing the lives of these Nubian farmers. In recent centuries Nubia had been an impoverished smudge on the map.

Nubian men had been fleeing north to Cairo for work as servants, footmen and soldiers since the 1700s. The Nubian empires that people spoke of today were long gone. And yet: The Nile and the date palms that drank from it had allowed these people to maintain their culture and native language in the face of a larger culture that preferred they either assimilate or disappear.

Some days after leaving Sebo, while watching HBO in the comfort of a five-star hotel in Aswan, I received a text message from Waleed Arafat: "I am so sorry to tell you that the Kajbar case has entered a bloody stage," he wrote. Dam authorities had started plowing under fields and cutting down palms. A group of protesters had marched out from the village of Jeddi to close the dam site and were met with tear gas and gunfire at the same pinch in the Dongola road where the police had been trapped two months before. Seven villagers were killed, nineteen injured and some, including women and children, were missing after they leaped into the Nile to escape the onslaught. Waleed and Moez were beaten by police in Khartoum while leaving a demonstration against the massacre. And five hundred soldiers from the Dams Implementation Unit's special security force had taken up permanent residence in Sebo.

In the morning I caught a bus to Wadi Halfa, squeezed between the driver and the left-hand door. Four women in full face-covering niqab, two wearing elbow-length gloves, were crowded to his right. This bus was a first cousin of the schooner that had brought me from Melut to Renk—no reclining seats or video amusements, just angry gears and hot wind. It took two days to make the three hundred miles to Halfa. We spent the night at a way station not far from the Nubian village of Dal at the Nile's second cataract, where yet another dam was planned. From there to Wadi Halfa the Nile became an eighty-mile stretch of rapids, boulders and islands of granite holding fast against the coursing water. Unlike the nearly flat river of southern Sudan, here the Nile dropped more than a foot a mile. It seemed just a matter of time before that energy would be tapped and a last piece of Nubia submerged. The Nubians had seen this before, when Old Halfa was destroyed by the High Dam at Aswan.

Wadi Halfa was a ghost, a dusty broken valise of a town. It clung to the edge of Lake Nubia, unreal and untethered, a permanent refugee camp. But it wasn't always that way. The real Halfa, now under water, had been a bustling if dusty frontier town of eleven thousand, the hub for transport and trade between Egypt and the Sudan. The locals lived off this trade, supplementing it with small farms and remittances from Nubians working abroad.

Despite initial resentment of the overbearing Egyptians, Sudan's government in 1959 consented to the construction of the Aswan High Dam, Nasser's grand monument to Egyptian progress. As many as 120,000 Nubians were displaced, and while Egypt's resettlement of the Nubians was carried out in an indifferent but generally humane manner—new villages were created on the Nile north of Aswan, where communities could remain intact—Sudan's response was disastrous. A model city, New Halfa, was erected near the Ethiopian border, and Old Halfa was evacuated. Most residents complied, but a group of families defied the government of General Abboud and refused to leave their city. They moved as the waters rose and in the mid-1960s reestablished Halfa at the edge of the new reservoir.

"We are one family from the first cataract to Dongola," said Sawi Bitek, a Nubian elder statesman, when I met him outside a small dry goods shop in Wadi Halfa. "When the High Dam came, some of the people were transferred by force. We, the five hundred families, insisted to die here. Four times we moved to escape the water. We were exposed to heat and cold. Fortunately there came the revolution of October '64 against the regime of Abboud and we were recognized. Before that we were outlaws."

"It's been more than forty years since the High Dam," I said. "And, I'm just a visitor here, but things don't look very good. What are you looking for? What do you want?"

"Our main point is how to keep our culture," he said. "We are a minority. We have no lands. The Nubian feels a man without land is not a citizen. He is just a wanderer." As the Nubians were being pushed off the land, newer, more politically reliable groups were talking their place.

"They are encouraging Islamists into the area," Bitek said. "Five or six months ago the *Al Waan* newspaper reported that Jews were fomenting revolt in Halfa! We oppose the dam, so we are Jews. The normal people don't like us. You can see it, from antiquity to today. They imagine a Nubian problem will rise one day. We are real Muslims, not Muslims for show. We are not hypocrites. During the Nimeiri years they wanted to start a Comboni school here—the rich and the powerful all send their children to the Comboni school in Khartoum. But the authorities said, 'No, they are weak Muslims. They will change.' They said that when the Comboni Brothers come we will all be making the sign of the cross. I was here before God. When did you come here? I was here six thousand years. Before religion. Before God."

I mentioned that Mohammed Wardi, the Nubian singer, had talked about armed resistance in Nubia. Bitek shook his head.

"I respect Mahatma Gandhi. Mr. Nehru, he sees a cow, he bows down. That's his belief. Those who speak of armed resistance should come and see. Come and see the situation here. Where are the people? This area is not suitable for guerrilla warfare." Halfa was a Nubian city, he said, but its institutions—the banks, the police and the major businesses—were all in the hands of the Muslim Brotherhood. "They control the economy."

"Has the peace treaty had any affect on the north?" I asked.

"The CPA is a gift from the south to the north," he said. The Comprehensive Peace Agreement contained provisions for political pluralism that affected the entire country. "Before, we would both be arrested for speaking out in the open like this," he said, "though there might still be a report. Everyone wept here when Garang died."

I spent three days in Halfa, sleeping at an open-air flophouse with dozens of others waiting for the ferry to Aswan, and breakfasted each morning at an outdoor restaurant in the back, eating *ful*, bread and tea with customs officers and local businessmen. Behind us two big orange diesel trucks, ten-wheeled passenger rovers with rows of aircraft-style seats, awaited a shipment of European tourists from Egypt to be borne through Sudan, Ethiopia and Kenya south to Cape Town. The trucks and their crewmen—a mix of white and black South Africans, an Australian and three Kenyans—had been waiting in Halfa for two weeks. They had planned to take the vehicles into Egypt and bring their wards south from Cairo, but something had gone wrong with their paperwork; the trucks would stay in Halfa while the tourists were transported south on Egyptian charter buses. The Kenyans were especially disappointed; they'd hoped to see the pyramids.

One evening, as I sat smoking with them, a solitary figure appeared at the edge of their encampment, a broad black man who stood on thick bare feet in a soiled robe. The cook at the restaurant brought him a metal cup of water and a piece of bread. Standing, he ate the bread and drank the water and carried the cup back to the cook without speaking. He walked slowly to our table and sat down but didn't utter a word. "He's an absolute mystery," one of the South Africans said. "No one knows where he came from. Been here for months. He's twice—twice—walked to Egypt across the desert, been caught and sent back here over the border. No passport, no documents, nothing. He doesn't speak."

The locals had given up trying to reach him in Arabic and

Rotana, the Nubian language. The Kenyans and the South Africans had tried English, French, Afrikaans, Xhosa, Swahili, Baganda and Luo, with no success either. He lacked the height, the leanness and the ritual scars of the Dinka, Nuer and Shilluk. And he appeared bigger, thicker, than the Equatorians I had met. A response to French might have traced him to the Central African Republic, the Congo, Rwanda or Burundi, but he didn't respond to French. And he clearly wasn't Ethiopian or Somali. His features were softer than those I associated with the people of the Horn. Handed a pen, he drew birds, not words. What was he seeking in Egypt? I imagined him on a quest to Mount Sinai or Jerusalem itself, maybe fulfilling a vow to a wasting relation back in Brazzaville, Bangui or N'Djamena. "Where you from, man?" I asked. "Where's your family?" Bare forearms on the table, he leaned forward and looked at me with his mouth just a little bit open, dark eyes speaking patience and humor, the way an adult might receive an infant's babble.

CHAPTER TEN

The Wednesday ferry to Aswan carried me and three hundred other passengers north over the submerged minarets of Old Halfa. We'd boarded like cattle, driven over a steel gangplank and crammed in a bickering line through the ship's double doors. The second-class passengers crowded into the open seating belowdeck to stake out plots among the rows of plastic chairs in the low-ceilinged chamber, dragging their children and baggage down the aisles. I walked up a flight of stairs to find my first-class stateroom, a clean enough private nook with a bunk bed and a roaring air conditioner that filled the cabin with a wet Shetland chill. Two life vests hung from a coat rack in case the twenty-hour journey turned desperate.

The ferry, maybe thirty yards long, its sides dotted with orange lifeboats, made for an uninspiring little ship but it was the *Queen Mary* compared with the boat Schon and I had rowed to Lake Kyoga or the barge Alexandre and I had hopped to Malakal. There was even a snack bar belowdeck that sold fried fish, chicken and *ful.* One flight up from the private rooms, the main deck was a bright daytime promenade where the few foreigners mixed easily

with the steerage class, cooing at the babies and sharing cigarettes with their parents. I met a vacationing French bureaucrat
who had come to Wadi Halfa via Djibouti, Ethiopia and the
railroad from Atbara. Graying and trim, he was stunned by the
recent election of Nicolas Sarkozy to the presidency. "Ségolène,
I worked with under Mitterrand," he said. "She is nothing. She
deserves to lose. But this man, this *little* man—this is not a president." He sat in the shade of the pilothouse chatting with a Sudanese Nubian communist who was returning to his home in Cairo
after visiting family in Khartoum. "It was me who broke the lock
on Kobar prison when Nimeiri fell," he said. Among the political prisoners he claimed to have freed was Hassan al-Turabi, the
man behind the National Islamic Front's military coup in 1989
and its subsequent reign of terror. "It is my greatest regret." While
he had second thoughts about cutting loose the country's leading Islamist, the communist retained the confident myopia that
afflicted so many northerners when it came to the civil war. He
refused to believe the south would ever secede from Sudan. To the
contrary, he said, "Just watch. In twenty years, the south will be
entirely Muslim. Now they are free to choose, and they will choose
correctly."

At night the promenade became a village; families emerged
from the sultry passenger hold to jockey and menace one another
for a breezy patch of deck on which to sleep. I was dozing in my
spot by a hanging orange lifeboat, having forsaken my room for
a view of the moon-licked waters, when a mustached man in a
brown robe and turban wordlessly prodded me awake with his
stevedore hands to make way for three doughy peasant women.
They together would bed down where I alone had been sprawled.
I picked my way through the sleeping bodies and crawling infants
toward the aft staircase to find it clogged with men and boys. They
filled the stairs and the small rear gangway, dozens and dozens
packed together in a rough circle around a skinny blind boy, maybe

eight or nine, and an older man who carried a wide and shallow drum. They sang in call and response, the boy standing erect, eyes closed, his right hand in the air, his left clutching the drummer's *jallabiya*, shouting out short religious verses in a piping and insistent voice that were answered by the assembly with long droning choruses. Teenage boys joined in from the upper deck. Some hung from the rail, their legs hooked around the painted bars so they might bring their faces closer and lend their voices to the Saharan wind.

Camera in hand, I apologized my way down the steps, cursing the near-total darkness, and made a right onto the port side walkway, past a row of rectangular portholes. The last of these was open, bleeding light, and I poked my head in to find a man bent over a microscope on a stained white countertop. Dressed in the same garb as the grizzled fathers corralling their families belowdeck, he was in fact a medical technician checking the blood of sick passengers for malaria. He and a physician were assigned to the ship by the Egyptian health ministry. Egypt, while home to untold mosquitoes, was malaria-free, and the government meant to keep it that way. Any passenger with a fever was tested on board, and if the results were positive, treatment began on the lake with follow-up in Aswan. I was impressed. Foreigners who spend any amount of time in Egypt return home with florid tales of colossal misgovernance—the ferry that went down in the Red Sea hours before authorities managed to mount a rescue party, the shortages of drinking water in five of the country's twenty-six provinces, the contaminated blood bags distributed to public hospitals. But some things did in fact work, and here was one. Egypt had all but beaten malaria, something that couldn't be said for its wealthier and more dynamic peers like India and Malaysia.

I returned to the icy cabin and met my roommate. He was a *saidi*, a traditional southern Egyptian farmer, dressed in an earth-colored *jallabiya* and white turban, with a heavy wool scarf around his shoulders and neck (an accessory worn no matter what the temperature). He sat on the bottom bunk carving a tomato with a knife whose blade had been ground into a crescent by untold sharpenings, the slices to be eaten with pieces of onion and Sudanese bread that rested on his lap inside a plastic shopping bag. I said hello and he nodded and we didn't speak again. I climbed into my bunk, wrapped my shoulders in a thick blanket and willed myself to sleep with the lights on. It was a false sleep, and I woke a few hours later as the ferry stopped and was met by another boat. We were boarded. I slipped my feet into sandals and crept out to see what was happening. A group of men were shaking hands outside the ferry's café. Their manners were easy and informal, but their uniforms didn't match. Then I got it. The Sudanese officials were leaving the ferry; Egyptians were taking their place. We had reached the 22nd parallel, the Egyptian border. Sudan was over. Lake Nubia was now Lake Nasser.

While the Aswan High Dam could trace its lineage to decades of British, German and Egyptian engineers and their evolving and competing plans for control of the Nile, this modern wonder had but one true father, and he was neither an engineer nor a colonial overlord. Colonel Gamal Abdel Nasser was a soldier, and he set his heart on building the dam, among the biggest in the world, within two months of seizing power in 1952. Never mind Egypt's empty treasury, its meager technical resources and a deep national malaise. ("The creative impulse was absent from Egypt" when Nasser and the other Free Officers staged their bloodless coup, the British author Tom Little wrote.) In the three-mile-long High Dam, Nasser found an act of creation to rival the pyramids, one that would tame the mighty Nile and free Egypt from its millennia-old dependence on the river's annual flood. The dam was as critical as any military strategy or secret arms deal. Millions of Egyptians were on the verge of being born, and they would need ground to till and food to eat.

That was the secret of the High Dam in those early days of revolution and socialist Arabism. Though it was publicly portrayed as the cure to all of Egypt's present and future ills, Nasser and his peers knew the stunning achievement would be, in its most vital incarnation, just a stopgap. Yes, it would one day provide cheap electricity to power new industries. Yes, it would allow Egypt's farmers to plant three crops a year instead of two. But in 1952, Nasser and his advisers were above all in a race against Egypt's breakneck birthrate. The billion-dollar High Dam ($6.5 billion in today's money) would provide just enough arable land to keep Egypt from starvation until new development came on line. And it worked, but not without cost.

Beneath the ferry lay more than 150 billion cubic meters of fresh water. When prolonged drought hit East Africa during the 1980s, the dam and the lake saved Egypt from thirst that devastated Sudan, Ethiopia and Kenya. In the 1990s, when heavy Indian Ocean monsoons sent massive flows barreling down from Ethiopia, the dam held back the crushing water, preventing floods that would have been calamitous in an earlier era.

The trade-offs for this security were environmental, financial and psychic. Surrounded by desert and pounded by the cloudless North African sun, Lake Nasser loses about ten billion cubic meters of water each year to evaporation, enough fresh drinking water for twenty million Egyptians. The dam prevents the volcanic silt nutrients of the Ethiopian highlands from reaching Egyptian soil, so while farmers can now plant three crops a year, they and their government must now shell out cash for chemical fertilizers that damage the soil and bring lower yields. This miracle silt, some five billion cubic meters of it (visualize, if you can, two thousand great pyramids of Cheops), sits at the bottom of the lake. In 2004 researchers floated the idea of mining the lake bottom for the life-giving muck, using electric slurry pumps and floating pipelines to vacuum the lakebed clean. Should such a plan come to pass, the

farmers of Egypt and Sudan will presumably be handed the privilege of paying to obtain what the Nile used to give them for free.

The human cost of the dam was also great. While the international community donated $87 million ($620 million today) to salvage the antiquities of Nubia, including moving the grand temples
of Abu Simbel out of the water's reach and crating the entire eight-
hundred-ton temple of Dendur off to the Metropolitan Museum of
Art in New York, less than a third as much was spent to resettle
Sudan's Nubians, an effort that left them hundreds of miles from
the Nile's banks, on land claimed by nomadic tribes of herdsmen,
and where large extended families were expected to live happily in
cramped "modern" houses. It was no wonder that Midhat seethed
and Mohammed Wardi spoke of armed insurrection. I was curious
to see how the Nubian Museum in Aswan, built with funds from
the United Nations, portrayed the inundation of Nubia.

The scientific, archaeological and ethnographic literature
examining the impact of the High Dam runs for miles. What is
missing is a psychic record of what happens to a people when
you literally change their calendar. For five thousand years Egypt
marked its seasons by the Nile flood. And then, quite suddenly, it
didn't. (Though some farmers still use three calendars—Islamic,
Christian and pharaonic.) Wouldn't that kind of disruption produce some measurable or observable cultural dissonance, a civili-
zational jet lag?

In the morning I slid down from my bunk, wet my face in the
crowded common washroom and stepped outside into a wall of
daylight. Vertigo hit me and I pressed myself against the bulkhead,
sure that I would topple over the rail into a blinding sea. The turbulence passed as my eyes adjusted and my lenses darkened. Schon
would have loved fishing off the side, I thought, though the absence
of beer might have driven him mad.

I prowled the ferry with my Nikon shooting the children as they scamped and posed for the stranger's camera. There was one family that had caught my eye the night before. They were Arabs, with a man, two women, a boy and a beautiful little girl maybe eight years old. She had bright bronze skin, amber eyes and long, messy hair that hung to her shoulder blades in two ragged braids. She smiled easily, a happy girl, and leaned amiably against a luggage-scuffed wall belowdeck, her dress flickering with rows of golden polka dots.

There was another, older girl who clung to the shadows while I took her young companion's photo. She was with the family but clearly not of it. She was a black African, maybe eleven or twelve, at ease with the little girl and her people and wary of others, including me. In time she joined us. She was long and thin, her short frizzy hair brushed in a forward swoop in the front and with a pert flip in the back. She wore a pretty calf-length red dress with two white ruffles that ran down from her shoulders and met at her waist. But there was something off about this girl: Why was she traveling with this family? Was she a friend, a servant, a slave? That question was pushed aside by a more immediate dissonance. Physically, something wasn't right, and as she turned away from my attention to speak with the smaller girl it finally registered: She had only one ear. The whole of her external right ear, what doctors call the pinna, was gone. Still, when I asked to take her photograph she posed in the stairwell with pride, looking directly into the camera, lit by little more than her own energy. I shot a hopelessly dark frame of her there, and asked her name. She replied in a shy mumble, and I asked again. She mumbled again, though it sounded like she had said "Mariam." I wanted to tell her that was my sister's name, Miriam, but to be sure I asked her again and as she answered without volume I automatically, instinctively cupped a hand to my ear. At this she bolted like a doe back to the passenger hold, where she crouched by a wall and glared through the doorway. My heart sank to the muddy bottom of Lake Nasser.

In the early afternoon we approached the elegant three-mile curve of the High Dam and the ferry turned east toward the Aswan port. The passengers were ordered to line up and present themselves to officials waiting inside the ship's café. All three hundred of us, once so happy on deck, were packed and stacked, dank cheek by sweaty jowl, with luggage and dependents, in the narrow halls and gangways and on the stairs while the name of each was checked against a list of known terrorists and insulters of the president. Foreigners had their passports inspected and stamped; those of the Egyptian and Sudanese passengers were held until every last potential dissident had been screened. One by one a family's name would be called, and the father would have to claw his way through and over the others to collect his papers.

There was a heat in Aswan that equaled the deserts of northern Sudan and the jungles of Equatoria. The sun peeled back my clothes and then my skin and seemed to braise what muscle lay underneath. It provoked a keen sense of entitlement. I was now back in some version of civilization. The Aswan port had been a real port, unlike the dockside pile that had seen the ferry off from Wadi Halfa. The train to town had been a real train, made in France. I was, for the first time in my journey, in a tourist town, where alcohol was served, with dozens of clean budget hotels to choose from, but in the heat I felt I deserved more.

The Old Cataract beckoned. Presidents, prime ministers and proconsuls had all stayed at the Old Cataract. Churchill, of course. A wasting François Mitterrand, just a week from death, jetted in for a final look at the Nile and the sunrise over the black boulders and pharaonic ruins of Elephantine Island. I extracted a credit card from a hidden cache in my rucksack, stepped over a metal barricade and walked up the long driveway for two nights of luxury.

But the Old Cataract's high-thread-count sheets, enigmatic

views (even the bathroom had a balcony), liveried room service and, by God, wine list, were not enough to cushion the shock of Egypt. If I had been asked to describe the northern Sudanese in one word, I would have said "cool." Strangers, even friendly ones, carried with them a formality, a seriousness that I found appealing. I never once in northern Sudan heard one adult raise his voice to another. On my first walk through Aswan I encountered a bellowing match between two taxi drivers competing for the same half-naked German fare, and the equally perplexing sight of one man slapping another's face during an argument outside an electronics shop. As curious as this open-air aggression—which surely would have led to someone's death in the Sudan—was the sense that the participants didn't really mean it. The slapped man continued his argument without slapping his opponent back, much less breaking his jaw.

In Sudan, which sees few foreign visitors, my shambolic presence was met with indifference in both cities and villages. In Aswan I was persistently tailed by taxi drivers, felucca captains, child beggars and touts offering "smoke-hash-boy-girl." Some were charming, with well-worn raps—odes to "Beel Clington," curses for "Geeeorg Boosh, no good"—but the spiels got old and the offers kept coming. I walked uphill, deeper into Aswan and away from the river until they lost interest. Here the city was more like a dense collection of villages. Brick buildings sat atop one another like blocks in a crumbly grayscale version of Tetris. A group of women in black abayas squatted against a wall selling vegetables; they ignored me. A cluster of men smoking and drinking tea nodded politely. This was more like it. I was nobody again.

Still, attractions beckoned. The Nubian Museum's collection of artifacts included a full equine suit of armor and life-size recreations of traditional Nubian homes, but Egypt's historical discomfort with this tiny minority had leached into some of the displays. The Nubian conquerors who established ancient Egypt's

25th Dynasty were described as fighting "under rulers of Egyptian origin." Heaven forbid a darker race might conquer the motherland without some Egyptian DNA to explain it. A photo exhibit on the salvage of Nubian and pharaonic antiquities before the raising of the High Dam made no mention at all of the dam's impact on the Nubian people themselves. It was as if they had mysteriously disappeared from the Nile Valley, leaving behind only these temples and tombs.

I hired a felucca, a tall-masted wooden Egyptian sailboat, to tour the waters off Aswan and visit Elephantine Island. There I descended into the island's ancient stone Nilometers—beautiful ancestors of the cement markers Schon and I had seen after our first day on the White Nile—and admired its piles of ruins and bones left by various pharaohs, Greeks, Romans and Christians.

Sailing off Elephantine, we took in the smaller Nile islands and the rapids south of the city, with giant black stones coated in the rind of thousands of years of flowing volcanic silt. Their burnished swoops and hollows lent each a distinctly organic, gnome-like appearance among the rusted steel towers that rose from the water every thirty yards. These were guideposts driven into the riverbed to help boat traffic in the days before the High Dam lowered the water level and left the boulders permanently exposed. Weaving through these, my felucca captain, Fony Badien, brought me to an island in the Nile that had been in his family's possession for generations. A hundred yards long and maybe thirty yards at its widest, the island was an unintended gift from Nasser. The property had been a seasonal destination in the days before the dam went up, submerged during the Nile flood and visible during its low period. Fony kept a cool mud house on his side of the island and dreamed of one day opening an inn there. His older brother farmed the other half, the island having soaked in Ethiopian silt for a thousand years or more, and spent his afternoons smoking from a water pipe under a straw-roofed hut. From there, on the island's southern tip, Fony pointed out a cluster of houses set above the water on the river's western bank. A large-boned white woman in capri pants was stepping out of a battered skiff with the help of a turbaned boatman. She walked casually up to the house as the boatman pushed the boat out and rowed away.

"She lives there?" I asked.

"She is from Europe," Fony said. "A bunch of those ladies, from England or Germany, they live here part of the year with Nubian husbands. They get the younger man here, not like in England. That's like their own village."

Fony's felucca offered a chance to regain the river and travel by water for the first time since Moses Malueth's barge dropped me in Malakal those many months before. Fony said it would take five days and three hundred dollars to reach Luxor, a hundred miles to the north. "You will see the Nile, the desert, some temples. I will cook and we will sleep in my felucca," he said in his lilting, high-pitched voice.

"Who else is on the river?" I asked.

"It is only tourists," he said. "Feluccas with the tourists. Regular people don't sail the Nile. Some fishermen will go here and there, but they don't actually go to places. They fish nearby and then come home." I had started my Nile journey to learn about an almost hidden world—the developing and dynamic communities on the African Nile. Here in Egypt, the river had been trammeled by five thousand years' worth of writers, explorers and sybarites; their observations filled the libraries and travel blogs. I decided to avoid the wordy wake of Gustave Flaubert, Florence Nightingale and William Golding and headed north in a second-class rail car.

With my departure from Aswan I left Nubia behind. Ahead lay the treasures of Luxor, the hardscrabble towns of Upper Egypt and Cairo itself. Almost everywhere along this route a glorious past lay just below the surface of the present. Take the village of Qurta, located just south of Edfu. It was near here that in 1962 Canadian researchers found, etched into the overgrown sandstone cliffs, a riot of artwork depicting bulls and other animals. The engravings bore an uncanny resemblance to etchings inside the caves of Lascaux in France and Altamira in Spain. Could it be, the Canadians diffidently suggested, that these Egyptian works were just as old—and therefore just as significant to the story of human development—as the Paleolithic treasures in Europe? The scientific community's answer was a scornful no. Art was born in Europe, and that was that. It was more than forty years before another team of archaeologists visited the area and found even more bull engravings, and, in the ruins of Paleolithic encampments, the horns of those same bulls, now extinct. Egypt was producing art well before the pharaohs. The reliefs and carvings showed care and attention to detail—the wrinkles on the neck and mouth of a hippopotamus, the slight lilt to the head of a bull as it appears to walk across a sandstone cliff fifty feet above the Nile. As the new archaeologists showed, Egypt's oldest known artworks were fifteen thousand years old—no less significant than those in Lascaux and Altamira.

Our next stop was Esna. Known today as a minor stopover for tourists en route to see the Ptolemaic temple at Edfu, Esna bore a much darker distinction in the late nineteenth century. Unknown to the visitors who flocked Esna's tourist market, it was here that young African boys captured during tribal warfare and sold into slavery were brought for castration. The Coptic Christian priests of Esna had cornered the market in minting eunuchs, and over the years they mutilated thousands of black-skinned boys from Sudan and Ethiopia, most of them between seven and nine years old. "Their profession is held in contempt by even the vilest Egyptians," a European visitor wrote, "but they are protected by the government, to whom they pay an annual tax." Those boys who survived the operation—victims were immersed up to their chests in Nile silt to heal—were sent to Cairo for sale into the harems of Egypt, Turkey and Syria, where each would one day guard another man's concubines. I kept out of Esna and slept the rest of the way to Luxor as the train sliced through a rambling landscape of cement-block houses, irrigation ditches and palm trees.

In Luxor the dead lived very well. It would be impossible to quantify the volume of time, imagination, sweat and reverence the Egyptians of yore put into honoring their royal departed, and I found their obsession irresistible. The site of the ancient city of Thebes, Luxor boasted what might be the world's biggest-ever religious complex: the 247-acre ruins of the temple of Karnak. Across the river lay the Valley of the Kings, the Valley of the Queens and the rest of the west bank necropolis. It was on the west bank, at the temple of Hatshepsut—the queen who ruled Egypt in the guise of a man—that fifty-eight foreign tourists and four Egyptians were slain by Islamist militants in 1997. The attack set off a no-holds-barred war between the state and its insurgents. It's estimated that twenty-five hundred people were killed by radical gunmen, while more than ten thousand suspected Islamists were sent to prison without trial. Most were tortured as a matter of bureaucratic course. By the end of the nineties the Gamaa Islamiya—the Islamic Group—had declared a cease-fire with the government, and a second group, Al Jihad, had gone underground. Al Jihad's leader, a doctor named Ayman al-Zawahiri, fled to Afghanistan, where he joined Osama bin Laden to declare the International Islamic Front Against Jews and Crusaders, better known as Al Qaeda.

The grisly history of Egypt's Islamist insurgency was all but forgotten in Luxor, where the city fathers were more concerned with emulating the Luxor casino in Las Vegas than in predicting another militant attack. I crossed to the west bank and let the

ancient world blow my mind for most of the 105-degree day before
returning to the pedestrian present. A half mile from the temple
of Hatshepsut, a barren earthen plain ran down from the sandstone Theban hills, its surface marked by the shells of a few crumbled mud-brick houses. Their walls were painted an incongruously
gay aquamarine, the landscape broken by dozens of sloping trapezoidal holes. This had, until a few months before, been Gurna,
a collection of hamlets created and later undone by archaeology.
People had always lived among the pharaonic west bank ruins,
but the population began to swell with Bedouins after the arrival
of foreign treasure hunters in the early nineteenth century. They
had found foreigners willing to pay good money for garbage—the
old bones and carvings that littered and sprang from the ground.
Tombs were scattered among the hills of Gurna, and the Bedouin
shrewdly built their homes atop them.

In time the archaeological community and the Egyptian government came to view the settlement as a menace to the underground
treasures, the hunger of Western collectors and museums for their
contents notwithstanding. In 1948 the government decided the
people of Gurna would have to be moved. The acclaimed architect Hassan Fathy, author of *Architecture for the Poor*, planned
a holistic model community to replace the larcenous village. The
homes of New Gurna would be made in the cool Nubian style of
inexpensive local materials, with a mosque, a souk, an outdoor
amphitheater and a school, but the effort wasted away and old
Gurna persevered. In 1998, the government tried to clear Gurna
again, this time by force, and several people were killed defending
their ancestral village. Nine years later, the state returned, offering
the sweetener of new "modern" homes for those who left, coupled
with the threat of prison for those who didn't. They cleared and
then leveled most of the houses. Gurna's thirty-two hundred families were moved to a new village a mile away, a new New Gurna,
with cookie-cutter stucco houses—the opposite of Hassan Fathy's

vision—that wouldn't have looked out of place in a suburb of Tucson or San Diego.

I stepped out of my taxi to shoot Gurna's remains and was interrupted by two young girls carrying water to a village farther down the road who invited me to take their photograph. I knew this would be followed by a demand for money, so I skipped that step and gave them each an Egyptian pound. They complained like angry birds—this was the off-season, and tips were scarce—before moving on. A man passed in a donkey cart and he too called out for me to take a picture. I turned away without answering and he brayed nothing good and carried on toward the river.

At an empty souvenir shop nearby, Mohammed Abdel Naeim sat in a wicker chair and denounced the government's dirty business. "If it was done professionally it would have been good," he said. "But they rushed everybody and they did the wrong thing. They spoke to the rich people. They spoke to the sheikh. But they don't know how the poor people live. And the poor weren't consulted." Abdel Naeim wore a smooth light green *jallabiya*. His nails were neatly trimmed and he wore a $3,000 Tag Heuer wristwatch, or at least a good knockoff of one. It had been a long time since this son of Gurna had pulled a mummy from the earth, assuming he ever had. Behind him a silent army of ibises, sphinxes, tomb cats, Nefertitis and King Tuts crafted from plaster, alabaster and wood lined the shelved walls from floor to ceiling.

"First of all, the new houses are bad," he said. "They're just bad. The foundations are bad. The columns are bad. You have no chance of building another level. The concrete is bad. You need six pieces of rebar in each column to build up and these have only four." In crowded Egypt, where land was scarce and families tight, every house was built with the expectation that a second and third floor would one day spring from the first. It helps to give the cities and towns their peculiar unfinished look—most houses have bare concrete columns sprouting from their roofs, the columns crowned by rusty spines of steel rebar, waiting for the day the money comes through to build again. It wasn't hard to imagine that the contractor responsible for building these had pocketed the savings on steel.

"Another thing," Abdel Naeim said. "A lot of people have animals. The yards at these new places are three by six meters. Some are three by ten. You need at least 175 square meters to graze a cow. But this new place isn't really a village. It's a complex—so you can't let animals out. Now, I have four sons. For my sons to get married, each needs a flat. Some families got more houses than they have sons. We got one house for everyone. My old house was mud brick, four rooms and a basement. It was a fantastic house—warm in the winter and cool in the summer. Now it's gone. Millions and millions of tourists come to Luxor, thousands come to the west bank every day. What have they done to help us? Nothing."

"From what I've read," I said, "the village was supported by tomb robbing. How long was that going to last?"

"*Ya ragul!*" he said. Come on! "You can't tell me there's a man riding a donkey and he's eating bread and salt and okra and he has all this money. Money shows. Look: In the future, when we set foot here it will be as strangers. It will all be tourists and businessmen. Don't be surprised if you see a tall hotel where Gurna used to be."

The new New Gurna had the plastic look of a planned community. Stuccoed houses of maroon and beige sat end to end; their wooden-shuttered windows opened onto wide and empty paved streets, with a streetlight on every short block. Skinny saplings rose from the curb every forty feet. At first it looked like a Potemkin village; there was no one to be seen, no sign of life. But it was hot—why would there be? I walked down the middle of the street like a sunstroked gunfighter until I found Umar Khalifa sitting in the meager shade of his front porch. He rose slowly to my greeting and offered me a chair. It was a difficult move to the new village, he said. "I told them I would leave when I was dead." That was three months ago. Now, he said, "My wife and I like it here." New blooms of bougainvillea were climbing a homemade trellis, and Khalifa's five-year-old granddaughter came outside to watch us speak and to play with a hose that had been left running in the dirt under the vines. For some, a little running water could go a long way. Khalifa was old and retired, and maybe a little wired. He and his wife, Afaf, had received a three-bedroom house even though their children were all grown and gone. Afaf even ran a little snack and soda stand nearby. I walked deeper into the set-tlement and found a few other villagers who said they were adjust-ing nicely to the indoor plumbing and plentiful electricity of their new homes, but they clammed up when a car appeared and parked about twenty yards away. A lone driver got out and watched our meeting without approaching. "We hass to go now," the taxi driver said. "He is bolise."

Bolise were indeed everywhere in Egypt. Young men in black woolen uniforms lounged outside the tourist sites pretending to screen visitors for explosives and guns. They manned the big inter-sections, breathing exhaust and sipping tea. They were like moss, gathering in shady alcoves outside the important hotels and build-ings, many dragging Kalashnikovs that one suspected had never actually been fired. In the alley behind my hotel I saw one police officer fooling with a little boy; they were playing tug-of-war with the officer's rifle. But this wasn't the kind of police that watched my foray into New Gurna. The uniformed police existed as a watery balm for tourist fears of terrorism. The plainclothes cops existed to protect Egypt from all critics, foreign and domestic. No threat was too small. That's why they tortured bloggers.

That evening I crossed again to the Nile's west bank for dinner with a friend of a friend who'd lived among the villagers for twenty years. A Coptic Christian doctor, he'd dropped out of the career race as a young man, preferring village life in Upper Egypt to the prestige and pressures that awaited his classmates in the hospitals of Cairo and Alexandria. He was sharp-featured, balding and thin, with a face like that of the French action hero Jean Reno. He drove me to a nearly empty outdoor restaurant that sat under gnarled shade trees, and waited for me to draw him out of his reticence and turn the duty of this social call into an actual conversation. He was both an outsider and a local, and I felt he might have a unique perspective on this strange city of the dead. I babbled uncomfortably for a half hour, and said at last, "I just don't understand how this place works. Even with millions of visitors, the entire city can't be employed by tourism. So how do people live?"

He nodded and drummed his long fingers against his forehead. "The work is farming and construction," he said. "But many of the farmers are not good farmers. They are Bedouins, they don't have the habit yet, it's too few generations. So they plant poorly. The building work is always around, because there is always need for new houses, because of population increase. The people have to eat, so there are shops for food and candies. There is more of that now than ever, more snacks and less nutrition."

I asked if he saw the effects of this new diet in his practice.

"Definitely. Malnutrition is a real problem. Their children eat as much Twinkie cake as they do bread. They take tea for breakfast, only tea. I tell them, you must have bread, some egg, something more than tea. The morning tea blocks the stomach from absorbing iron for the rest of the day. So there is malnutrition and anemia also. And the wrapped cakes are so cheap that people think they're as good as bread."

I asked him how the villagers interacted with the tourists—how did they view these legions of foreign visitors? "There is nothing beside the exchange of money," he said. "Sometimes a local man will marry a foreign woman—never the other way around—but it doesn't last. It cannot last here, in this environment. She will grow bored. Or she will get him a visa and they will live in England or

Germany. If they resolve to live here, the relationship lasts only until they have a child, and if they have a daughter it is a guarantee they will leave."

"She'll take the girl before the family can circumcise her?" I asked. Genital mutilation—"purification"—of girls, while less common than in the past, was still pervasive among both Muslim and Coptic Christian families, thanks in part to a belief that the clitoris, if left attached, will grow into a penislike appendage, leaving the woman unfeminine and indifferent to men.

"No," the doctor said. "The family won't touch the girl that way, they will respect the mother's opposition. It is *mental* excision they are fleeing. Because the girl will become like the other girls in the family and she will be cut out of her future. But even if they have a boy, the child will need a school, and the regular schools are horrible and the good private schools are expensive. By the time the child is school age they are back in Europe, or the mother leaves and takes the child with her."

"I saw a village in Aswan that my felucca captain said was built entirely by old European women who had married local men."

He flung his head back and brought it forward in a truncated nod. "You see that man over there?" The man in question looked to be in his late twenties, dressed in slacks and a rayon shirt, relaxing over bottles of 7-Up with his abayaed wife and three small children. "He has another wife besides this one. He is married to a foreigner, a Dutch. It's disgusting."

"Disgusting? Really? What's wrong with having a foreign wife? I mean, it's legal, isn't it?"

He thrummed his forehead again, exasperated. "This is not that kind of marriage, a love marriage. These women like he has married are old. And fat. And ugly. No one will touch them in their own country, so they come here and they get a young husband. She gives him money to build a house, and she sends money from Holland, and then she comes for a few weeks in the winter and he has to be with her. Several of my patients do this. They cry when they talk about it. They come and ask me for drugs. The only way they can perform is to get drunk. It is an old practice here that a man will sometimes put dust from one of the temples in his tea, to help with performance, but even the pharaohs' dust can't help these ones. Only liquor."

"And the Egyptian wives? They don't care?"

"They don't mind. It is allowed by the religion and by the law, and it gives them a good life."

Predatory foreign brides were the least of Egypt's hazards. As I ran by rail through Upper Egypt, the rustic belt of hard villages and bleak towns that separates Luxor from Cairo and the Delta, it was easy to see how a man could marry a stranger and how his true wife would support it. The ever more teeming box-brick towns of Sohag, Assiut, Minya and Beni Sueif gave a sense of generic poverty and unloveliness. But tucked away in the midst of this grim archipelago was a place where the ancient world inhabited the present. I got off the train at Sohag and, with the help of three interlocutors, one of whom I suspected was a police spy, convinced a nervous taxi driver to take me into the countryside. Just before Sohag the Nile runs hard by limestone cliffs riddled with the caves of hermits. A Coptic Christian stronghold, the area is home to some of the world's oldest monastic communities and is a living link between the pharaonic and Coptic traditions. Despite Egypt's approximately ten-to-one ratio of Muslims to Copts, the latter do not see themselves as a minority so much as the true community of indigenous Egyptians. The Arab invaders of AD 649 referred to their new conquest as *dar el Gibt*, "home of the Egyptians," and many Copts still hold fast to that distinction. When their masses are spoken in the pre-Arab vernacular, Coptic priests are not only speaking the language of Christianity's earliest days; they are evoking the speech of Ramses and Cleopatra, as surely as the Coptic cross is a descendant of the ankh, the symbol that pagan gods used five thousand years ago to restore life to the mummified worthies of Egypt.

This stretch south of Sohag was one of the rare sections of the Egyptian Nile where the banks were not marred by construction; the river here recalled the Nile I had traveled in Uganda and southern Sudan, one of tall reeds, papyrus and a marvelous absence of garbage. Sohag itself offered nothing to the eye, but its countryside seemed a place apart. Amid the fields and patches of date palms I saw clusters of mud-brick houses with tall castle-like dovecotes, pigeon towers built in an ancient style thought to be the oldest in the world. The mud homes were rambling constructions with new rooms added generation after generation to accommodate the ever-growing Egyptian family. But unlike in Uganda and Sudan, my ranging made people uncomfortable. After a couple hours the driver brought me back to the train station, demanding triple our agreed fee for the risk he'd taken. Foreigners aren't allowed to move around rural Egypt, though I could never figure out if it was because of banditry, the occasional clashes that took place between rural Muslims and Christians or simply a general fear for the fate of Westerners so far outside their element. I settled up with the driver and waited for the next train. My wife was meeting me in the capital. It had been a long time.

Cairo was a riot. A party. A slum. A traffic jam.

In Africa's biggest city, the elevated expressways were just another road. Working people and students scaled concrete barriers to stand on the highway and hail taxis and buses. Craft sellers piled their wares on blankets on the side of the slow lane, as low

Toyota pickups, their beds packed with cattle or sheep, swerved around them on the way to market. Overhead the billboards advertised Samsung mobile phones and luxury condos in Mecca.

At street level the nineteenth and twenty-first centuries collided with less irony and considerably more iron. In 1991, at the time of Saddam Hussein's invasion of Kuwait, Cairo had 2.6 million cars on its streets. Sixteen years later, there were seven million. Neither the traffic system nor driver education had kept up. Even with an average automobile speed of just six miles an hour, Cairo boasts the shockingly high rate of fifty-eight thousand road deaths a year. Riding in from the Ramses train station, my taxi missed by a sliver colliding with a gray BMW pushing its way into traffic, a disaster that might have brought the driver a beating in addition to financial ruin. "*Tawakilt ala Allah*," the driver said moments later as he punched the gas to fill a five-foot gap between us and the next car. "I put my trust in God." Cairo's taxi fleet was a polyglot collection dominated by stately black-and-white Peugeot 504s, with a handful of Fiats and Soviet-era Ladas thrown in. Some still ran on leaded gasoline while a few burned clean compressed natural gas. The traffic police, who direct cars the way stoplights do in other countries, have six times the globally accepted level of lead in their blood, more than any other group in the world save perhaps the men who actually mine the stuff. My driver and his brethren vied for space with an explosion of privately owned cars bound for gated satellite cities in the desert with names like Dreamland and Utopia, overloaded diesel city buses, sardine-packed minivan taxis, swarms of motorcycles and scooters and even the occasional and alarmingly brave bicyclist.

In the affluent island neighborhood of Zamalek where I stayed, the main east-west street was thick each morning with traffic and exhaust as local residents joined the flood of commuters heading into Cairo's even more crowded precincts for work. July 26 Boulevard had six lanes on the ground and four more on the expressway above. Each morning, I would turn my head after buying the *International Herald Tribune* and catch sight of a ghost floating through this honking congestion: a pale man, white as pearl, pedaling hard on a heavy black bicycle, one hand on the handlebars, the other steadying a six-foot-long wooden plank resting on his head like a surfboard, a tray piled with flat rounds of Egyptian bread. I saw this deliveryman more than a dozen times, his cheeks and brow spectral with flour, his concentration keen as an astronaut's, and never once did I see the traffic get the better of him. Not once did he have to stop and somehow recover a fallen piece of bread among the cars.

It was a city of near-miss artists. Drivers could calculate to the millimeter the amount of space that would keep them from collision. On the streets, beefy men fought in slapping matches like the one I'd seen in Aswan, a sight that never ceased to shock, and yet this too I came to see as a calculated avoidance of real violence. In a country with rising inflation and falling subsidies and wages, choking pollution and widespread underemployment, people needed to blow off steam. The powers that be watched the frustration grow and tried where they could to divert it. Eighteen million people were crowded here on the Nile, trapped by thirst and by a government that couldn't do much with efficiency but break heads. Police and internal security forces outnumbered the army. They filled the streets in black-uniformed phalanxes at the first sign of a mild liberal protest. The *rais*, President Mubarak, was very old. His son was gearing up to replace him and nobody could really think of an alternative regime that could actually govern the country—not that the country was being governed now. The liberals were crushed like beetles, and, as the only game in town for young comers, the ruling party vacuumed up most of the new political talent. The Western powers simultaneously tsked at and embraced this status quo.

While their cousins in Sudan completed their seventeenth year in power, the Muslim Brothers of Egypt were in a state of perpetual cull, their leaders facing trial before military tribunals even as hundreds of thousands depended on them for social services the government was too incompetent to provide.

This standoff between the authoritarian government and those few bold or organized enough to challenge it was an old one, and that's what stung about Egypt, the sense of a place trapped in amber—though amber at least acts as a preservative. Egypt felt like some slow-decaying element.

It was all a bit difficult to contemplate, what with the young man wagging his ass in my face.

He was a doughy boy, maybe eighteen, and a half hour of dancing inside the humid confines of the riverboat nightclub had cast a dark vertical band of sweat down the cleft of his cream dress slacks. The young man wore his hair in short oily curls and his tongue on the outside of his mouth. While his bottom shook to a complicated rhythm that would intimidate a Cuban bandleader, the boy's arms sliced through the air in a fast but simple one-two beat. Nearby a thirty-piece band was playing a rhythm and blues instrumental that sounded thoroughly Egyptian, with its tiny cymbals and fretless lute—and also, with its ripping tenor sax, indistinguishable from the music of James Brown's backup band, the legendary JB's.

There were dozens of other boys gyrating among the crowd. They wore matching suits and each moved as if possessed by an especially lascivious *djinn*. The audience of upper-class Egyptians—necktied fathers, bejeweled and headscarfed mothers, girls in their finery, little boys in little tracksuits—was transfixed; some of the women sported grins of mild embarrassment, others of absolute wickedness. And then the music stopped and the dancers froze and there was a thunder of drums from the ten-man percussion section. A booming chant of *"Salaam aleikum"* filled the room. Saad El Soghayar had arrived, illuminated by a single spotlight pointed down from the VIP balcony. In contrast with the formal garb of his eighty-odd dancers, drummers and sidemen, Egypt's most popular *shaabi* singer sported a yellow T-shirt and tight no-brand blue jeans. He took the stage in punctuated steps, a wireless microphone in his right hand. Short bursts of machine-gun lyrics popped from his mouth as the dancers went wild again.

Shaabi has been described as Egypt's version of hip-hop. The comparison, while inapt, is the nearest available. It was slum music—low culture infecting high. Played with speed and brevity, its topics were at times naughty and uncomfortably political in a country where the reins of culture had been in the hands of the government since Nasser's day. It didn't seek to extol the nation or set an example. It was earthy and fun and consequently banned from the national airwaves. But not even a five-decade national security state could keep a good beat down. Despite its absence from the radio, shaabi was in demand, and so here was Saad performing in front of the swells, who had paid more than the average Egyptian's monthly salary to see him. It was past three in the morning and this was his sixth show of the night. Five weddings had preceded it.

Across the table from me, facing the stage, sat my host, a lanky man with straight white hair, pale blue eyes and a smile that said he'd seen it all and still enjoyed most of it. I didn't know Miles Axe Copeland III when I was a boy, but I loved his work: As the founder of IRS Records, Miles had brought the world The Police, R.E.M. and Wall of Voodoo. Miles's father, a jazz trumpeter from Alabama, had a successful career manipulating, advising and overthrowing Middle Eastern governments as one of America's legendary spies (and wrote a dictionary of colloquial Syrian Arabic along the way). Now his son was marketing Arabic popular music to the West, and Saad was one of his discoveries. Copeland was back in

Egypt looking for new talent and had stopped by to say hello to
Saad, who was just now prowling the audience, standing on tables
and singing *"Al Hantour"* (The Carriage).

> *Hey, you there! Hey you there on the carriage!*
> *Hey you, swaying back and forth!*
> *Whoa! Yeah! How I wish to ride in the carriage*
> *And sway back and forth.*

And who wouldn't? The song contained a few simple metaphors
for sex and also lyrics of almost courtly romance ("I'd put her hand
on my arm and we would link arms and sway/and we would stop
on either side [of the road] and get down to eat grilled sweet potatoes") and the beat kept on its *bum bim! bum-bum-bum-bum
bum-bum bim!* rhythm of drums and tambourine. Saad shimmied
and come-hithered the women with wolf eyes until, quite without
warning, he plopped down on my lap, straddling my left thigh, and
began to grind his pelvis into my leg with a pole dancer's enthusiasm. The spotlight followed. When Saad grew bored of embar-
rassing me, he leapt up, spun around, looked my wife in the eye
and gave his right nipple a twist, posed for a photo with Miles and
moved on to the next verse and victim.

It was only a matter of time before Saad and his band eroded the
audience's middle-class reserve. Some of the fathers, a few bearing
the raised forehead callus that marked Egypt's Muslim devouts,
stood up to dance spastically beside their seated wives. A half dozen
little girls took the stage to show off their belly-dance moves. They
were cleared off after a few minutes save one, maybe nine years
old, dressed in a white terrycloth pantsuit, who seized the spotlight
and arched her back so her long black hair might touch the floor,
hands held out level with the stage, her child hips moving *ta-ta,
ta-ta*. Miles shook his head. "People in America wouldn't understand this," he shouted across the table. "They think the Middle

East is nothing but veiled women and angry men. That's the image they get—violent shrews who don't have any fun." We stumbled out of the club after six in the morning, got into a taxi, waited while the driver tipped a police officer with a Cleopatra cigarette for the privilege of idling there and sped into the dawn on nearly empty streets, swerving near the Four Seasons Hotel to pass a donkey cart hauling chickens in wooden cages.

Egypt hadn't fought an armed conflict since the October War of 1973 but the Delta was still considered a strategic area. I traveled north with a pass from Egypt's Supreme Council of Antiquities. It gave me permission to visit the Delta's archeological sites, a badly needed cover to explain my presence to police and other snoops in areas off the tourist track. The Delta was Egypt's agricultural and industrial heartland. Here the Nile split into its eastern and western branches, each feeding a complex network of irrigation canals and waterways. It was here that the silt of the ages had been deposited, creating a fertile 9,600-square-mile triangle between Cairo and the Mediterranean. It was here that the electricity from the High Dam had been put to use irrigating the land and powering the looms. Nasser's land reforms had turned serfs into small landowners and his factories had created employment for two generations of workers. Now factory towns like Zagazig, Mahalla and Kafr el-Dawwar were in foment. A wave of wildcat strikes was shaking the great state-owned textile mills, where workers were spooked over low wages, high prices and threats of privatization. A populace conditioned to expect everything from the state was now being told to fend for itself, and it was buckling under the strain.

The government too was buckling. It tried to manage the bigger threats, like the industrial strikes, applying force and sometimes compromise as it felt the situation warranted. But the state's true

face appeared in its reaction to smaller irritants, as when a sixteen-
year-old girl at a Delta high school found herself being interrogated
by the education ministry after she criticized the American invasion of Iraq in a school essay. What secret organization, the under-
secretary of education wanted to know, had told her to write such
things? The girl, Alaa Farag Megahed, was told she would have
to repeat the entire school year, a sentence that was repealed once
news of the scandal broke. "This is a public offence, which is punishable under Law 41 for the year 2000," a ministry official told *Al-
Ahram Weekly*. "The essay asked students to describe reasons for
the environmental problem of desertification—what has this to do
with President Bush and the Egyptian regime?"

The Delta itself was sinking under the weight of modern Egypt.
The region was one of mud stacked on mud, and each year it sank
a little bit. This reduction in elevation had been countered by the
annual Nile flood and the silt it left behind, but silt hadn't reached
the Delta since the High Dam went up. Without it—those five billion cubic meters now on the floor of Lake Nasser, the Delta was
falling and the sea was invading. Geologists say the Nile Delta has
now entered its "destruction phase."

Still, the only sinkage I could discern was metaphorical. My
train north took me past dusty company towns and emerald fields
where water buffalo pulled plows. Thick with the human, agricultural and industrial waste of Egypt, the Nile water here was as
brown as the water at Lake Victoria was clear. A young Winston
Churchill famously imagined a day when the Nile waters would
be "equally and amicably divided among the river people, and the
Nile itself, flowing for three thousand miles through smiling countries, shall perish gloriously and never reach the sea." The waters
were now divided, not equally, though almost amicably, and the
smiles were surely forced. But the last part of Churchill's predic-
tion has nearly come true. Its flow slowed by the High Dam, its volume bled by miles of canals, the Nile struggles to completion.

I got off at Damietta, a prosperous port city near the mouth of the Nile. It is known for its furniture workshops and as the meeting place, in 1219, of Saint Francis of Assisi and Sultan Malik al-Kamil of Egypt during the Fifth Crusade. It was said that Damietta had no unemployment. Its sixty thousand furniture workshops imported timber from Europe and sent it back in the form of wooden chairs, tables and divans, all hand-carved in a classic nineteenth-century style. Damietta had a clean, seaside feel and its narrow streets and alleys rang with the blows of untold hammers and chisels. The people seemed to move with a relaxed sense of purpose that was missing from the frenzied streets of Cairo. There, a workingman had to carry two or three jobs to scrape by—a government job during the day, a taxi at night and maybe a weekend shift at a cigarette stall. The people of Damietta made things with skilled hands and sold them; they seemed healthier for it.

A few miles north was Ras al Bahr on the Mediterranean coast. With this resort town the sea truly began. It was late afternoon and the big, high-bowed fishing boats were coming back inland for the evening. The water's surface rhythm was complex, a meeting of river and sea. I stopped to chat with three men walking along the riverside promenade. "It is in the Koran, you know," one said.

"What is?"

"This place, where the river stops and the sea begins." He pulled out his Nokia, punched a few keys and the verse came out reedy and, I had to admit, a little magical, through the tiny polyphonic speaker. Sura 25, Verse 53: "And He it is Who hath given independence to the two seas (though they meet); one palatable, sweet, and the other saltish, bitter; and hath set a bar and a forbidding ban between them." The Mediterranean and the Nile met at Ras al Bahr, the verse implied, but they didn't mix.

I took a taxi ninety miles across the Mediterranean coastline to Rosetta, where the Nile's western branch made its exit, and paid a captain to take me there on his fiberglass motor launch, an open-air tourist boat in a town with no tourists. Rosetta, home to some lovely Ottoman-era homes, lacked the bustle of Damietta, but its outskirts hummed with industry. Three layers of economy were visible from the boat. The water was crowded with fish farms. Floating wooden platforms, some of them supporting little shacks with guard dogs, overlooked square netted enclosures that dotted the river for miles. Up and down the shore, fat triple-decker yachts and pleasure boats were being built from the ground up of imported wood for sale to wealthy Gulf Arabs. And just inland, dozens of brick kilns pricked the clear Delta sky with their smokestacks. We rode the last of the river to the chopping sea and turned back without fanfare. I had spent more than six months tracing the Nile from the shores of Lake Victoria and had expected to be happier at the end of the line. Down the length of the Nile people lived and even thrived under extraordinary constraints. But Uganda and Sudan were dynamic, changing. There, the future was unwritten and—however unevenly—the horizon was growing. It seemed the opposite held in Egypt: Here, your fate was obvious and you would never be free.

On a railway platform south of Rosetta, waiting for a train connection back to Cairo, a young man in the uniform of the pious—skullcap, high-water pants, a thin but untrimmed beard— approached and tried to share with me the good news of the Prophet and his revelation. He had a cleft palate and innocent eyes and clearly not a dime to his name, and I listened with a courteous false attention as he produced cassette tapes of sermons by preachers he admired. He ran his finger across the words on the cover of one, sounding it out for me: "Ishh-lam. Ishh-lam." I thanked him and apologized for not speaking better Arabic, and he said that was all right and gave me a stack of tapes to take home with me. I reached into my pocket to give him some money, and he pushed my hand away. "*Salaam aleikum,*" he said, and left me again to myself.

The train would be coming soon. I walked to the other end of the platform in search of a bottle of water, and saw the young fisher of men in agitated conversation. He was moving his hands quickly, explaining something to two police officers. The train pulled up, and I stepped in and continued to watch through the open doors. One officer was looking through the cassettes in the boy's plastic shopping bag. The other, sweating under his black beret, looked away, a winding up of the torso, and then turned back to the boy with an extended arm and open palm, connecting hard with the right side of his face. It sounded like a popped balloon. The train gave a lurch and pulled away. I took my seat and was gone.

AUTHOR'S NOTE

The names of some people in chapters 4, 6, 7, 8 and 9 have been changed to preserve their privacy and security.